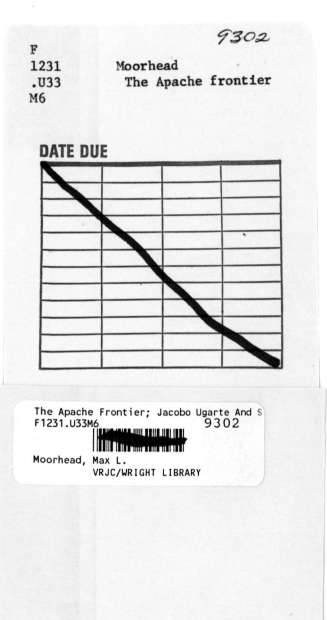

THE APACHE FRONTIER
*Jacobo Ugarte and Spanish-Indian Relations
in Northern New Spain, 1769–1791*

THE APACHE

MAX L. MOORHEAD

FRONTIER

Jacobo Ugarte and Spanish-Indian Relations in Northern New Spain, 1769–1791

UNIVERSITY OF OKLAHOMA PRESS : NORMAN

By Max L. Moorhead

Commerce of the Prairies, by Josiah Gregg (Editor) (Norman, 1954)

New Mexico's Royal Road: Trade and Travel on the Chihuahua Trail (Norman, 1958)

The Apache Frontier: Jacobo Ugarte and Spanish-Indian Relations in Northern New Spain, 1769–1791 (Norman, 1968)

Library of Congress Catalog Card Number: 67–64449

Copyright 1968 by the University of Oklahoma Press, Publishing Division of the University. Composed and printed at Norman, Oklahoma, U.S.A., by the University of Oklahoma Press. First edition.

PREFACE

When the frontier of Spanish settlement moving north from central Mexico reached the range of the Apache nation, it was abruptly halted in what is now the American Southwest. No other Indians so successfully resisted Spanish penetration in North America. No other Indians so completely wrested the offensive from the *conquistadores*. In the past the Spaniards had overrun and enserfed one Indian nation after another, but now they themselves became almost tributary vassals. For two centuries marauding Apaches swooped down on the thin line of Spanish settlement in hit-and-run raids, which baffled the defending troops and exacted an almost regular toll in persons and possessions from the terrorized colonists.

It is the purpose of this book to examine in detail the most critical period of this long and bloody struggle, that is, the turning of the tide in favor of the Spaniards during the military administration of Jacobo Ugarte y Loyola. Without inquiring into the actual results, historians have merely assumed that the beginning of the end of Apache ascendancy was the enunciation by Viceroy Bernardo de Gálvez of a brilliant new Indian policy in 1786. Putting such a complex program into practice, however, was no easy matter. The present account attempts, for the first time, to reveal how Commandant-General Ugarte faced this problem and the extent to which he was able to solve it. This, then, is intended to be a history of the influence of a man and of the conflict between two peoples.

A word to the racially sensitive: My purpose is to glorify neither the Spaniard nor the Indian. There were heroes and villains aplenty on both sides. For all his faults, the Spaniard was struggling to extend civilization; and, for all his virtues, the Apache was struggling to preserve his way of life, however limited. If my interpretation fails to do justice to the Apache, it is not owing to malice but to this truth and also to the nature of the evidence on which the historian must rely. The Spaniard left written records; the Apache did not. And such oral tradition as might have arisen from the era in question has long since passed from memory. Nor can the conscientious historian read into the Spanish records what is not there but perhaps should be. Fortunately for the Apache case, however, some Spaniards were critical of others, and several were at times even sympathetic with the Apaches, and so the admissible evidence is not entirely one-sided.

I must also explain an obvious imbalance in the amount of space I have assigned to each of the several Apache tribes. There are two chapters on the tribes of the Eastern division of the nation and only one on the Western. There is also far more attention given to the Mescaleros than to any other single tribe. In regard to the Eastern Apaches I must point out that the Spaniards were able to collect more information about them simply because they more frequently sought peace and association than did the Western tribesmen. As for the Mescaleros, it is my own judgment that their pact with the Spaniards, although short-lived, was the very cornerstone of Ugarte's grand strategy to pacify the entire Apache nation. Upon the success or failure of the Mescalero peace rested the result of his total effort.

Although this study is based very largely on archival materials, I am indebted to a dozen or more scholars whose basic research has clarified several aspects of Spanish-Indian frontier history in North America. I have recognized their important contributions in my footnotes and bibliography. An exception is Luis Navarro

Preface

García's *José de Gálvez y la Comandancia General de las Provincias Internas del Norte de Nueva España* (Sevilla, 1964), a major work, which came to hand after I had completed my own study. Although based on Spanish rather than Mexican archival sources, it reaches conclusions regarding Ugarte's administration that are surprisingly similar to mine.

I wish also to acknowledge and express my sincere gratitude to the Faculty Research Committee of the University of Oklahoma for generous grants-in-aid spread over the last seven years, which have borne the costs of microfilming many tomes of manuscript materials, of essential stenographic service, and of the cartographic work. The eight maps were drawn especially for this study by Mr. George P. Zech of Edmond, Oklahoma.

I am also indebted to a score or more people who have helped make materials available to me. Deserving special mention are Miss Nettie Lee Benson, of the Latin American Collection at the University of Texas Library; my colleague, Mr. Arrell M. Gibson, and Mr. Jack Haley, both of the Division of Manuscripts at the University of Oklahoma; Mrs. Alice Timmons, of the Frank Phillips Collection at the University of Oklahoma Library; Mr. F. J. Dockstader, of the Museum of the American Indian, New York City; Mr. Bert Fireman, of the Arizona Historical Foundation at Tempe; Mr. Sidney B. Brinckerhoff, of the Arizona Pioneers' Historical Society, at Tucson; and Mr. John Barr Tompkins, of the Bancroft Library at the University of California at Berkeley. I wish also to thank Mrs. Josephine Soukup and Mrs. Norma Jane Baumgarner for a most painstaking effort in typing the manuscript and to thank my wife, Amy, for her patience and care in helping me proofread it. Such errors as may have survived are mine alone.

Max L. Moorhead

University of Oklahoma
April 10, 1968

ix

CONTENTS

ILLUSTRATIONS AND MAPS

All maps were prepared by George P. Zech

LIST OF ABBREVIATIONS

AGI   Archivo General de Indias, Seville, Spain
AGN Archivo General de la Nación, Mexico City
CV   Correspondencia de los Virreyes
PI   Provincias Internas

THE APACHE FRONTIER
*Jacobo Ugarte and Spanish-Indian Relations
in Northern New Spain, 1769–1791*

CHAPTER I

THE APACHE FRONTIER

Stretching generally to the north of the present border between the United States and Mexico, from the upper reaches of the Colorado River of Texas to the headwaters of the Santa Cruz River of Arizona, ranged a nomadic people known to their neighbors as Apaches. The land they inhabited was characteristically arid, but otherwise it was surprisingly varied. From the grassy plains of the Texas Panhandle it merged into the juniper-and-pine-clad mountains of New Mexico, the sandy valley of the Río Grande, and the crusty expanse of sterile desert stretching westward into Arizona. The monotony of this latter landscape was relieved at great intervals by dark forested mountains, billowing sand dunes, limestone-capped mesas, statuesque sandstone pinnacles, glistening salt flats, and deeply etched arroyos. It was a harsh land, supporting only a sparse population.

The Gran Apachería, as the Spaniards sometimes called it, was 750 miles in breadth—from the 98th to the 111th meridian—and in some areas as much as 550 miles in depth—from the 30th to the 38th parallels. The main range of the Apaches was what we now call the desert Southwest, but when they were bent on plunder or revenge, they extended their murderous raids deep into what are now the Mexican states of Nuevo León, Coahuila, Chihuahua, and Sonora.

Linguistically and—to a lesser extent—culturally the scattered Apaches constituted a single nation, but politically they did not.

3

Neither the Eastern nor the Western Apaches recognized a general government, and although the several tribes of each were somewhat more cohesive, even these subdivisions broke up into virtually autonomous bands. Although the bands were united by kinship and controlled, at least in wartime, by recognized chieftains, they dissolved into isolated clans or families whenever convenience dictated. Among all the Apaches love of liberty was stronger than ties of kinship or kind. Apache groupings shifted with time and space, and anthropologists and ethnohistorians have been hard pressed to trace the relationships and nomenclature of their amorphous affiliations. In fact, there is some disagreement as to who were Apaches and who were not.

Essentially, the Apaches were a people of the Southern Athapaskan language stock; they were nomadic and predatory, but they were not immune to the cultural influences of neighboring peoples. The Navahos, for instance, were originally Apaches, speaking a dialect of the same language and linked by kinship with the Gila Apaches to the south. By the close of the eighteenth century, however, when their village sites became more fixed, their farms more productive, and their herds more numerous, they began to be distinguished as a separate nation. On the other hand, the Jicarillas developed similar industries after becoming isolated from their parental tribe, the Faraón Apaches, but they retained their original identification. Neither habitat nor mores was a clear-cut determinant. In the eastern area the Apaches pitched leathern tipis on the grassy plains; in the western area they fashioned crude wickiups of scrubby tree branches and placed them in the craggy mountains. Most of the tribes relished horse and mule meat, but the same flesh was taboo among the Lipanes.

After more than a century of long wars and short truces with the Apaches, the Spaniards managed to gather a rudimentary knowledge of these people. According to a description written near the close of the eighteenth century by a veteran army officer, there were then nine distinct Apache tribes. To the west of the Río Grande in New Mexico were the Mimbreños, the Navahos,

4

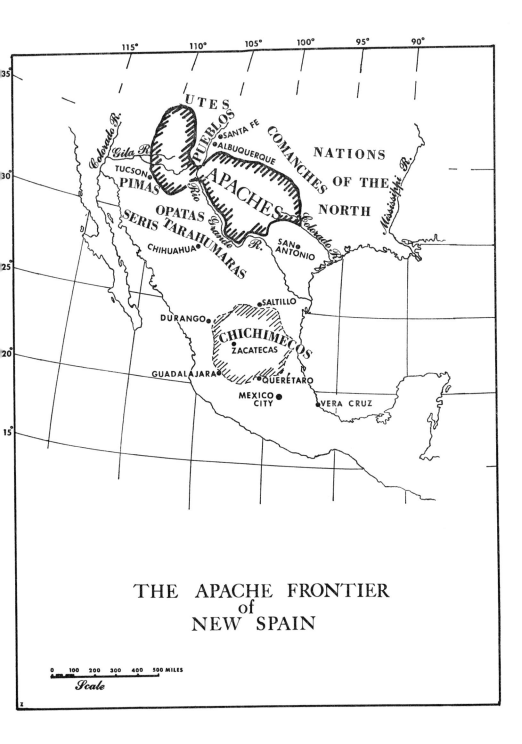

UTES

Colorado R.

Gila R.

PUEBLOS

SANTA FE

ALBUQUERQUE

COMANCHES

NATIONS

TUCSON

PIMAS

APACHES

OF THE

Rio

NORTH

OPATAS

Grande

Mississippi R.

SERIS TARAHUMARAS

R.

CHIHUAHUA

Colorado R.

SAN
ANTONIO

SALTILLO

DURANGO

CHICHIMECOS

ZACATECAS

GUADALAJARA

QUERÉTARO

MEXICO
CITY

VERA CRUZ

THE APACHE FRONTIER
of
NEW SPAIN

0   100   200   300   400   500 MILES

Scale

the Gileños, the Chiricahuas, and the Tontos or Coyoteros. To the east ranged the Faraones, the Mescaleros, the Llaneros (Natagées, Lipiyanes, and Llaneros proper), and the Lipanes. Although these tribes were alike in some of their customs, usages, and tastes, they were different in others. They spoke the same language, but their accents varied, and each employed a local terminology. All recognized a Supreme Being, or Creator, named *Yastasitasitan-ne*, but he was neither benevolent nor punitive and was therefore not worshipped. Rather, they endeavored to appease the Evil Spirit, who controlled their livelihood and destinies. Generally, however, they lived for the present with little regard for the hereafter.[1]

Physically the Apaches were endowed with exceptionally robust constitutions, seemingly insensible to the rigors of the seasons; they were as agile, nimble, and indefatigable as horses, and even superior in rugged and rocky terrain. They moved about continuously in search of new game and natural fruits for subsistence, and they abandoned their camps when these became contaminated by sickness or accumulated refuse. Extremely gluttonous when food was abundant, they were nevertheless able to withstand great hunger and thirst without losing their strength.[2]

For meat the Apaches stole Spanish horses and cattle or hunted deer, antelope, bear, wild pig, panther, and porcupine, but their common food was the prickly pear, yucca, saguaro, acorns, pine nuts, and especially mescal. The latter was the heart of such cactus as the century plant, desert spoon, soapweed, and small agave, which the Apaches baked in pits. They also reaped the seed of certain grasses and made it into a kind of grits, and with minimal effort they raised some corn, beans, squash, and tobacco.[3]

Peevish in temperament, the Apaches were astute, distrustful, inconstant, bold, proud, and especially jealous of their liberty. They usually dwelled in the most rugged and mountainous re-

[1] Daniel S. Matson and Albert H. Schroeder (eds.), "Cordero's Description of the Apache—1796," *New Mexico Historical Review*, Vol. XXXII (October, 1957), 335–56.
[2] *Ibid.*
[3] *Ibid.*

gions, where they found abundant water and wood, natural fortification, wild fruits, and nearby game. The men generally dressed in deer or antelope skins fitted around the body but not covering their arms, a bonnet of the same material sometimes adorned with feathers or horns, and high-topped moccasins. They also wore ear pendants of shell, feathers, or mouse skins, which, along with their faces, arms, and legs, they painted with chalk and red earth. The women also dressed in skins, but with a short skirt tied at the waist and loose at the knees, with a shirt drawn over the head and hanging to the waist. They wore moccasins like those of the men, but had no head covering except an animal-skin bag supporting the hair, which they tied into a bun. The women wore strings of deer and antelope hooves, shells, fish spines, and fragrant roots around their necks and arms, and the more affluent adorned their clothes and shoes with borders of porcupine quills or latten brass bells.[4]

The only duty of the men was to hunt, fight, and make such paraphernalia as was necessary for those activities. They armed themselves with lances and bows and arrows. These they preferred to firearms, although some of the Eastern Apaches carried guns. The women cared for the horses, made the utensils they needed, cured and tanned hides, carried water and firewood, collected seeds and fruits, made bread and cakes, and sowed and reaped the few crops on which they depended. They also accompanied the men on their expeditions and served as drivers of stolen livestock, as sentinels, and in other such tasks. Both men and women were esteemed in proportion to the strength they possessed to carry out their respective obligations. Many remained active far into old age. Each man had as many wives as he could support and gained prestige from the number of huts occupied by his clan. The Apaches, however, congregated in huge encampments only when hunting, or gathering in the same area, or when mobilizing for war against a common enemy.[5]

When embarking on a war party, the braves left their families

[4] *Ibid.*
[5] *Ibid.*

in a secluded camp with a small escort and set out in small groups, usually on foot, in order to avoid leaving a trail. Rendezvousing near the enemy, they would send out a few decoys to steal cattle and lure the pursuers into an ambush. When pursued in force, they fled with amazing speed, even when making off with a large number of animals. Crossing rugged mountains and waterless deserts to avoid capture, they killed what livestock impeded their escape when they were overtaken by superior forces. When their pursuers were inferior in number, they set ambushes and massacred those who fell into them. Finally, when they were beyond reach, they divided their booty, and each party returned to its own camp. Such were the Apaches as seen through Spanish eyes.[6]

Flanking and infiltrating the Gran Apachería were a number of other Indian nations, some equally nomadic and belligerent, but all as hostile to the Apaches as to the Spaniards who approached their ranges. To the southeast were the several Caddoan nations—the Taovaya, Wichita, Kichai, Iscani, Tawakoni, and others—whom the Spaniards called the Nations of the North, being north of the Texas settlements.[7] These numerous warriors stoutly resisted the encroachments on their domain of the Lipán and other Eastern Apaches, who in turn were being pushed south-

[6] *Ibid.* A military observer in 1766–68 called attention to the extreme cruelty of the Apaches, who reportedly tore off and ate the living flesh of Spaniards who fell into their hands and slashed the bodies of pregnant women, pulled out the unborn infants, and beat them to death. He also remarked on their indolence, attributing their thievery of Spanish livestock to the fact that this took less effort than hunting wild game or raising crops. According to the same observer, the Apaches habitually went about naked except for a breechclout and a bonnet trimmed with feathers or small horns, but donned leathern clothing when entering Spanish towns on peaceful missions or attending their own festivals. Nicolás de Lafora, *Relación del viaje que hizo a los presidios internos situados en la frontera de la América septentrional perteneciente al Rey de España* (ed. by Vito Alessio Robles), 83–84. For an English translation, see Lawrence Kinnaird (ed.), *The Frontiers of New Spain: Nicolás de Lafora's Description, 1766–1768,* 79–80.

[7] Herbert E. Bolton (ed.), *Athanase de Mézières and the Louisiana-Texas Frontier, 1768–1780,* I, 23–24, *et passim*; Elizabeth Ann Harper, "The Taovayas Indians in Frontier Trade and Diplomacy, 1719–1768," *Chronicles of Oklahoma,* Vol. XXXI (Autumn, 1953), 268–89.

ward from the buffalo plains by the more powerful Comanches. It was probably the contest for control of the buffalo herds that made both the Comanches and Nations of the North implacable enemies of the Eastern Apaches. Pressing from the north were also the Utes, who preyed not only on the Jicarillas in northeastern New Mexico but also on the more numerous Navahos to the west of the Río Grande.[8] The several Pueblo nations, mostly settled along the upper Río Grande, lived in fortified villages for protection against the Apaches and other enemies, although at times they carried on a peaceful commerce with these more primitive peoples. Pueblo-Apache animosity seems to have increased after the Spanish occupation of New Mexico.[9] In the west the sedentary Moqui (Hopi) and Zuñi were intermittently at war with the Apaches as were also several nations to the southwest, in Sonora, especially after they were reduced to Spanish mission life. Indeed, had it not been for the pressure from the Indian enemies of the Apaches, the Spaniards would have been overwhelmed by the Southern Athapaskan warriors.

The Spaniards who moved into this desolate and savage land were themselves a hardy breed. Although softened by the civilizing influences of Roman law, Moorish luxury, and Christian religion, they carried with them the heritage of the centuries-long reconquest of their homeland, the epochal conquest of Mexico, and a pioneering urge that was at once economic, religious, and adventurous. All within a few years a few hundred of their soldiers of fortune had overcome the mighty Aztec confederacy, humbled that magnificent civilization, and mastered the teeming thousands who occupied central and southern Mexico. But when their descendants moved northward against the far less numerous and advanced Apaches, they met a much more formidable resistance. After 200 years of bloody effort, they were still unable

[8] See Alfred B. Thomas (ed.), *After Coronado: Spanish Exploration Northeast of New Mexico, 1696–1727* and *The Plains Indians and New Mexico, 1751–1778* for a discussion of Apache-Comanche relations in this quarter.

[9] For Apache-Pueblo relations to the close of the 1600's, see the revisionist study of Jack D. Forbes, *Apache, Navaho, and Spaniard*, 24–30, *et passim*.

to crush those savage tribes. It was the old story of a technologically-advanced military power frustrated by primitive guerrilla warfare.

Hernán Cortés and his soldiers of fortune had encountered among the Aztecs a sophisticated Indian civilization concentrated in a relatively small area, tied by religious devotion to permanent temples, by economic dependence to tilled fields and established market places, and by social organization and sentimental attachment to fixed townsites. The defenders could not retreat. The invaders, moreover, had certain distinct advantages: horses for mobility; cannon for destruction; armor for personal protection; the strangeness that inspired fear; and a talent for creating confusion. But most important of all, in the seething resentment among the tributary nations of the Aztec "empire" itself, they had allies in sufficient numbers to match the massive armies of Montezuma. Dramatic and daring as it was, the conquest of Mexico followed a classical pattern. The Spaniards sowed the seeds of discontent, allied with the dissidents, spread confusion with rumor and insinuation, laid siege to the stronghold, let starvation and disease take its toll, and then closed in for the kill.[10]

In 1521 the fall of Tenochtitlán, now Mexico City, ended the resistance of the Aztec confederacy to the Spanish invasion. Within a few more years most of the outlying lands and peoples, formerly tributary to the Aztecs, were also under Spanish control. There was one great rising against the conquerors, the so-called Mixtón War, but after heavy losses to both sides, Spanish troops —supported by Aztec, Tlaxcalan, Tarascan, and other Indian allies—suppressed it ruthlessly. The Mixtón War (1541–42) is best remembered as the conflict in which the reckless Pedro de Alvarado lost his life. It is more significant, however, for the resultant enslavement of thousands of defeated Indian rebels, for the aid given them by the nomadic tribes of the north, and for the beginning of the Spanish practice of arming their native allies

[10] All the well-known histories of the Conquest—the contemporary accounts of Hernán Cortés and Bernal Díaz as well as the latter-day studies of William H. Prescott and Hubert H. Bancroft—offer abundant evidence of these decisive factors.

with European weapons.[11] The Spaniards occupied southern and central Mexico with comparative ease.

As the Spanish frontier extended northward, however, resistance stiffened. With each step northward the expanse of land broadened, and as the frontier widened the line of Spanish settlement became thinner. With each advance the climate became progressively more arid and the soil less productive. Finally, with each push northward the natives became more nomadic, and Spanish military control became correspondingly less effective. The Spaniards received a taste of what they were to find when they reached the Apache frontier as they penetrated land of the Chichimecos. For several years Spanish occupation was held back in the north, as that of the Aztecs had been in the past, by the more primitive but bellicose nomads in that quarter. The Gran Chichimeca was a hostile plateau country stretching between the eastern and western Sierra Madres, from just north of Querétaro and Guadalajara in the south to Durango and Saltillo in the north. It was inhabited by four major nations—the Pames, the Guamares, the Zacatecos, and the Guachichiles—and one-half dozen lesser ones. These hardy tribesmen had little or no farmland, no fixed abodes, and no permanent temples to defend. They could attack, retreat, regroup, and strike again as often as occasion demanded.[12]

When Spanish explorers discovered rich silver deposits in the mountains of the north, especially in the vicinity of Zacatecas, a rush of miners, ranchers, farmers, and merchants penetrated the forbidding land, and by 1550 half a century of warfare with the Chichimecos was under way. It was during this bloody conflict that the authorities of New Spain evolved a policy for dealing with the *indios bárbaros* of the north.

Relying on traditional methods, the Spaniards at first merely established military garrisons and defensive towns at strategic places, peopled by both themselves and friendly Indians; they

[11] For a detailed treatment of the causes, course, and results of the Mixtón War, consult Hubert H. Bancroft, *History of Mexico*, II, Chapter XXIV.

[12] The most authoritative treatment of the half-century of conflict between the Spaniards and the Chichimecos is Philip W. Powell, *Soldiers, Indians, and Silver: The Northward Advance of New Spain, 1550–1600*.

regulated all traffic into the hostile zone and furnished it with escorting troops; and, occasionally, they mounted retaliatory attacks against the predators in order to discourage their raids on the mines, missions, ranches, and towns. The Spaniards were aided by Otomí and other Indian allies, but when the hostile Guachichiles and Zacatecos joined forces in 1561, the Chichimecos gained the upper hand. By 1570 the viceroy at Mexico City declared a full-scale war against the predatory tribes, but the increased military effort merely incensed the nomads to further resistance and retaliation. More troops were recruited, more presidial garrisons were established, and more money was appropriated for the war effort, but the situation got even farther out of hand. Poorly paid even with double salary for combat duty, soldiers were recruited by allowing them to capture Chichimeco tribesmen and sell them into slavery. Officers entered into the sordid traffic, squandered military appropriations for personal benefit, and directed their operations toward profit rather than victory. As a result Chichimeco raids increased in intensity, reaching a climax between 1580 and 1585. By this time their inspired warriors were mounted on stolen Spanish horses. Finally, when the tide of war was turned, it was due to a shift in Spanish policy rather than to an intensification of military effort.[13]

When the Marqués de Villamanrique arrived in Mexico City as viceroy in 1580, he reappraised the deteriorating situation, consulted expert advice, and reversed the practices of the past. Striking at the heart of the problem, he prohibited further enslavement of war captives, freed or placed under religious care those already taken, and prosecuted those found guilty of engaging in that traffic. He also eliminated unauthorized expeditions into the Gran Chichimeca, required a stricter audit of military expenditures, reduced the number of garrisons and troops serving in that theater, and launched a full-scale peace offensive. He reduced the troops operating in the hostile land to thirty under a single captain, and this company was sent over the country offering aid in exchange for peace. With the inducements of food, clothing,

13 *Ibid.*

lands, religious instruction, government protection, and agricultural tools and instruction, the olive branch proved more persuasive than the sword. By 1589 hostility began to subside, and some
Chichimecos began to come in voluntarily to ask for peace. The
policy of peace by persuasion and purchase was continued under
the next viceroy, Luis de Velasco. He sent Franciscan and Jesuit
missionaries to replace troops in the field, kept an ample military
force in reserve, and spent more money on provisions for the
Chichimecos than on military effort. He also recruited some 400
families of Tlaxcalans from the south and settled them in about
eight model towns within the Gran Chichimeca. This encouraged
the predatory nomads to settle down in a similar manner and
enjoy the blessings of tranquility. Velasco's successor, the Conde
de Monterrey completed the remarkable transformation. He attracted Chichimecos to mission life and established a language
school at Zacatecas to teach the missionaries the various Chichimeco dialects and thus speed their efforts at converting them to
Christianity. By the end of the century the bloody Chichimeco
war was over. Some resistance continued in the high Sierra
Madres and in Nueva Vizcaya, but most of the vast area was now
safe for Spanish occupation.[14]

When Spanish settlements reached the Apache frontier, they
encountered a similar barrier. This time, however, there was no
economic incentive to invade the hostile domain. No fabulous
silver strikes, no farming or grazing lands lay beyond to attract
the covetous settlers. There was, of course, the long tongue of
land irrigated by the upper Río Grande and occupied by the
agrarian Pueblos, which the Spaniards occupied in 1598, but the
Apaches could pretend to nothing but a commercial interest in
that territory. Perhaps it was the Spanish occupation of the
Pueblo country that set off the Apache wars. Certainly the Spaniards diverted much of the Pueblo produce from Apache to Spanish hands and when the Apaches resorted to raiding the Pueblos,
the Spaniards joined in defending the lives and property of the
latter. Perhaps it was the slaving raids of early Spanish mining

[14] *Ibid.*

13

communities to the south that antagonized the Apaches. Regardless of whatever was the original cause, it was eventually lost to the memory of either side and the death and destruction of endless retaliation continued under its own momentum.[15] Perhaps the desultory war may have had no other fundamental cause than the mutually antagonistic cultures of sedentary and nomadic societies.

The Spaniards and their Indian vassals labored in their mines, fields, and shops to produce the essentials of their livelihood. They valued and protected property, whether in the form of land, livestock, goods, or money, the personal possession of which was sanctioned by law. The Apaches, on the other hand, valued freedom and survival above controls and aggrandizement. Theirs was a marginal economic existence, alternating between feast and famine, and if the survival of the clan, band, or tribe depended upon plundering its neighbors as well as upon hunting and gathering, necessity took precedence over property rights. They may have looked upon Spanish crops and livestock as they did natural fruits, wild deer, and buffalo. By the same token, the possessive Europeans probably felt little compassion for the plighted natives who violated their laws, no matter what need may have inspired the transgression. Whatever the origin of the conflict, it was an established fact that the aspirations of civilization and the Apache ways of life were in sharp conflict, and peaceful coexistence lay far in the future.

Unlike other Indians whom the Spaniards had encountered in their northward advance, the Apaches had almost nothing of their own that the Spaniards coveted. What the Spaniards wanted most of all was peace and security for their lives and possessions in the settlements adjacent to the Apache country. But peace was impossible without an enforceable treaty, and the Apaches had no government with which an effective treaty could be negotiated and enforced. The fragmented nature of the Apache nation reduced peace pacts to mere truces; what the Apache people held as

---

[15] Forbes, *Apache, Navaho, and Spaniard,* blames the Spaniards for the continuation of hostilities.

liberty the Spaniards considered license. And so the war went on.

If the amorphous Apache groups were lacking in central authority, the more unified Spaniards were lacking in central policy. They did have a national government in structure, but in operation it allowed for such a large measure of local autonomy that no concerted attitude or action was possible, at least until 1772. Until that year provincial governors and local garrison commanders dealt with hostiles almost independently. One governor might negotiate peace with an Apache band or tribe, grant it protection, and provide it with food and clothing. But this merely gave security to the women and children while the warriors rode off to raid in a neighboring province where no such pact was in force. And when these marauders returned, they were not only safe from pursuit and punishment, but were also free to barter their booty and ransom their captives among the obliging provincials with whom they were at peace. If they should choose to break their treaty, they were free to do so in the full knowledge that another provincial government would grant them the same protection. In a sense the Apaches held the Spanish frontiersmen in tributary vassalage, extracting from the settlers and their subject Indians a never-ending subsidy. Yet neither side was satisfied with the arrangement, and both preyed upon the other when occasion permitted. Until the Apache nation could unite under a central authority with sufficient power to bargain for and enforce a just and lasting peace, it could survive only by continuing its predatory practices. Until the Spanish frontiersmen could formulate and conform to an over-all policy for dealing with their adversary, they too would have to remain on a military footing and in a precarious existence.

The Spaniards were the first to take corrective measures. In 1724 the Marqués de Casa-Fuerte, viceroy of New Spain, dispatched a general inspector to investigate conditions in the so-called Provincias Internas del Norte, the frontier provinces of the northern interior. Then, on the basis of Brigadier Pedro de Rivera's recommendations, the Viceroy published a general order designed to place the frontier presidios—the permanent garrisons

—on a sounder military basis. Apparently Rivera's inspection coincided with a comparative lull in hostilities, for his recommendations called for the reduction rather than the expansion of the frontier army. Moreover, the Viceroy's *Reglamento de 1729* also recognized an essentially pacific situation. Or perhaps it intended to establish the same policy of peaceful persuasion that had solved the Chichimeco problem of the late 1500's. Anyway, the general order prohibited attacks on friendly, neutral, or even hostile tribes until all efforts to pacify them by persuasion had failed. It prohibited the frontier authorities from siding with one pagan nation against another unless one of the two had specifically requested such assistance. It enjoined the soldiers from creating unrest in Indian villages, exploiting them economically, or dividing the families of hostiles whom they had captured in war. Whenever enemy Indians sued for peace, moreover, the frontier authorities were required to accept the offer, but only under a signed, written agreement.[16] The *Reglamento de 1729* set a precedent for a uniform policy in the Provincias Internas, but the specific instructions were unavailing, for in the next forty years hostilities actually increased.

When the Marqués de Rubí returned from a three-year inspection of the frontier in 1768, he proposed a number of startling changes. Distinguishing between the real and imaginary territory under Spanish control, Rubí proposed a single outer line of defense to restrain the marauding invaders. He identified the Apaches as the only really implacable enemy on the entire frontier, proposed peace and an alliance against them with all non-Apache tribes, and recommended an all-out war to the extermination or exile of that nation. Only when the Provincias Internas

[16] *Reglamento para todos los presidios de las provincias internas de esta Gobernación*, reproduced in part in Vito Alessio Robles (ed.), *Diario y derrotero de lo caminado, visto, y observado en la visita que hizo a los presidios de la Nueva España Septentrional el Brigadier Pedro de Rivera.* For additional information consult Lawrence C. Wroth, "The Frontier Presidios of New Spain: Books, Papers, Maps, and a Selection of Manuscripts Relating to the Rivera Expedition of 1724–1729," *Papers of the Bibliographical Society of America*, Vol. XLV (1951), 191–218.

were entirely free of Apaches, he felt, would they be safe for Spanish civilization.[17]

It was while the Viceroy and the king were considering these sanguinary recommendations that Colonel Jacobo Ugarte y Loyola arrived in New Spain to assume the military governorship of one of the frontier provinces. Fortunately for his own more charitable inclinations, the crown decided to water down the bitter medicine that Rubí had prescribed for the northern scourge. The *Reglamento de 1772*, which superseded the ineffective policy of 1729, set down a uniform and realistic procedure. It was the most brutal Indian policy ever sanctioned by the king of Spain, but it fell short of Rubí's extreme demands. It required an active and incessant war against the declared enemy Indians, but also a more humane treatment of those captured. Generally, these were to be interned near the presidios or in the far interior, where the women and children were to be converted and educated, and all were to be provided with the same rations that were issued to the friendly Indian auxiliaries. Prisoner exchanges were to be required before hostilities would cease, and frontier military officers could grant only armistices. It was up to the viceroy to fix the conditions for a permanent peace. On the other hand, every effort was to be made to maintain good relations with neutral and peaceful nations, to persuade them to receive missionaries, and to induce them to submit to the authority of the king. Their minor transgressions were to be overlooked and their more serious ones punished with minimum force, but in no case were

[17] Digttamen que de orden del Exmo. señor Marqués de Croix, Virrey de este Reyno, expone el Mariscal de Campo Marqués de Rubí, en orden a la mejor Situazion de los Presidios para la defensa y extensión de su Frontera a la Gentilidad en los Confines al Nortte de este Virreynatto, Tacubaya, April 10, 1768, AGI, Audiencia de Guadalajara, Legajo 511 (hereinafter cited as Rubí, Dictamen, Tacubaya, April 10, 1768, AGI, Guadalajara 511). Another copy is in AGN, Ramo de Historia, Tomo LI (hereinafter cited as AGN, Historia 51). Rubí's recommendations are summarized in Kinnaird, *The Frontiers of New Spain*, 36–40; Herbert E. Bolton, *Texas in the Middle Eighteenth Century: Studies in Spanish Colonial History and Administration*, 380–82; and Carlos E. Castañeda, *The Mission Era: The Passing of the Missions, 1762–1782* (*Our Catholic Heritage in Texas, 1519–1936*, IV, ed. by Paul J. Foik), 256–58.

those arrested to be placed in servitude.[18] Ugarte arrived at his frontier command more than two years before the *Reglamento de 1772* was in force.

[18] *Reglamento e instrucción para los presidios que se han de formar en la línea de frontera de la Nueva España, resuelto por el Rey Nuestro Señor en cédula de 10 de Setiembre de 1772*, reproduced and translated from the México, 1834, printing in Sidney B. Brinckerhoff and Odie B. Faulk, *Lancers for the King: A Study of the Frontier Military System of Northern New Spain*, 11–67.

CHAPTER II

THE GOVERNOR OF COAHUILA
1769-1777

The impact of Jacobo Ugarte y Loyola on Spain's Apache policy was neither catastrophic nor dramatic. Rather, it was gradual in its development and then doggedly persistent in its application. During Ugarte's early years on the northern frontier his influence was minor. But by the time he was elevated to the office of commandant-general of the Provincias Internas, he was the most fully prepared, at least in point of previous military and administrative experience in the region, of all who had held that position. He had spent forty-five active years in the royal service, fifteen of these as provincial governor within the viceroyalty of New Spain, and thirteen of them in the northern frontier provinces. While attaining this valuable practical experience, the veteran soldier had also developed certain personal characteristics that were to set him apart from an ordinary administrator in the Spanish service. As early as his first assignment in America, as governor of Coahuila, Ugarte had begun to demonstrate an independence of judgment and an initiative in action that sometimes bordered on outright insubordination. In fact, this characteristic trait may well have been responsible for the slowness of his promotions. But whether owing to influential patrons in high places or to ultimate recognition of his ability, the promotions were always forthcoming.

Definite information on Ugarte's lineage and relationship with persons of influential office is distressingly elusive. Almost nothing of this nature appears in his service records or in other papers, which he submitted from time to time in support of his applications for advancement. Shreds of evidence in these and other documents do hint, however, that Ugarte was favored by something other than his own energies and accomplishments. It is quite possible, for instance, that his own family was of influential Basque nobility.

The heads of the Ugarte households in the province of Vizcaya were *hidalgos de sangre*, and several who bore that surname had been knighted in Spain's most exalted military orders.[1] On the maternal side, the Loyolas in the province of Guipúzcoa were even more distinguished.[2] There were many Ugartes and Loyolas, of course, but an aristocratic lineage of Jacobo is suggested by several interesting circumstances. In the first place, while it would have been a matter of course for both his parents to have been of noble descent, since intermarriage among the titled aristocracy was normal, an alliance between two commoners of noble surname would have been an unusual happenstance. In the second place, Jacobo received special dispensation for his minority when he enrolled as a cadet in the Regiment of Royal Guards,[3] a concession not unusual for the sons of nobility, but rare and without reason for those of common lineage. In the third place, while Jacobo was a mere lieutenant in the king's army, the minister of war addressed him as *don* and alluded to his "accredited ancestors."[4] Finally, Ugarte's retention of office and successive promotion in the face of his repeated provocation of immediate superiors suggests that he was protected by high-level favoritism,

[1] Ugartes were made knights in the Order of Santiago in 1525, 1638, 1653, 1671, and 1783; in the Order of Calatrava in 1566 and 1691; and in the Order of San Juan de Jerusalén in 1625. Julio de Atienza, *Nobilario español: diccionario heráldico de apellidos españoles y de títulos nobilarios,* 30, 732.

[2] Ignatius Loyola had founded the all-powerful Jesuit Society; one of his cousins, who was also a descendant of the Inca dynasty of Peru, was made Marquesa de Santiago de Oropesa in 1614; and other members of the family had been knighted in the Order of Santiago in 1651 and 1664; *ibid.,* 496.

[3] Ugarte, Escala de Ascensos, May 8, 1788 (cert. copy), AGN, PI 112, Expediente 2.

[4] Juan Gregorio Muniain, endorsement, El Palacio, December 28, 1766 (copy), AGN, PI 112, Expediente 2.

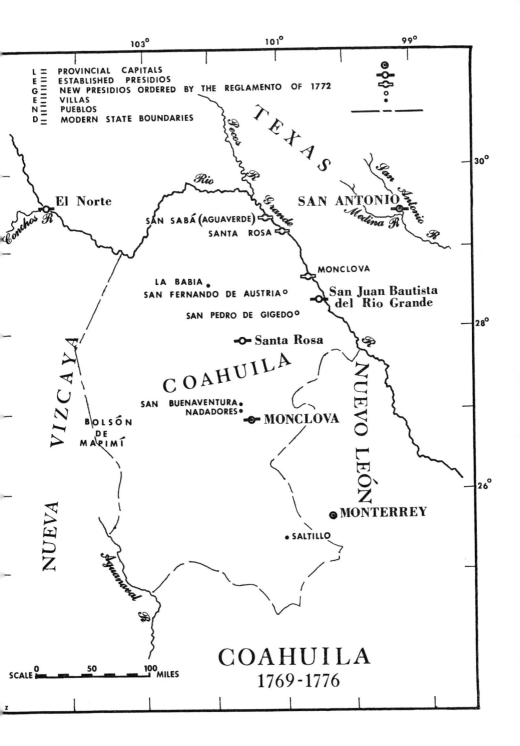

103° 101° 99°

Pecos R.

T E X A S

San Antonio

Rio

El Norte

Conchos R.

Grande

30°

SAN ANTONIO

Medina R.

SAN SABÁ (AGUAVERDE)
SANTA ROSA

MONCLOVA

San Juan Bautista
del Rio Grande

LA BABIA
SAN FERNANDO DE AUSTRIA
SAN PEDRO DE GIGEDO

28°

Santa Rosa

R.

C O A H U I L A

SAN BUENAVENTURA
NADADORES

MONCLOVA

V I Z C A Y A

N U E V O   L E Ó N

BOLSÓN
DE
MAPIMÍ

26°

N U E V A

Aguanaval R.

MONTERREY

SALTILLO

SCALE 0   50   100 MILES

COAHUILA
1769-1776

z

a condescension ordinarily accorded only members of distinguished families. Yet, if he was of noble lineage, he must certainly have been a younger son, not an heir to any privileges, for the only titles to which he himself pretended were those of his military rank.

Ugarte's service records and other available papers are studiously secretive about his age or date of birth. In all probability he was born sometime after 1717 and must have been less than fifteen years of age on April 15, 1732, for on that date he enrolled as a military cadet while still below the requisite age. He may have been even less than ten years at the time, for he remained a cadet for eight years and did not enter the regular Spanish army until 1740.[5]

Records are also silent regarding his formal education, except for what he might have received as a cadet, but they are more revealing about his military career. After five years in the regular service Ugarte volunteered and was accepted for active service in the Italian campaigns of the war of the Austrian succession. With the Spanish Regiment of Royal Guards he participated in the sieges of Casale and Milan and, on June 16, 1746, in the bloody nine-hour battle of Piacenza. Ugarte was wounded in this latter action and again two months later in another. Meanwhile, on April 7, 1746, he was promoted to the rank of ensign (*álferez*) and, on April 6 of the following year, to that of ensign of grenadiers. Other advancements followed at intervals of four and five years, and as a lieutenant of fusiliers during the Portuguese campaigns of the Seven Years War, he participated in the successful siege of Almeida, from August 15 to August 25, 1762. After the war, when popular riots broke out in the Basque province of Guipúzcoa against the high cost of bread, Lieutenant Ugarte distinguished himself by restoring order in the city of San Sebastián. The minister of war took notice of his accomplishment and recommended him for special consideration. As a reward for this serv-

[5] Ugarte, Escala de Ascensos, *loc. cit.*; Ugarte to the King, Valle de San Bartolomé, September 29, 1788, AGN, PI 77, Expediente 11.

ice, Ugarte received a skip in promotion, on January 11, 1767, to colonel of infantry and also received his first American assignment, on March 10, 1767 to the political and military governorship of the province of Coahuila.[6] Thus, after twenty-seven years in the Spanish army, Ugarte entered upon an administrative career in America, which was to last for another thirty-one years, until his death in 1798.

It is not clear just when Colonel Ugarte sailed for the New World nor when he arrived at Mexico City for his viceregal instructions. It is known, however, that after spending a considerable period of time at the capital of New Spain, he was still there on June 8, 1769. In addition to conferring at length with the viceroy, the Marqués de Croix, Ugarte had to study the voluminous reports and recommendations concerning Coahuila. From these he learned something of the several Indian tribes that had been attacking the province from three directions, of the three presidios that were attempting to defend it, and of the rosters and budgets of these garrisons. According to the reports he was poring over, Coahuila suffered more from Indian hostility than any of the other frontier territories.[7] The Marqués de Rubí had concluded his inspection of the northern frontier and submitted his general recommendations for reform during the previous spring. Whether Ugarte had any reservations or misgivings about this report at the time is not evident, but shortly after reaching his assigned office he found himself in violent disagreement with the inspector's urgings, especially as they pertained to the location of the presidios. The *Reglamento de 1772* was still being formulated, but a drastic change of one kind or another was already expected, and the new Governor of Coahuila faced something more than a routine administration. Ugarte planned to leave Mexico City in June, but he probably did not do so until October, for the trip northward ordinarily took high officials, who traveled

6 Ugarte, Escala de Ascensos, *loc. cit.*; Ugarte to the King, September 29, 1788, *loc. cit.*; Muniain, endorsement, December 28, 1766, *loc. cit.*

7 Ugarte to the Viceroy Marqués de Croix, México, June 8, 1769, AGN, PI 24, Expediente 1.

at a leisurely rate, about four months, and Ugarte arrived at his seat of government on December 5, 1769.[8]

Immediately on reaching the Villa de Monclova, Governor Ugarte was escorted to the government buildings. These he found to be in a most deplorable state of repair. Their original construction, begun in 1690 and completed in 1694, was shoddy in itself. The adobe bricks were of poor quality and without mortar; the timbers were rough and of odd sizes; and the earthen roof was leaky. Ugarte considered the buildings totally unfit either for his own repose or for the safekeeping of military supplies. Within a month of his arrival he had to throw away many items that had been damaged by rain dripping in from the roof and he was still looking for a dry place to put his bed. The rains of the two previous years had caused the roof of the storeroom to cave in, and the presidial gunpowder had been so dampened and caked that new supplies had to be borrowed from the garrison at Santa Rosa. It would cost 7,254 pesos to rebuild the dilapidated structure with adobe and another 1,788 pesos if stone were used instead. The only revenue available for repairs or reconstruction was the revenue from the local real estate tax, which amounted to only 80 pesos a year, and this had already been mortgaged far into the future by a previous governor. Ugarte, therefore, appealed to Viceroy Croix for assistance.[9]

Finding no treasury funds for the purpose, Viceroy Croix advised Ugarte to assess the householders of Monclova for the cost. Ugarte, however, felt that the residents of the town were already overburdened. If funds from the royal treasury were not supplied, he informed Croix, he would resign himself to living in the unrepaired quarters, exposed as they were to the elements.[10] Just how the Governor saw to his comfort and the preservation

[8] Ugarte to Croix, Monclova, April 17, 1770. In his letter to Viceroy Croix of January 19, 1770, Ugarte errs in recording his arrival as January the fifth of the new year instead of December the fifth of the old—AGN, PI 24, Expediente 1.

[9] Ugarte to Croix, Monclova, December 14, 1769, January 19 and February 7, 1770; certified estimate signed by Nicolás Thadeo Hernández, Joseph Manuel de la Zerda, and Juan Manuel Flores de Valdés, Monclova, April 14, 1770, AGN, PI 24, Expediente 1.

[10] Ugarte to Croix, Monclova, April 17, 1770, AGN, PI 24, Expediente 1.

of military supplies during the remaining eight years of his administration is not at all clear. The next viceroy, Antonio María de Bucareli, also refused to make treasury funds available for repairs or reconstruction, and Ugarte was still reluctant to assess the local citizenry for the costs. Finally, however, Bucareli, after hearing opinions from all quarters, ruled in October of 1776 that the citizenry of the several districts of the province should be assessed in equitable proportions and by collectors acting with the utmost prudence and gentleness.[11] Considering the deliberate pace with which such matters usually proceeded, it is doubtful that the government buildings were ever renovated before Ugarte surrendered his office in November of 1777.

It is quite possible that the dampness of Ugarte's official quarters contributed to the illness from which he suffered throughout his term. Ten months after he reached Coahuila he was complaining that he had contracted a malady which he called "flatulent hypochondria," the major symptom of which was known locally as *latido* (panting or palpitation). He had summoned a doctor, but he could offer no remedy, for there were no supplies of drugs within 400 miles.[12] After Ugarte had been in Coahuila four years he found the climate so unsuited to his nature that he petitioned the king for a new position in a more temperate region.[13] The state of his health on the eve of a major military campaign in 1773 so concerned the viceroy that he asked Ugarte for a formal statement on the subject. Ugarte replied that he was fit for a campaign at any time except winter, for he had suffered from a nervous depression during that season for the last four years. Although this affliction did not force him to bed or disturb the performance of his administrative duties, it did induce him to stay in out of the cold, and it caused him to miss attending mass several times.[14]

If Governor Ugarte's health was vulnerable to the rigors of the

---

11 Ugarte to Melchor de Peramas, Monclova, November 10, 1773; Viceroy Antonio María de Bucareli to Melchor Vidal de Lorca, México, October 23, 1776 (draft), AGN, PI 24, Expediente 3 and Expediente 4.
12 Ugarte to Croix, Monclova, October 22, 1770, AGN, PI 24, Expediente 1.
13 Ugarte to the King, Monclova, April 23, 1773, AGN, PI 24, Expediente 3.
14 Ugarte to Bucareli, Monclova, June 6, 1774, AGN, PI 24, Expediente 3.

elements, his province was even more vulnerable to the incursions of the Apaches. Coahuila embraced a vast terrain stretching from the Medina River of Texas on the northeast to the Arroyo de la Pendencia, which divided it from Nuevo León on the southeast; from the Big Bend region of the Río Grande on the northwest to the Bolsón de Mapimí on the southwest. Scattered over this immense semidesert, wherever available water permitted, was a civilized population of about 800 Spanish and mixed-blood families. These were clustered together in four chartered towns, three formal military garrisons, and sixteen rural settlements. There were also four towns of civilized Indians, mostly Tlaxcalans from central Mexico, and from six to nine missions serving the less stable Indian tribes native to the province. The major towns of Coahuila were the *villa* of Santiago de Monclova (present Ciudad Monclova), the *villa* of San Pedro de Gigedo (present Villa Unión), and the *villa* of San Fernando de Austria (present Ciudad Zaragoza). To protect the civil population and missions from marauding Apaches, there were only three garrisons during Ugarte's administration: the presidios of Monclova, San Juan Bautista del Río Grande (present Villa Guerrero), and Santa Rosa del Sacramento (present Ciudad Múzquiz).[15]

Vast stretches of arid land and protruding spurs of jagged mountains isolated the settlements, but what made the province particularly vulnerable to attack and what most frustrated military defense was the Bolsón de Mapimí. This extensive longitudinal basin on the western edge of Coahuila gave the Apaches easy access to the centers of population and a secure asylum from

[15] The rural settlements included the población of San Buenaventura; the haciendas of Castaño, Carmen, Quatro Ciénegas, Sardinas, Las Encinas, El Alamo, and La Cauciera; the *estancias* of Santa Tecla, San Pablo, San Miguel, and Santiago; and the *ranchos* of San Vicente, La Casita, El Chocolate, and San Matías. The Tlaxcalan towns were the pueblos of Nadadores and San Francisco, and those with Tlaxcalan and other Indians were in the Valle de la Candela. The *misiones* were San Miguel de Aguayo, San Bernardo, San Juan Bautista, Nombre de Jesús, San Francisco de Bizarrón, and San Josef del Carrizo. Ugarte, Estado de los presidios, villas, lugares, pueblos, misiones, haciendas, estancias, y ranchos . . . de Coahuila, Monclova, November 27, 1771, AGN, PI 24, Expediente 2. See also Lafora, *Relación del viaje*, 195–200.

pursuit by the troops. A series of almost sterile sierras bordering the great depression seemingly offered pasturage and water only for the Apaches and their mounts and allowed them to slip through its forbidding wastes and strike the interior of either Coahuila or Nueva Vizcaya without detection. Its terrain favored ambush of small patrols and wore out more horses on reconnaissances in force than the military could spare. To the north, just beyond the Río Grande, ranged the Lipán, Lipiyán, Natagée, Llanero, Faraón, and Mescalero Apaches, the most frequent intruders, but Coahuila was also invaded on occasions by the western tribes of the same nation. When the Marqués de Rubí inspected the province in the summer of 1767, he found the Apaches in comparative peace, committing only an occasional raid on livestock.[16] But in the spring of 1770 Governor Ugarte was sounding a general alarm.

Some 3,000 Apaches had been encamped for several days across the Río Grande from the presidio of San Juan Bautista, he reported, and smaller bands were making repeated incursions along the entire northern frontier of the province. The troops of the three presidios, 115 in number, were maintaining a continuous operation against them, but they were unable to check the raids. The settlers therefore had to protect their own lives and property. Being few in number, poor, and, above all, unarmed, they petitioned the Governor for weapons, and Ugarte asked the viceroy for 300 muskets with corresponding powder and ball for their use.[17] The situation got worse, however, before the firearms arrived. Within a year the terrorized settlers were beginning to flee the province. In July, 1771, the emboldened Apaches attacked the presidio of Santa Rosa at high noon while the Governor himself was there. They killed 1 soldier, wounded 3 others, and made off with over 600 horses. Ugarte mobilized 54 troops from two presidios, and these pursued the raiders for more than 180

---

16 Lafora, *Relación del viaje*, 197. For a detailed description of the Bolsón de Mapimí, see Vito Alessio Robles, *Coahuila y Texas en la época colonial*, 559–68.
17 Ugarte to Croix, Monclova, April 17, 1770, AGN, PI 24, Expediente 2.

miles, but they eventually wore out their horses and had to return. Again Ugarte urged the viceroy to send the additional muskets and ammunition.[18]

By November the arms for civil defense had still not arrived. Ugarte now appealed to Bucareli, the new viceroy, asking not only for 300 muskets, but also for the same number of swords. The inhabitants, he warned, were in great consternation. At one ranch the Apaches had killed twelve men and women and had carried away more than ten children as well as a large number of horses. No troops were available to pursue the offenders. Ugarte did send a number of poorly-armed civilians and Tlaxcalan auxiliaries, but these arrived too late to retaliate. During the same month 700 hostiles were reportedly gathering to attack the presidio of Santa Rosa and its environs.[19]

By April of 1772 Ugarte had identified the hostiles as Lipán Apaches and had decided to mount a full campaign against them. Viceroy Bucareli applauded the idea, but required the Governor to await further advice. He had just appointed Lieutenant Colonel Hugo O'Conor as commandant-inspector with orders to coordinate military operations along the entire frontier of the northern provinces, and Ugarte's proposed campaign would have to be approved by this officer. Bucareli had finally called for the delivery of the muskets for civil defense, but he had ordered only 200 of these and no swords. Worse, the red tape and officiousness of the royal armory staff was such that four months later the muskets had still not arrived.[20] The arms seem finally to have been delivered in February of 1773, almost three years after Ugarte had requested them, for the Governor was then complaining that the citizenry was too impoverished to pay for them. Bucareli insisted that the full cost be collected so as not to embarrass the royal treasury, but, as in the case of the assessments for repairing

---

[18] Ugarte to Croix, Santa Rosa, June 8 and July 21, 1771, AGN, PI 24, Expediente 2.

[19] Ugarte to Bucareli, Coahuila, November 4, and Monclova, November 27, 1771, AGN, PI 24, Expediente 2.

[20] Bucareli to Ugarte, México, June 16 (draft), and Ugarte to Bucareli, Monclova, October 25, 1772, AGN, PI 24, Expediente 2.

the government buildings, he recommended that the money be raised by gentle and delicate measures. Ugarte apparently never collected the full amount due, for nine years later the treasury still noted a shortage of 2,225 pesos in this account. In failing to tax the citizenry sufficiently, Ugarte had to assume the deficit personally.[21]

In their raids on Coahuila the Apaches were aided and abetted not only by the confounding topography, inadequate troops, dispersed settlements, and official red tape, but also by disloyal Indians in some of the missions. The Julimeños, especially in the mission of San Francisco Bizarrón, could no longer be trusted as guides and scouts. Reportedly they were informing the Apaches of troop movements, collaborating with them in some of their raids, and even slipping away from the missions to commit robberies and attacks on their own. Ugarte could recommend no remedy to this problem but removing them to the interior where, far from contact with the barbarous Apaches, they might be subjected to a peaceful and law-abiding life.[22] The Julimeños, Ugarte reported, were causing even more damage than the Apaches, but it was impossible to prove their guilt except on circumstantial evidence. They were known to be in possession of stolen goods, but the worst of their alleged crimes was the bad example they set for other friendly Indians by engaging in scalp dances and other acts of idolatry.[23]

Before Viceroy Croix would consider removing the Julimeños to the interior, he required Ugarte to draw up a full report on them, documented with testimony from the missionaries themselves. Ugarte felt that such information would be prejudiced in favor of the converts, but he collected the testimony and submitted the report anyway. The evidence against the Julimeños that Ugarte amassed was drawn largely from the historical past rather than the present, but he nevertheless recommended that

21 Bucareli to Ugarte, México, March 9, 1773, and Viceroy Martín de Mayorga to the Caballero de Croix, México, September 6, 1782 (drafts), AGN, PI 24, Expediente 3 and PI 79, Expediente 6.
22 Ugarte to Croix, Monclova, December 31, 1769, AGN, PI 24, Expediente 1.
23 Ugarte to Croix, Monclova, January 19, 1770, AGN, PI 24, Expediente 1.

they be shipped to the government's factories at Havana as a "pious punishment" for their "enormous guilt."[24] When Croix failed to take such drastic action, Ugarte made the same recommendation to the next viceroy, and as late as 1776 he was still complaining of Julimeño complicity in Apache raids and atrocities of their own.[25]

On November 4, 1771, Ugarte's alarming report of Apache invasions was accompanied by an urgent appeal for more troops. Bucareli was not impressed. In passing along the request to the minister of the Indies, the Viceroy noted cynically that "the maxim of the captains of presidios is to increase the number of men in their garrisons" and that "their respective allotments always seem small."[26] The presidio of Monclova had 33 soldiers, 1 sergeant, and 1 lieutenant—all directly under the command of the governor, who served as its captain. The companies of Santa Rosa and San Juan Bautista, each with 48 soldiers, one chaplain, and 3 officers, had their own captains. Although subordinate to the governor, their two captains exercised personal management over these troops and their ratings, salaries, equipment, and provisions.[27] Thus, the province could theoretically rely on 137 officers and men, but at times there were as few as 115.

Such a thin line of troops could never hold back the Apache tide, least of all when morale was low, and in the face of shameful exploitation by the presidial captains, little *esprit de corps* could be expected. Before 1772 frontier soldiers were paid from 380 to 420 pesos a year, had to buy much of their own military equipment, and obtained food, clothing, and other provisions for themselves and their families on credit from a company store operated by their captain. The captain jealously protected his

[24] Ugarte to Croix, Monclova, April 17, 1770, with enclosures, AGN, PI 24, Expediente 2.

[25] Ugarte to Bucareli, Coahuila, November 4, 1771, and August 14, 1776, AGN, PI 24, Expediente 2 and Expediente 4.

[26] Bucareli to Julián de Arriaga, México, November 26, 1771, in Rómulo Velasco Ceballos (ed.), *La administración de D. Frey Antonio María de Bucareli y Ursúa, cuadragesima sexto virrey de México,* I, 14–15.

[27] Ugarte to Croix, México, June 8, 1769, AGN, PI 24, Expediente 1; Lafora, *Relación del viaje,* 178–79, 182, 237.

monopoly by preventing private merchants from entering the presidios as competitors, and, as it worked out, the enlisted men, charging purchases against their annual salaries and exhausting their credit before the end of each year, received no money at all and actually went into debt. In effect the troops were paid in goods instead of cash. The practice not only demoralized the troops, but also the military service itself, for the captains, fearing the loss of what was owed them, were reluctant to commit their troops to hazardous engagements with hostile Indians. Herein lay a major cause of the ineffectiveness of the presidial defensive force. The situation also discouraged civilian migration to the frontier, for the troop subsidy, which was paid in coin, was collected only by the commercially-involved captains, and since they made their purchases in the interior, this money did not circulate in the frontier communities where it could have primed the local economy.[28]

An attempt to reform the corrupt practices in presidial administration was made while Ugarte was governing Coahuila, but the *Reglamento de 1772* also reduced the pay of the soldiers to a mere 300 pesos a year. The new regulation did require the election of a member of each company as an *habilitado,* or paymaster, who would replace the captain as provisioner and bookkeeper, and this representative was encharged with selling goods at cost and keeping an open accounting of all transactions. Under this arrangement the common soldier usually came out with a balance from his annual salary of from 30 to 100 pesos.[29]

As captain of the presidio of Monclova, Governor Ugarte justified the previous abusive practices before they were reformed. Since the royal treasury was almost as stingy in paying the officers as the enlisted men, he felt that a captain should be allowed some personal profit from the supply service, especially since the king himself, in a decree of July 30, 1731, had sanctioned the practice.

[28] Enrique González Flores and Francisco R. Almada (eds.), *Informe de Hugo O'Conor sobre el estado de las Provincias Internas del Norte, 1771–1776,* 73–76.
[29] *Ibid.*; Reglamento e instrucción . . . de 10 de Setiembre de 1772, Título XIV, reproduced in Brinckerhoff and Faulk, *Lancers for the King,* 44–48.

This royal dispensation had noted the low salary of captains and recognized the necessity for providing them with additional compensation even though it placed reasonable limits on profiteering by establishing an official maximum-price list at each presidio. Ugarte also took note of the losses that the captains sometimes suffered from excessive freight rates, taxes, breakage, and occasionally from having to sell the commodities at less than cost.[30] The peculiar perquisite of the captains was not merely a matter of pecuniary concern, he insisted, but one of honor and justice as well. He referred to the case of the captain of the presidio of San Juan Bautista who died in 1772 leaving a debt to the mission fathers and to a purchasing agent, which amounted to from 7,000 to 8,000 pesos for money he had borrowed to purchase provisions for his troops. Since most of the goods he had purchased were now consumed and could therefore not be attached to cover the debt, the little that the captain's widow owned was all that could cover the amount due. Since she had children to support and would have been left "absolutely in the street," Ugarte requested that the viceroy apply a portion of the troop pay for that year to cover the debt she had inherited.[31] Some of Ugarte's concern for the welfare of the captains was purely selfish, however, for while the provisioning of the troops remained in the hands of that officer, he tried to acquire the captaincy of the presidio of Santa Rosa and benefit from it as well as from that of Monclova, which he already held. Three times he petitioned for this sinecure —in 1769, 1770, and 1771—but after the *Reglamento de 1772* deprived the captains of their profitable enterprise, he gave up the attempt. Moreover, after the reform was adopted, Ugarte complained that together with his low salary and large expenses it was causing him to go farther and farther into debt.[32]

On the other hand, Ugarte was not completely unmindful of

[30] Ugarte to Croix, Monclova, February 7, 1770, AGN, PI 24, Expediente 1.
[31] Ugarte to Bucareli, Monclova, February 16, 1772, AGN, PI 24, Expediente 2.
[32] Ugarte to Croix, México, June 8, 1769, Monclova, October 22, 1770, and Monclova, November 4, 1771, and to Bucareli, Monclova, November 29, 1774, AGN, PI 24, Expediente 1, Expediente 2, and Expediente 3.

the misery of the enlisted men. When the local priest, from whom the soldiers had borrowed heavily to make ends meet, presented them with the bill and demanded payment in cash, Ugarte insisted that he accept goods instead. In justifying his position, he pointed out that the soldiers had actually been paid for their services in goods instead of cash, that they were excessively burdened by the cost of baptizing, marrying, and burying their children, and that they very rarely escaped falling into debt to the parish priest.[33] Likewise, when the viceroy insisted that soldiers as well as civilian householders be assessed for the repair or reconstruction of the government buildings at Monclova, Ugarte complained that the frontier soldier not only had to feed and clothe himself and his family from his meager pay, but also had to provide at his own expense his horses, weapons, and other military equipment, and to maintain them in readiness at all times for sorties and campaigns.[34]

The *Reglamento de 1772* not only reformed the internal administration of the frontier garrisons, but also ordered their realignment to form a defensive cordon along the northern limits of the provinces in keeping with Rubí's recommendations of 1768. The viceroy's council that drew up the new regulation also raised an armed force of 300 men to operate on the border of Coahuila's neighboring province, Nueva Vizcaya, created the office of commandant-inspector to co-ordinate military operations along the entire northern frontier, and vested this authority in Lieutenant Colonel Hugo O'Conor, who relieved the *Comandante de Armas* Bernardo de Gálvez. O'Conor was given the additional responsibility of putting into effect the changes ordered by the *Reglamento de 1772*.[35] In Coahuila the presidios of Santa Rosa and Monclova were to be moved to positions on the Río Grande, downstream from San Juan Bautista, which was already on that river. A fourth presidio, Aguaverde, had been recently established at San Fernando de Austria with a garrison, which had been orig-

[33] Ugarte to Croix, Monclova, February 7, 1770, *loc. cit.*
[34] Ugarte to Croix, Monclova, April 17, 1770, *loc. cit.*
[35] Bucareli to Ugarte, México, April 15, 1772 (draft), AGN, PI 24, Expediente 2; Bernard E. Bobb, *The Viceregency of Antonio María Bucareli in New Spain, 1771–1779*, 133–34.

inally stationed at San Sabá, in Texas, and this was also to be moved northward to the Río Grande. Bucareli's council provided each presidial captain with 3,000 pesos to cover the expense of transferring his company and building a fort at its new station. The Governor was ordered to supply the new Commandant-Inspector with whatever he requested to effect the removal of the presidios.[36]

From Ugarte's correspondence there appears little doubt that he, a full colonel, was miffed at being subjected to the orders of a mere lieutenant colonel (and an Irishman at that!), but his subsequent reluctance in complying with O'Conor's orders and with the articles of the *Reglamento de 1772* stemmed from his own practical knowledge and superior sense of defensive strategy as well as from his hurt pride. Ugarte's obdurate opinions, although condemned by Bucareli, were supported at the time by most of the presidio captains, by O'Conor's successor of superior rank (Commandant-General Teodoro de Croix), and eventually by the former *Comandante de Armas* Bernardo de Gálvez when he became viceroy of New Spain.

As an argument for keeping the presidios situated near the population centers instead of removing them northward to an outer line of defense, Ugarte called attention to the widespread depredations of the Apaches in Coahuila. In May of 1772 he reported that more than 300 Lipán Apaches had suddenly attacked the haciendas of Sardinas, Posuelos, and San Miguel, the *ranchos* of Los Menchacas and Santa Gertrudis, and the pueblos of Nadadores and San Buenaventura. These raids, spread over more than 200 miles of terrain and perpetrated in the short span of less than two hours, had taken the lives of twenty-three persons, and the hostiles had also carried off twenty-two men, women, and children together with 954 horses and mules. The damage would have been worse, Ugarte insisted, if he had not arrived from Monclova with troops as soon as he did. He argued

[36] Bucareli to Ugarte, México, April 15, 1772, *loc. cit.;* "Instrucción para la nueva colocación de presidios," Paragraphs 14–18, Reglamento e instrucción . . . de 10 de Setiembre de 1772, in Brinckeroff and Faulk, *Lancers for the King,* 56–58.

that if the presidios should be removed to the Río Grande the citizens would then be left with even less protection, for the Apaches found no difficulty in fording the river and hiding in the interior sierras to avoid detection. In their present position the presidios could protect the settlements more effectively, at less risk to the inhabitants, at greater savings to the royal treasury, and with less frustration to the spiritual conversion of the peaceful Indians. Bucareli, however, found these arguments much less convincing than Rubí's recommendations of 1768, and so he ordered O'Conor to proceed with the removals.[37]

In his response to Ugarte, Bucareli defended Rubí's *dictamen*, the reports on which it was based, the *Reglamento de 1772*, and the decisions of his own council. He then reminded the Governor that it was not within his province to oppose the new alignment of presidios, but only to aid O'Conor in establishing it.[38] Not the least chastened, Ugarte continued to remonstrate against the removal of the garrisons, and it was necessary for the Viceroy to admonish him to confine his opposition to the hostile tribes, which were invading Coahuila, and to cease questioning superior orders.[39]

Ugarte did bow to the Viceroy's requirements. He agreed to suspend his own proposed campaign against the Apaches, subject himself to the orders of the Commandant-Inspector, and co-ordinate his operations with those of his new superior.[40]

[37] Bucareli to Arriaga, México, June 26, 1772, with attached summaries of provincial reports, in Velasco Ceballos, *La administración de Bucareli*, I, 52–59. Ugarte's objections to the proposed relocation of the presidios appears to have been based, in part at least, on an extensive survey made in 1748 by Captain Joseph de Berroterán, an officer of considerable experience and knowledge, who had reported to the viceroy that the Río Grande was an indefensible frontier, that even if presidios were established along its banks every thirty miles the hostile tribes could still cross the river and invade the settled region to the south, and that the sterility of the soil along the river would not support crops to sustain the troops or pasturage for the horses. Alfred B. Thomas (trans. and ed.), *Teodoro de Croix and the Northern Frontier of New Spain, 1776–1783*, 23–24.
[38] Bucareli to Ugarte, México, July 1, 1772 (draft), AGN, PI 24, Expediente 2.
[39] Bucareli to Ugarte, México, September 15, 1772 (draft), AGN, PI 24, Expediente 2.
[40] Ugarte to Bucareli, Monclova, July 11, 1772, AGN, PI 24, Expediente 2.

O'Conor had organized a large-scale campaign against the Apaches, and to this effort Ugarte dutifully contributed seventy officers and men from the presidios of Monclova, Santa Rosa, and San Juan Bautista, all equipped with munitions of war and provisions for more than three months. The campaign was to be launched on November 20, 1772.[41]

O'Conor's campaign of 1772–73 was directed against the invading Mescalero Apaches, who were hiding out in the desolate Bolsón de Mapimí. It was successful in dislodging them from this basin, in driving them northward, and in achieving even more notable results in neighboring Nueva Vizcaya.[42] While it was in progress, however, Ugarte continued to resent his subjection to O'Conor, who had now been promoted to full colonel, and to his allegedly unwise decisions. Although unimpressed by the Governor's pretensions, Bucareli remained remarkably patient. Reminding Ugarte of his three admonitions to comply with O'Conor's orders, the Viceroy now appealed to pure reason. The royal service could never be improved if such jealousies and representations continued, he explained, and it would be most reprehensible if the other captains in Coahuila followed Ugarte's example of insubordination. This spirit of discordance could bring funestral results, and Bucareli hoped that he would not have to remind Ugarte of his obligations again. Finally, in October of 1773, the Governor announced that he would comply fully with the Viceroy's instructions and would order his captains to do likewise.[43] By June of 1774 Ugarte seems to have reconciled himself to his new subordinate position. He even made a special trip to meet the Commandant-Inspector at one of the new presidio sites, and he came away ostensibly in accord with O'Conor's plans.[44]

[41] Ugarte to Bucareli, Monclova, December 11, 1772, AGN, PI 24, Expediente 2.
[42] Alfred B. Thomas (ed.), *Forgotten Frontiers: A Study of the Spanish Indian Policy of Don Juan Bautista de Anza, Governor of New Mexico, 1777–1787*, 6.
[43] Ugarte to Bucareli, Monclova, April 23 and October 4, and Bucareli to Ugarte, México, September 28, 1773 (draft), AGN, PI 24, Expediente 3.
[44] Ugarte to Bucareli, Monclova, June 6, 1774, AGN, PI 24, Expediente 3.

All did not go well, however, for Bucareli was complaining in October of 1774 that even though construction of the new presidios in Coahuila had started six months before those of Nueva Vizcaya, the work was almost finished in the latter while it was far behind schedule in Coahuila. The Viceroy was disgusted with the delay and urged Ugarte to get on with the program. The delay, Ugarte explained, was due to the fact that the new forts for Monclova and Aguaverde (San Sabá) were being built of masonry rather than adobe, which took more time; that there was a scarcity of laborers in Coahuila; and that a water shortage had caused a three-month stoppage of work at the new site for Monclova. The walls were now being finished with adobe brick so as to speed up construction, and Ugarte could point with pride to the fact that the new *villa* of San Carlos, in the Valley of La Candela, was being established, as required by the *Reglamento de 1772*, and that the new *villa* of San Antonio de Bucareli would be finished in another four months. He thought it might be difficult to find settlers for the latter town, however, for people were fearful of moving to Coahuila.[45]

By the spring of 1775, O'Conor had progressed sufficiently with the rebuilding of frontier defenses along the new line to plan a new and more comprehensive offensive against the Apaches. The Commandant-Inspector's original plan to mobilize 2,000 troops from the several frontier provinces had to be scaled down, however, for New Mexico had lost too many horses to hostiles to equip its complement of troops and the Viceroy had ruled out the use of regulars from Sonora since these were needed for a colonizing expedition to Upper California. For his part Ugarte was to prepare for the campaign 325 men from his three presidios, a company of Spanish regulars now supplied by O'Conor, several armed settlers, and Indian auxiliaries. With this force Ugarte was to march northward beyond the Río Grande to the former site of the presidio of San Sabá, veer westward to the Pecos River, join forces with the company of San Juan Bautista,

---

[45] Bucareli to Ugarte, México, October 19 (draft), and Ugarte to Bucareli, Monclova, December 14, 1774, AGN, PI 24, Expediente 3.

and then continue up the Pecos. His forces were to drive the Apaches westward where the troops from the presidio of El Norte, in Nueva Vizcaya, would attack them in the mountains of the Big Bend country.[46] Thus, the Governor's main purpose was merely to penetrate the Apache lands north of the Río Grande and either drive or frighten the Apaches westward, where it was hoped they would be annihilated by other forces.

The grand campaign was launched in September and concluded in December. With the militia of Sonora deployed to receive the fleeing enemy in the mountains along the Gila River of southwestern New Mexico, and with the troops of New Mexico preventing them from escaping to the north, O'Conor, with the main force from Nueva Vizcaya, managed to drive the Apaches into the western trap. In a series of encounters his forces killed 138 warriors, captured 104 other Apaches, and recovered 1,966 animals.[47]

Ugarte's contribution to the combined operation was more strategic than tactical. With eighty-nine presidial troops, fifty-four militia, sixteen Tlaxcalan auxiliaries, and twenty-nine unarmed men, Ugarte began his march up the Río Grande from San Juan Bautista on September 22, 1775. Ten days later, about seventy miles upstream, an Apache chieftain with two warriors approached his camp, but he turned out to be Cabello Largo, the principal chief of the Lipanes, with whom O'Conor had solidified a peace the year before and to whom Bucareli had sent the title of "General of the Lipán Apaches."[48] Assured that the troops were not marching against his people, Cabello Largo and his two braves slept in the camp that night and sent for other Lipán chiefs—Poca Ropa, Boca Tuerta, El Cielo, El Flaco, Panocha, Rivera, Javielillo, Pajarito, and Manteca Mucha—who arrived for a visit the next day. On October 6 the march was resumed, and on passing the main camp of the Lipanes, Cabello Largo supplied Ugarte with two braves to serve as guides. The only

[46] Thomas, *Forgotten Frontiers*, 10–11.
[47] *Ibid.*
[48] Bucareli to Arriaga, México, September 26, 1774, in Velasco Ceballos, *La administración de Bucareli*, I, 178–81.

other Indians encountered on the march were hostiles. Reconnoitering the upper reaches of the San Pedro, a tributary of the Pecos, the troops sighted Indians on December 22. Ugarte sent a lieutenant with fifty men who caught up with about the same number of warriors, but they managed to kill only three and wound another three before dispersing them. In the brief encounter two militiamen were killed, one mortally wounded, and another soldier was less seriously injured.

Except for eliminating three Apache warriors, inducing the other hostiles to flee westward, and reconnoitering a large amount of territory along the Pecos River, Ugarte had nothing to show for the march by 188 men of approximately 740 miles during a period of three and one-half months.[49] One of his detachments covered another 460 miles in reconnoitering the Guadalupe Mountains in western Texas and eastern New Mexico, and another, scouting the upper reaches of the San Pedro, marched almost 300 miles. The expedition, therefore, covered almost 1,500 miles in all.[50]

Ugarte's troops returned to their presidios in January of 1776 with their horses exhausted, and in February a caustic letter arrived from the Viceroy. Over four months had passed since Ugarte had begun his march, and neither Bucareli nor O'Conor had received a report on his operations.[51] This, Ugarte felt, was easily explained. As far as he was concerned, his campaign had not ended until he returned to the presidio of Santa Rosa on January 21. Ten days later he had sent the Commandant-Inspector his report and diary by regular patrol riders, and if these had not reached O'Conor, he felt that he was not to blame. Further, he saw no reason to report separately to the Viceroy, since this

[49] Ugarte, Diario de lo executado por el Destacamento mandado del Governador de la Provincia de Coahuila, Monclova, January 14, 1776, AGN, PI 24, Expediente 4.

[50] See the diaries of Vicente Rodríguez, captain of the presidio of San Juan Bautista, November 1, 1775–December 2, 1776, and Alexo de la Garza Falcón, Ensign of the Presidio of San Sabá, December 26, 1775–January 9, 1776, AGN, PI 24, Expediente 4.

[51] Bucareli to Ugarte, México, February 28, 1776 (draft), AGN, PI 24, Expediente 4.

was O'Conor's function as the superior officer. He did admit to the meager results of his campaign, but this also was easily explained. The Indians of the mission of Carrizo, who maintained trade and communication with the Apaches, had reported the departure of his troops and thus forewarned the enemy. This was why he was unable to overtake and inflict significant losses on them. He had, however, fulfilled the essential requirements of his mission by causing the hostilities to move westward toward O'Conor's prearranged trap.[52]

Captain Rafael Martínez Pacheco, commandant of the new presidio of La Babia and leader of a separate operation with the remaining troops of Coahuila, had already reported to the Viceroy, and some of his remarks were highly critical of Colonel Ugarte's disappointing accomplishments. This caused Bucareli to require O'Conor to reprimand Pacheco for his disrespect toward a superior officer, but also to ask the Commandant-Inspector for a high-level appraisal of Ugarte's operations. Without affirming or denying the miscarriage of Ugarte's campaign, O'Conor eulogized the Governor in a letter of April 5 and explained that he had conducted his operation with the honor for which he was noted and with the most ardent desire to achieve the ends intended. Bucareli forwarded this information to Spain so as to set the record straight and avoid any prejudice against Ugarte that the king might have received from the preliminary reports.[53]

Actually, all hostile Apaches on Coahuila's frontier were not driven into the western trap laid by the Sonora forces. Some seem to have eluded Ugarte's army and hidden out in the mountains north of the Río Grande, for their raids into Coahuila were resumed shortly after the troops returned from the campaign. In scattered forays during the first six months of 1776, the enemy Apaches killed twelve persons, captured three children, and ran off several herds of horses, mules, and cattle.[54] In July they at-

[52] Ugarte to Bucareli, Santa Rosa, April 6, 1776, AGN, PI 24, Expediente 4.
[53] Bucareli to Minister of the Indies Marqués de Sonora (José de Gálvez), No. 2294, México, May 27, 1776, AGI, Guadalajara 515.
[54] Ugarte to Bucareli, Santa Rosa, July 9, 1776, AGN, PI 24, Expediente 4.

tacked the mule trains carrying supplies to two presidios. Some of these raids, however, seem to have been made by the Lipanes, with whom O'Conor had made peace in 1774, for Ugarte reported that this tribe had again offered to make peace in July of 1776. One of the Lipán chiefs, Poca Ropa, who disclaimed any guilt of his people for the recent marauding, had offered to permit the Spaniards to inspect the tribal horse herds, but Ugarte still felt certain that the Apaches who had attacked the presidial supply trains were Lipanes and that they could easily have concealed the stolen animals.[55] Hostile incursions continued throughout the year and the number of settlers and livestock in Coahuila dwindled steadily. The toll for October was seven persons killed, three wounded, two children captured, and more livestock run off. In December three more people were killed and several animals were stolen. The nerves of the settlers were wearing thin.[56]

Commandant-Inspector O'Conor directed another major campaign against the Apaches in 1776. This time he sent them scurrying to cover in the Guadalupe and Sierra Blanca Mountains and along the Colorado River of Texas, but the *coup de grace* was administered from the north by the Comanches. These powerful and traditional enemies of the Apaches found three hundred families butchering the buffalo they had slain in a recent hunt and killed them all.[57]

Meanwhile Governor Ugarte's five-year term had drawn to a close, and while awaiting his successor, he was looking to his own future. He had never relished his assignment in Coahuila, for neither the climate nor the pay was suitable. As early as November of 1771 he had asked the Viceroy to intercede with the king for an appointment to the vacant presidency at Guadalajara of the audiencia of Nueva Galicia, and in April of 1773 he had appealed directly to the king for either that appointment or the soon-to-be-vacated governorship of Nueva Vizcaya. Recount-

55 Ugarte to Bucareli, Coahuila, August 14, 1776, AGN, PI 24, Expediente 4.
56 Ugarte to Bucareli, Monclova, November 7, 1776, and January 16, 1777 (copies), AGN, PI 24, Expediente 4.
57 Thomas, *Forgotten Frontiers*, 63–64, citing O'Conor to Bucareli, Carrizal, December 20, 1776.

ing his own military service since 1732, he called attention to the debts he had contracted in order to reach America and take over the command in Coahuila. He had not taken advantage of his position to satisfy his creditors at the expense of the citizenry, he professed, but was counting instead on the increased income that would accompany a higher office.[58] By December of 1773 he had declared himself bankrupt. The royal treasury was charging him personally for the firearms he had distributed to the settlers for their protection against the Apaches, since he had refused to assess them for the cost, and he was unable to cover the amount himself. He had gone farther into debt for other services to the province, which he had not reported, and he still owed for his expensive trip from Spain. Only another, more remunerative office would permit him to emerge from his burdensome financial obligations.[59] It was even more difficult for him to satisfy his creditors now that he, along with other presidio captains, had been denied the profitable perquisite of provisioning the troops, and especially since his salary was less than that of other governors of the frontier provinces. The governors of Texas and New Mexico each received 4,000 pesos a year, while his salary was only 3,000 pesos. In June and again in November of 1774 he appealed to the Viceroy for an equitable adjustment. In February of 1775 he pleaded with Bucareli once more, this time complaining that his needs were becoming daily more urgent.[60] Finally, in July of 1775 the Viceroy informed him that the treasury officers of the audiencia had agreed to raise his salary to the standard 4,000 pesos and that this decision had been sent to the king for his approval.[61]

Bucareli had reported to the king's minister in January of 1775 that Ugarte had completed his five-year term and that even

[58] Ugarte to Bucareli, Coahuila, November 4, 1771, and to the King, Monclova, April 23, 1773, AGN, PI 24, Expediente 2 and Expediente 3.
[59] Ugarte to Bucareli, Monclova, December 31, 1773, AGN, PI 24, Expediente 3.
[60] Ugarte to Bucareli, Monclova, November 29, 1774, and February 21, 1775, AGN, PI 24, Expediente 3.
[61] Bucareli to Ugarte, México, July 26, 1775 (draft), AGN, PI 24, Expediente 4.

though he considered him qualified by merit and fitness for the office, he thought it best to remove him to another position. According to Bucareli, Ugarte had embarrassed the Commandant-Inspector's administration, had done little to advance the removal of presidial companies and construction of new forts in spite of repeated viceregal admonitions, and had been reluctant to subject himself to O'Conor's orders in this matter. The governor of Texas, Baron de Ripperdá, was guilty of the same insubordination.[62] Four months later, when Bucareli received O'Conor's favorable report on Ugarte's performance in the campaign of 1775–76, he had to tone down his criticism of the Governor so as not to prejudice his appointment elsewhere, but he still wanted him replaced by someone who would carry out the Commandant-Inspector's orders.[63]

In August of 1776, when Ugarte acknowledged word from the Viceroy that his successor had been named, he intimated that certain persons were about to cast suspicions on his administration in Coahuila. He wanted to come to Mexico City and bring with him documents, which would refute all such charges. Bucareli, however, assured the Governor of his own high opinion of him and instructed him to remain at his post until his successor arrived.[64]

The new governor did not reach Coahuila until late the following year. Then, on November 23, 1777, Ugarte surrendered his office to Colonel Juan de Ugalde.[65] There is no apparent basis for the assertion of one scholar that the rancor that eventually developed between Ugarte and Ugalde stemmed from the former's jealousy over being replaced by the latter.[66] Ugarte had asked three times for another assignment. Although the two were

[62] Bucareli to Arriaga, México, January 27, 1775, No. 1697, AGI, Guadalajara 301.

[63] Bucareli to the Marqués de Sonora, No. 2294, May 27, 1776, *loc. cit.*

[64] Ugarte to Bucareli, Coahuila, August 23, and Bucareli to Ugarte, México, September 11, 1776 (draft), AGN, PI 24, Expediente 4.

[65] Alessio Robles, *Coahuila y Texas en la época colonial*, II, 436.

[66] For this contention, see Al B. Nelson, "Juan de Ugalde and the Rio Grande Frontier, 1777–1790" (unpublished Ph.D. dissertation, University of California, 1936), 42.

bitter rivals in later years, the jealousies and antagonisms developed from other and subsequent circumstances.

In evaluating Ugarte's administration in Coahuila even the most partial biographer would be hard pressed to find it eminently successful. The records themselves indicate that the Apache menace was not seriously reduced at the end of his five years, and he himself admitted in 1777 that the only solution to the problem would be to round up the entire Lipán tribe, which had repeatedly violated its peace treaty, and ship it overseas.[67] In comparison with the subsequent aggressive campaigns of Governor Ugalde, Ugarte's military operations against the hostiles amounted to little more than patrol activity and small-scale pursuit of localized raiding parties. Except for the expedition up the Pecos River in support of O'Conor's campaign of 1775-76, he seems to have spent very little time in the saddle himself. He did, however, manage to put firearms in the hands of the civilian settlers so that they could better defend themselves and even spared them the normal tax to cover the cost. He had defended the troops against the exactions of moneylenders, but he had profited personally from their provisioning until the paymaster's office was established in 1772. He had lived beyond his means and accumulated ruinous debts, although some of his private expenditures were actually for public purposes. Finally, his administration seems to have been distinguished primarily by his own reluctance to carry out orders from higher authority. There was a saving grace to this stubborn independence and near insubordination, however, for subsequent developments did prove the wisdom of his most tenacious convictions.

[67] Thomas, *Teodoro de Croix*, 26, citing Croix to José de Gálvez, Nos. 47 and 48, May 26, 1776.

44

CHAPTER III

THE GOVERNOR OF SONORA
1779-1782

In 1776, the last full year of Ugarte's governorship of Coahuila, the administration of the frontier provinces underwent a major shake-up. In that year the king separated these northernmost provinces from viceregal control, created the independent *comandancia general* of the Provincias Internas del Norte, and appointed Teodoro de Croix as its executive officer. As *Comandante General* the Caballero de Croix, a nephew of former Viceroy Croix, superseded Commandant-Inspector Hugo O'Conor, who was transferred to Guatemala. The contentious Ugarte, however, was retained in the frontier service. Viceroy Bucareli passed the news of the reorganization on to Ugarte on December 24, 1776, and ordered him to report to the Caballero de Croix as soon as he arrived in his new command.[1]

After studying the reports from the northern provinces in the viceregal archives at Mexico City, the new *Comandante General* decided to appoint Ugarte to the,governorship of New Mexico. The king, however, had already assigned that position to Colonel Juan Bautista de Anza, the outgoing military governor of Sonora. Therefore, on July 26, 1777, Croix recommended Ugarte for the latter office. This met with royal approval but the

[1] Ugarte acknowledged the order in a letter to Bucareli from Monclova, January 18, 1777, AGN, PI 24, Expediente 5.

minister of the Indies insisted that Ugarte remain on in Coahuila until his own successor arrived.[2]

As a matter of fact, at Croix's request, Ugarte stayed on in Coahuila for a few weeks after Colonel Ugalde relieved him. Croix had asked the principal officers of the provinces to meet in a council of war at Monclova to discuss the Indian problem and arrive at a uniform policy toward the hostiles. As the foremost authority in point of rank, years of service, and practical knowledge on the subject, Ugarte attended the session, from December 9 through December 11, 1777, and contributed to its decisions.[3]

The deliberations at Monclova and at another council at San Antonio de Béjar, Texas, in January of 1778 (which Ugarte did not attend) were reviewed and co-ordinated by similar but more important sessions held in Nueva Vizcaya in June and July of the latter year. Convened in the council of war at Chihuahua were the most distinguished military officers of the entire northern frontier: Colonel Ugarte, now on his way to govern the province of Sonora; Colonel Anza, en route from Sonora to his new governorship in New Mexico; Colonel Felipe Barri, the governor of Nueva Vizcaya; and Croix's new commandant-inspector, Joseph Rubio. Also in attendance were several presidio captains and prominent civilians of Nueva Vizcaya. As in the council at Monclova, Ugarte found himself in agreement with the majority on the major decisions. Additional troops would be required for an effective war on the Apaches. If these were not forthcoming, the presidios, which had been moved to Rubí's outer line of defense, should be withdrawn to positions closer to the settlements, for the relocation of the presidios under O'Conor's direction had been responsible in part for the increased damage inflicted by the Apaches during the last five years. It was also agreed that peace treaties with the Apaches had never been of lasting dura-

[2] José de Gálvez to Teodoro de Croix, Madrid, December 21, 1777, AGI, Guadalajara 416; Thomas, *Forgotten Frontiers*, 19.

[3] Details of the deliberations of the council at Monclova appear in Bolton, *Athanase de Mézières*, II, 147–63, and Thomas, *Teodoro de Croix*, 35–36, *et passim*.

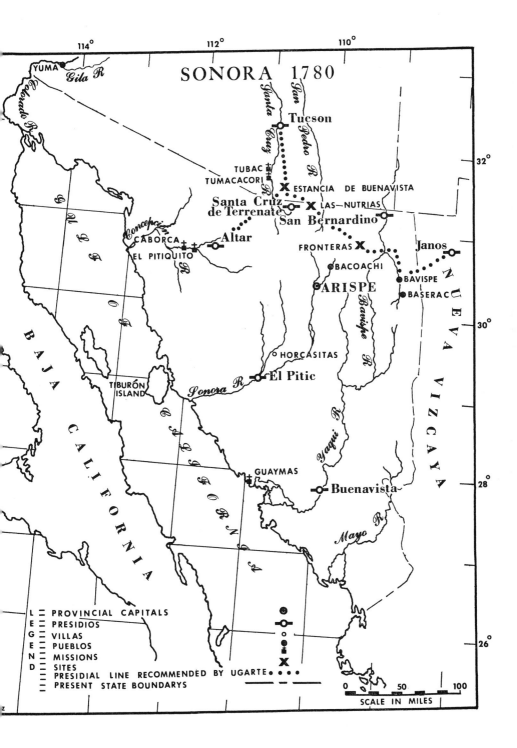

SONORA 1780

YUMA
Gila R.

Tucson

TUBAC
TUMACACORI
ESTANCIA DE BUENAVISTA
Santa Cruz
de Terrenate ✗ LAS—NUTRIAS
San Bernardino

CABORCA Altar FRONTERAS ✗ Janos
EL PITIQUITO
BACOACHI BAVISPE
ARISPE BASERAC

N
U
E
V
A

HORCASITAS

TIBURÓN
ISLAND *Sonora R.* El Pitic

V
I
Z
C
A
Y
A

B
A
J
A

C
A
L
I
F
O
R
N
I
A

G
O
L
F
O

D
E

C
A
L
I
F
O
R
N
I
A

GUAYMAS

Buenavista

Mayo R.

L ≡ PROVINCIAL CAPITALS
E ≡ PRESIDIOS
G ≡ VILLAS
E ≡ PUEBLOS
N ≡ MISSIONS
D ≡ SITES
≡ PRESIDIAL LINE RECOMMENDED BY UGARTE
≡ PRESENT STATE BOUNDARYS

0   50   100

SCALE IN MILES

tion, but that an alliance with the Mescaleros would be more secure than one with the Lipanes.[4]

With the adjournment of the council, in July of 1778, Ugarte was free to leave for his new post, but he remained at Chihuahua until the following spring with the intention of accompanying Croix, who was scheduled to make an inspection trip to Sonora at that time. Meanwhile the temporary governor of that province, Pedro de Tueros, became alarmed over the threat of another revolt of the Seri nation. Croix could not leave Chihuahua because of a serious illness, which he suffered in May, and so Ugarte went on without him. On July 31, 1779, the new Governor of Sonora reached Arispe and replaced Tueros in that office.[5]

As governor of Sonora, Ugarte found himself with even less authority than in Coahuila, where he had been under O'Conor's command. In the first place he was now not only subordinate to Croix, but after November of 1779, when the *Comandante General* arrived in Sonora, he was under his personal supervision and remained so for the rest of his administration. In the second place Ugarte was merely the military governor. The civil authority was vested completely in Intendant-Governor Pedro de Corbalan. Finally, Ugarte's active administration, such as it was, lasted only three years, from his arrival at Arispe on July 31, 1779, to about August 26, 1782, when he received orders to terminate his gubernatorial office. On the basis of his curtailed authority in Sonora, it would appear that his star was in its decline. On July 10, 1779, he had been promoted to the rank of brigadier,[6] but by this time it was apparent that the old soldier (now in his thirty-eighth year of service) was no longer fit for the rigors of field command. Even as military governor of Sonora he left the per-

---

[4] Articles 2, 6, 10, and 16, transactions of the council at Chihuahua (copy accompanying Croix to Gálvez, Chihuahua, June 29, 1778, No. 217), in Thomas, *The Plains Indians and New Mexico*, 190–213. See also Thomas, *Teodoro de Croix*, 36.

[5] Croix, General Report of 1781, Arispe, October 30, 1781, in Thomas, *Teodoro de Croix*, 71–243, Paragraphs 282–84.

[6] Ugarte, Escala de Asensos (cert. copy), May 8, 1789, AGN, PI 112, Expediente 2.

sonal conduct of campaigns against the Apaches to a subordinate, Captain Joseph Antonio de Vildósola.[7]

The major problems confronting Ugarte as military governor were the pacification of the rebel Seri nation, a reconnoissance of the frontier with a view to revising the presidial line, the organization of a presidial company composed of loyal Opata Indians, and the establishment of a military colony among the Yumas near the junction of the Colorado and Gila Rivers to protect the new supply road to Alta California.

Former Governor Anza, while attending the council at Chihuahua, had given Croix a gloomy report on conditions in Sonora. The Seris had revolted in 1777, as they had several times in the past, and, although Anza had crushed this rising, there was still grave unrest among these Indians. Anza had also reported that they were in league with the Gila Apaches, whose raids from the northeast into the very heart of Sonora neither he nor Governor Tueros was able to stem.[8] Therefore, Croix called upon Ugarte to convene with Tueros and Intendant-Governor Corbalan and then make a secret report on the situation, setting forth his own opinion in minute detail and clarity as to what was necessary to free Sonora from these hostilities and the royal treasury from the expenses they were entailing. Ugarte's report pulled no punches.

Among all the Indian nations known in Sonora, Ugarte declared, the Seris were without doubt the most shiftless, inconstant, ungrateful, and cruel. Their many acts of hostility were both notorious and undeniable. By robbing the poor inhabitants of their most essential goods and continually letting their blood, the Seris had reduced the province to a most unhappy state. They had fought with unimagined fierceness and used poisoned arrows from which the slightest wounds were fatal. Fourteen times the king had pardoned their rebellions, allowing them to live with security in well-regulated villages, but they had repeatedly abused this privilege. Frequently they had absented them-

[7] Croix, General Report of 1781, *loc. cit.*, Paragraph 552.
[8] *Ibid.*, Paragraphs 280, 283, 287.

selves from these villages, committed robberies and murders, and then returned in a few days to reside in the utmost serenity. By maintaining an uninterrupted contact with the Tiburones and Tepocas, who were rebel branches of their own nation, they had become even more dangerous to the province than were the outlying hostile tribes. Ugarte saw no hope for their subjugation and conversion to Christianity. Whenever Spanish peaceful intentions, gentle treatment, and magnanimous oversight of their past errors appeared to have induced the Seris to act as faithful vassals, they actually became daily more vain, cruel, and inhumane. The king had generously provided them with everything of sustenance they needed or desired, but this contributed only to the impression that the Spaniards feared them. In itself this notion might be tolerated, especially if there were any hope for their conversion, but they had profaned the residences of the priests, put the sacred chalices to vulgar use, and even killed one of their missionaries. They were now so unruly that they looked upon the Spanish religion with great indifference and refused either to attend mass or attend to the explanation of the doctrine unless forced by the soldiers to do so. Many years of association with the Spaniards, vigilance of the missionaries, and even coercion by the military had failed to relieve them of their superstitions, cults, and paganism. Ugarte was convinced that as long as peaceful measures were employed with them, Sonora would never be free from their hostilities, the government from the grave problems they created, their own souls from the risk of condemnation, nor the troops from the continuous fatigue which prevented them from being more usefully enlisted against the enemy tribes on the frontier. Far from attracting the Seris to obedience and professed Christianity, peaceful measures had actually encouraged them to commit excesses and barbarities. Ugarte had reached the conclusion that the only means at Spain's disposal for solving the problem was to send all the Seris—men, women, and children—to Havana, or somewhere else overseas, and to wage the most energetic war on their rebel Tiburón and Tepoca kinsmen until

Military plaza, San Antonio, Texas.

From Emory's *Report on the . . . Mexican Boundary Survey*

The Plaza and Church of El Paso.

From Emory's *Report on the . . . Mexican Boundary Survey*

they were either exterminated or reduced to faithful obedience. Only this would bring about the king's pious intentions for the salvation of these ungrateful nations. Otherwise they would remain eternal, cruel, and incorrigible rebels.[9]

Although this extreme recommendation appears at first glance to have been born of mere frustration and to have been the same rash solution offered by Ugarte in respect to the disloyal Julimeños and faithless Lipán Apaches in Coahuila, it should be noted that Ugarte's predecessors and contemporaries in Sonora —Francisco Antonio Crespo, Juan Bautista de Anza, Pedro Tueros, Pedro de Corbalan, Joseph Antonio de Vildósola, and even the Caballero de Croix himself—considered the expatriation of the Seri nation imperative.[10] The king, however, decided that for the present such an undertaking would be too expensive and that exterminating them militarily would be both inhumane and contrary to religious law. Instead, he decreed that they should be attracted to peace by whatever pacific means possible and that their occasional acts of barbarism should be overlooked, since these were only the result of their lack of civilization.[11]

When Croix arrived in Sonora, he placed Ugarte in direct charge of controlling the restless Seri. On the recommendation of Ugarte, Corbalan, and the engineer Gerónimo de la Rocha, the *Commandante General* moved the presidial company of San Miguel de Horcasitas to the Pueblo of El Pitic, where the Seris were concentrated. By 1781, however, Croix had to admit that he and Ugarte had achieved no more success in pacifying Sonora than had Anza and Tueros. The Seris had revolted again after Ugarte's arrival, those of Guaymas joining the Tiburones and those at El Pitic fleeing their pueblo.[12] The problem actually outlasted both the *Comandante General* and the Military Governor. In 1784, Croix's successor prepared a major campaign against

[9] Ugarte to Croix, San Miguel de Horcasitas, January 15, 1780 (cert. copy), AGI, Guadalajara 272.
[10] Croix, General Report of 1781, *loc. cit.*, Paragraph 537.
[11] Eduardo W. Villa, *Historia del Estado de Sonora*, 128–30.
[12] Croix, General Report of 1781, *loc. cit.*, Paragraphs 286–88, 509–11, 522.

the rebels, but the insurgent chieftains surrendered before the attack could be launched.[13]

The greatest fear of continual Seri unrest was that these interior Indians were frequently in collusion with the ever-hostile Apaches of the Gila River region. By 1781 Gileño attacks had reached to the very environs of Arispe, where they had killed fifteen soldiers and fifty civilians, abducted another twenty-eight persons, burned a number of houses, and profaned a church, all in one day.[14]

In an effort to break up the suspected alliance between the Gileños and the Seris, to curb the invasion of the former, and also to secure the supply line to the new colonies in Alta California, Croix decided to form a more effective line of presidios than that which O'Conor had established in accordance with Rubí's recommendations and the *Reglamento de 1772*. Too ill to supervise the undertaking personally, Croix on April 15, 1780, commissioned Ugarte to reconnoiter the northern borderlands of the province. In company with the engineer Gerónimo de la Rocha, who was to map the terrain in some detail, Ugarte was to make a scrupulous and extensive inspection of the sites of both active and abandoned presidios and then in a full report to recommend the best possible positions for the garrisons. He was to keep in mind that the new sites would also have to support civilian communities, for these were eventually to take over the defense of some positions. Armed with the previous reports on the matter made by O'Conor, Colonel Crespo, Adjutant-Inspector Antonio de Bonilla, and the Franciscan Father Juan Díaz, Ugarte was to set out from Arispe on April 15, 1780, and return on July 16.[15]

Following a prescribed route, Ugarte began his inspection with a study of the situation of Fronteras, Sonora's easternmost presidio, on the western slope of the Sierra Madre. Then proceeding westward to the Río San Pedro, he reconnoitered the arroyos of Guachuca, Las Nutrias, and Terrenate. Following the San

[13] Ugarte, Informe General, Arispe, December 10, 1787, AGN, PI 254, Expediente 2.
[14] Croix, General Report of 1781, *loc. cit.*, Paragraph 289.
[15] Copy of the order in *ibid.*, Paragraphs 294–306.

Pedro northward, he next surveyed the terrain near its junction with the Gila. From there he marched southwestward to the presidio of Tucson, on the Santa Cruz River, then southward up that stream to the former site of Tubac and on southeastward to the active presidio of Terrenate. From Terrenate he proceeded westward to the presidio of Altar, reconnoitering along the route the valleys of Arive, Busanic, Sari, Tubutama, and other mission sites as far southwestward as El Pitiquito.[16]

In his report to Croix, Ugarte agreed essentially with that of De la Rocha's independent survey, that there now existed no real presidial line at all. The buildings for the new presidio of San Bernardino, which O'Conor had moved from Fronteras, were not even near completion, and the site itself was too isolated from Janos, Nueva Vizcaya's westernmost garrison, to collaborate with it in blocking the Apache invasions of either of the two provinces. The new post of Terrenate, which was supposed to be forty leagues from San Bernardino, was actually much farther, the route between the two was unsafe from the Apaches even for dispatch riders, and the troops at the new presidio were becoming panicky. Furthermore, the presidio of Tucson (formerly at Tubac) was well north of Rubí's recommended line, too remote to receive assistance from that of Altar, and too feeble to support Terrenate as fully as necessary. These four presidial sites formed a broken line of more than 360 miles in length.[17]

Ugarte recommended that a new presidio be established at Bavispe, which was on a major invasion route of the Apaches between the Sonoran and Nueva Vizcayan settlements, and that the company at San Bernardino, which was inadequate for its purpose, be withdrawn to its former position at Fronteras. He thought that the second fortress in the line should be at Las Nutrias, where the company of Santa Cruz de Terrenate was now encamped and which was only from sixty-five to seventy-five miles from Fronteras, depending upon the route taken. The third presidio, he felt, should be situated on the spacious mesa of Buena-

---

[16] *Ibid.*, Paragraphs 300–302.
[17] *Ibid.*, Paragraph 310.

vista, on the banks of the Río de San Antonio, where all of the resources existed for a successful colony and which was only about ninety miles from the interior presidio of Altar, about sixty-eight miles from outlying Tucson, and sixty-five from Las Nutrias, the site he recommended for the second presidio. A presidio there would protect the missions and pueblos of Calabazas, Tumaca-cori, and Tubac along the road between Buenavista and Tucson. These three presidios would form a more defensible line, and their sites would support civilian settlements adequate in themselves to defend the frontier. Ugarte felt that the presidio of Tucson, although far north of the line, should be preserved until a colony could be established on the Colorado River for the protection of the California supply road. He could not report with any certainty on the terrain around Tucson or along the supply route beyond it, for his reconnaissance did not include that remote region. He was sure, however, that the line should not follow the banks of the San Pedro, nor that any presidio should be located at the confluence of the San Pedro and the Gila, because of the remoteness and sterility of that land. Ugarte's presidial line provided for a series of fortresses within supply range of the interior, with arable land for their own support, and within easy reach of one another for mutual assistance and concerted operations. As to the interior presidios, those of Altar, Horcasitas, and Buenavista should remain at the present positions and with their present forces until the hostile Seris were transferred overseas.[18]

Although Croix did not rely wholly on Ugarte's reconnaissance and recommendations but also studied and compared others offering conflicting opinions, the presidial sites that he finally decided upon in order to reform the leaky and remote Rubí line were those recommended by his Military Governor. Beginning in the east, San Miguel de Bavispe was to be established as a new presidio, about sixty miles southwest of Nueva Vizcaya's presidio of Janos; San Bernardino (Santa Rosa de Coro de Guachi) was to be removed to Fronteras, its former site, seventy-five miles west of Bavispe; Santa Cruz de Terrenate was to be trans-

[18] *Ibid.*, Paragraphs 423–35.

ferred to Las Nutrias, sixty-five miles west northwest of Fronteras; a new presidio was to be established at the *estancia* de Buenavista, near the headwaters of the Santa Cruz River and fifty-five miles northwest of Terrenate; and Tucson, like the three interior presidios of Altar, Horcasitas (now at El Pitic), and Buenavista (on the Yaqui River), was to remain at its present site.[19]

The new presidio of Bavispe, although proposed at an early date, was established by Governor Ugarte. The idea originated from a petition from Sonora's most loyal Indian nation. Opata warriors had served several presidial companies as explorers and were generally considered by the Spaniards as the only Indians wholly suitable for use in formal military operations, although others were useful as allies and auxiliaries. O'Conor had failed to pay either them or the Seris for their services in the general campaign against the Apaches in 1775, and Anza had reported in 1777 that the Opata were complaining bitterly of ill-treatment by the missionaries and military officers.[20] Croix had then directed Anza to compensate the Opata at once and take measures to suppress the Seri rebellion, and this had appeased the former. Their "general," Don Juan Manuel Varela, was paid in full and given political authority over the Pueblo of Baserac and the rest of the Opata nation. He was also authorized to see that the Father Provincial of the missions impressed the friars with the necessity of treating the Opata well. It was probably with a view to insuring that the Opata auxiliaries were paid regularly in the future that "General" Varela petitioned Croix to organize them into a formal presidial company situated at one of their pueblos, either Baserac or Bavispe. Croix endorsed the proposal even before he arrived in Sonora, and the king approved it on July 18, 1778.[21]

A year later, on July 12, 1779, Croix ordered Ugarte and Intendant-General Corbalan to work out the details. They were to study the situations of Baserac and Bavispe and recommend which would be the more suitable site, and they were to deter-

---

19 *Ibid.*, Paragraphs 506–507.
20 *Ibid.*, Paragraph 328.
21 *Ibid.*, Paragraphs 325–26.

mine whether the new unit should be constituted as a presidial or mobile company. Whichever the case, the company was to be established in accordance with the *Reglamento de 1772* except for the number, composition, and organization of its troops. Two veteran Spanish officers of subaltern rank were to be in charge, one as company commander and the other as paymaster and supply officer. The corporals and other lesser officers, however, were to be Opatas. Since there was no special appropriation for the purpose, it was determined that the salary budget for the entire company would not exceed what was already being paid for the seventy-five Opata scouts who were then employed by the several presidios of Sonora. If these Indian troops should volunteer for general campaign duty, however, they were to be paid additionally, not in cash, but in the fruits of the province. After all, the purpose of the Opata company was to defend their villages without neglecting their agricultural pursuits.[22]

Corbalan, reporting on August 31, 1779, without having actually reconnoitered the sites, recommended that the Opata presidio be situated at Bacoachi, where some gold placers were expected to attract a large population. Ugarte, having explored the terrain, preferred the fertile and spacious valley of Bavispe because of its superior resources, the abundant water of the Yaqui River, its strategic position for the protection of all of the Opata pueblos, and its shorter distance from the garrisons at Janos and Fronteras. In collaboration with these two presidios, a garrison in the valley of Bavispe could readily block the invasion route of the Apaches into either Sonora or Nueva Vizcaya and also dislodge the hostiles from the mountains bordering the valley itself. In short, it would better serve the new presidial line than would Bacoachi. Croix finally agreed with Ugarte's recommendations. A shortage of supplies delayed the establishment of the new presidio, but by October of 1781 the site had been determined, the best Opata warriors selected, and the Spanish commandant and paymaster appointed.[23] The new presidio at the *estancia* de

[22] *Ibid.*, Paragraphs 330–31, 333–34, 338, 340.
[23] *Ibid.*, Paragraphs 349–65.

Buenavista was also manned by Indian troops, but the company there was a combination of Opatas and Pimas.[24]

Without doubt the most important single event that occurred during Ugarte's military governorship of Sonora was the revolt of the Yuma Indians, which destroyed the new settlement at the confluence of the Colorado and Gila rivers. For many years the Franciscan friars had urged the establishment there of missions under military protection. A prominent chief of the Yumas, Olley-quotequiebe, whom the Spaniards had christened Salvador Palma, also favored the idea. Palma had accompanied Anza to Mexico City in 1776, and after being baptized, indoctrinated, and regaled with sumptuous gifts there, he returned and convinced his people of the material advantages of the Spanish establishment among them. Each spring for the next three years Palma appeared at a Sonoran presidio to request such a colony. Croix himself was eager to form a settlement there so as to protect the California supply road, which Anza had just explored. Unfortunately, however, the three interested parties—missionaries, Indians, and military government—favored the project for different and conflicting purposes, and, worst of all, the plan finally adopted was an impractical compromise of the three distinct interests. The missionaries were given spiritual control over the Yumas, but all temporal authority was vested in the military. Yet, the military protection of the site was shared by civilians, and the Yumas themselves were incorporated into the civilian colony.[25]

Croix had originally planned to transfer the presidios of Horcasitas and Buenavista to the strategic site, but the Seri uprising required their continued presence in the interior, and Ugarte's reconnaissance had convinced him that no site on the Gila would support a full presidio. Moreover, after 1779 the war with Eng-

[24] Adjutant Inspector Roque de Medina, Extractos de Revistas, Compañías presidiales de la Provincia de Sonora, Buenavista, November 26, 1785, AGI, Guadalajara 521.
[25] Jack D. Forbes, *Warriors of the Colorado: The Yumas of the Quechan Nation and Their Neighbors*, Chapters 5–6; Charles E. Chapman, *The Founding of Spanish California: The Northwestward Expansion of New Spain, 1687–1783*, 408–409.

land limited the amount of money that could be spent for a garrison. Therefore, Croix economized by establishing two small civilian colonies among the Yuma and supporting them with only eighteen soldiers, one ensign, one sergeant, and two corporals, all drawn from the three interior presidios. The principal settlers were the families of the twenty-one officers and enlisted men, twenty civilian families, and a number of unconverted Yumas who voluntarily joined the colony. Each colonizing family was subsidized at the rate of ten pesos a month for a year or more and was supplied with twelve dependent laborers, whom they were to pay at the wage rates prevailing in Sonora. The lands and waters of the new site were divided among the soldiers, settlers, and Yumas. In all, it was to cost the government only 4,477 pesos a year, whereas a regular presidio would have required 18,998 pesos, and the treasury expected a further saving as soon as the settlers were able to support themselves. When the first settlers arrived in December of 1780, they were well received by Palma and his tribesmen, and both Indians and Spaniards set to work building their houses. It was hoped that the integrated community would not only attract the Yumas to Christianity and civilization, but would also encourage travel and commerce between Sonora on the one hand and both California and New Mexico on the other.[26] But Croix's bright hopes for its future were soon dashed.

The land was not bountiful. Spanish settlers allowed their livestock to graze on and trample Yuman crops. The Yumas, expecting more material assistance and gifts than were forthcoming, became disenchanted, and when provisions ran low they refused to share their produce with the Spaniards except at exorbitant prices. Father Francisco Garcés and Fray Juan Díaz restrained the Yumas from continuing in some of their heathen practices—including the waging of war on neighboring tribes—and the close association of Spaniards and Indians merely intensified the friction. Finally, a crisis occurred when Captain Fernando de Rivera y Moncada arrived with a large pack train and over 100 soldiers

[26] Croix, General Report of 1781, *loc. cit.*, Paragraphs, 517–52.

58

and recruits who were bound for the new settlements of California. Wintering at the Yuma colony so as to recuperate for the remainder of his march, Captain Rivera permitted his horses and cattle to forage on Yuma lands and to remain at the colony into the following summer. Then, on July 17, 1781, the Yumas rose in revolt, killed Captain Rivera, Father Garcés, Fray Juan Díaz, and 101 troops and colonists. They also carried off as captives 74 others.[27]

As soon as he learned of the massacre Croix summoned Ugarte and other officers to a council of war at Arispe. On its recommendations he then sent a large body of troops to the Colorado River. These forces managed to secure the release of the captives by ransoming them from the Yumas in September and November of the same year, but their attempt to punish the rebel tribesmen was much less successful. At a later meeting, in January of 1783, the council at Arispe endorsed Ugarte's earlier report that the banks of the Colorado and Gila were unsuitable for maintaining presidios, and on its recommendation all attempts to garrison the strategic junction of the two rivers were formally abandoned.[28] Croix attributed the disaster primarily to the unfortunate representations made by Governor Anza and Father Garcés to Viceroy Bucareli on the resources of the site, subsequently to his own inability to provide an adequate military force for the protection of the settlers, and ultimately to the failure of the officers of the colony to establish satisfactory relations with the Yumas.[29]

Meanwhile, as Ugarte's term as military governor was drawing to a close, he began to cast about for other employment. He was particularly interested in a position at Guadalajara or Mexico City, and on February 8, 1782, the king assured him that another appointment would be forthcoming.[30] Then, on February 28, a

[27] Forbes, *Warriors of the Colorado,* 188–205; Chapman, *Founding of Spanish California,* 408–409, 413, 442.
[28] Forbes, *Warriors of the Colorado,* 205–20; Joseph F. Park, "Spanish Indian Policy in Northern Mexico, 1765–1810," *Arizona and the West,* Vol. IV (Winter, 1962), 339–40.
[29] Thomas, *Teodoro de Croix,* 59–60.
[30] Viceroy Martín de Mayorga to Croix, México, January 13, 1783 (draft), AGN, PI 79, Expediente 6.

royal order was issued requiring him to terminate his duties in Sonora. This notice seems to have reached him on or shortly before August 26, for on that date the new commandant-general, Felipe de Neve, reported that Ugarte had surrendered his office. Neve also reported that Ugarte had been issued a conditional warrant for 1,000 pesos to cover his trip to the viceregal capital. Previously, as inspector general under Croix, Neve had asked the Viceroy for instructions as to what salary Ugarte should expect as a brigadier without office, and the Viceroy had replied on January 13, 1783, by sending a file on Ugarte's salary records and authorizing Neve to reconcile the matter as he saw fit. Neve was apparently well satisfied with the Military Governor's record, for on March 24, 1783, he sent the king's minister an "efficacious" recommendation of Ugarte's "good services, disinterest, and particular merit." This endorsement seems to have satisfied the king, for on October 15, 1783, he appointed the unemployed brigadier to the governorship of Puebla de los Angeles, in central New Spain. Furthermore, in view of Ugarte's poverty and indebtedness, the king approved Neve's provisional warrant for 1,000 pesos for Ugarte's trip to Mexico City and instructed the Viceroy to place him in immediate possession of his new office.[31]

Ugarte arrived at Puebla in January of 1784, took office on March 7, and served actively for two years, until March 26, 1786.[32] Since his duties in administering this interior jurisdiction were unrelated to the northern frontier, they may be dispensed with here. Very shortly after assuming this office Ugarte was being considered for still other employment. On August 20, 1784, the king ordered the audiencia of Mexico to pass on his merits for one of several vacant positions, and on May 7, 1785, this body certified that he was qualified for any of the offices he had solic-

[31] Felipe de Neve succeeded Croix on August 15, 1783. Marqués de Sonora to the Comandante General (Neve), San Lorenzo, October 15, 1783 (copy), AGN, PI 112, Expediente 2; Mayorga to Croix, México, January 13, 1783, loc. cit.

[32] Ugarte to the King, San Bartolomé, September 29, 1788 (copy), AGN, PI 77, Expediente 11; Villa, *Historia del Estado de Sonora*, 138–39.

ited except that of the presidency of the audiencia of Nueva Galicia, at Guadalajara. That office, it ruled, required a person with a degree and experience in law.[33] Five years later, however, without further legal training, Ugarte would succeed to that very same position. Meanwhile, in recognition of his meritorious services and of his having been without salary since he retired from the governorship of Sonora, Ugarte was favored by the king with exemption from the traditional half-annate assessment on his gubernatorial salary at Puebla.[34] Even with this relief, however, the impecunious old soldier could not live within his income. While at Puebla he went further into debt by lending money to the Indians there so that they could meet their annual tribute payments, but five years afterwards he was apparently reimbursed for this generosity.[35]

Also while at Puebla, Ugarte had the very good fortune to have a former officer of the Provincias Internas with experience and attitudes much like his own to be elevated to the office of viceroy of New Spain. Bernardo de Gálvez, formerly *comandante de armas* on the Apache frontier and later governor-general of Louisiana, was not only personally conversant with the frontier problems, but also unusually influential as a result of family ties. He was the son of Viceroy Matías de Gálvez, whom he succeeded in that high office, and the nephew of Minister of the Indies José de Gálvez, the Marqués de Sonora. As early as August 20, 1784, the Marqués de Sonora had asked the new Viceroy for a full report on Ugarte's merits and services and on the debts which he allegedly owed, and a year later the Conde de Gálvez, as the new Viceroy was known, forwarded these to his uncle with a recommendation that Ugarte be promoted to the rank of *mariscal de campo* (field marshal). In support of this recommendation, the

[33] Audiencia de México to the Conde de Gálvez (Bernardo de Gálvez), No. 427, México, May 24, 1785, AGN, CV 137, Foja 11.

[34] Conde de Gálvez to the Marqués de Sonora, No. 33, México, July 21, 1785, AGN, CV 137, Foja 190.

[35] Ugarte to the Conde de Revillagigedo, Chihuahua, September 10, 1790, AGN, PI 84, Expediente 1.

Conde called particular attention to Ugarte's thirty-five-year military career in Spain with service in the Italian and Portuguese campaigns and to his seventeen years in America as governor of Coahuila, Sonora, and Puebla. These fifty-two years of continuous service, the Viceroy declared, had been performed with "zeal, precision, and disinterest." Former viceroys and *comandante generals* had also endorsed the old soldier's solicitations for advancement, but he was still behind in his promotions and was indeed burdened with involuntary debts. It was owing to his unselfish conduct in office that Ugarte had been unable to emerge from these obligations while governor of Puebla. Therefore, the Conde de Gálvez declared, he was recommending Ugarte not only for the higher military rank, but also for whatever administrative position that might be vacant and sufficiently remunerative to enable him to escape from his financial embarrassment.[36]

What position Viceroy Gálvez probably had in mind was that of *comandante general* of the Provincias Internas, for Croix's successor, Felipe de Neve, had died unexpectedly in Nueva Vizcaya, and the commandant-inspector, Colonel Joseph Antonio Rengel, had been elevated to the vacancy only on a temporary basis. At any rate, two months after the Viceroy wrote in Ugarte's behalf, the king appointed him to that office. The appointment, dated October 6, 1785, alluded to Ugarte's "merit, service, and intelligence" as well as to his practical experience on the northern frontier, and although it specified that Ugarte was to hold the office only on an *ad interim* basis, he was actually retained for a full five-year term. On the one hand Ugarte was vested with the same powers that Neve had exercised, but on the other he was subjected in military, political, and economic matters to the Conde de Gálvez as long as the latter was Viceroy of New Spain. Confident in Ugarte's zeal, love for the royal service, and ability to discharge the duties involved, the king ordered him to take the oath of office from Gálvez and enter into possession of the commandancy-general immediately. His salary was to be the

---

[36] Conde de Gálvez to the Marqués de Sonora, Nos. 84 and 137, México, August 2, and 25, 1785, AGN, CV 137, Fojas 255 and 297.

same as Neve's, 20,000 pesos, and was to begin as soon as he entered on his duties.[37]

Informed of the appointment, Viceroy Gálvez notified acting *Comandante General* Rengel of the change, sent the royal *cédula* to Governor Ugarte at Puebla, and urged him to hasten to Mexico City in order to confer on important matters relating to the Provincias Internas del Norte.[38] On March 26, 1786, Ugarte turned over the governorship of Puebla to his successor and set out for the capital.[39] His gubernatorial salary continued until April 19, 1786, when he entered the jurisdiction of his new command, and although the Viceroy had been unable to grant his request that the new salary begin immediately after he surrendered his office in Puebla, he was able to advance the new *Comadante General* 10,000 pesos for travel and maintenance against his new salary.[40]

[37] Real cédula, San Ildefonso, October 6, 1785 (cert. copy), AGN, PI 15, Expediente 7. Another certified copy appears in PI 77, Expediente 5.
[38] Conde de Gálvez to the Marqués de Sonora, Nos. 406–407, México, January 27, 1786, AGN, CV 139 (no pagination).
[39] Villa, *Historia del Estado de Sonora*, 139.
[40] Conde de Gálvez to Ugarte, México, March 28 and 29 and May 24, 1786 (drafts), AGN, PI 78, Expediente 5.

CHAPTER IV

THE COMMANDANCY-GENERAL
1786-1791

The jurisdiction and authority of *Comandante General* Jacobo Ugarte y Loyola were much reduced from what they had been when the office was created and bestowed upon the Caballero de Croix in 1776, and these powers were further eroded in the years of his own administration. It was Ugarte's ill fortune to receive each of his frontier appointments on the eve of an administrative reorganization. Thus, shortly after he became governor of Coahuila, all military governors of the northern provinces were subordinated to the new office of commandant-inspector; by the time he was transferred to Sonora, his military governorship was under the direct authority of the more powerful *comandante general*; and by the time Ugarte rose to that superior office, it had been subjected to the authority of the viceroy. Moreover, what was left of Ugarte's authority was shortly divided again, first into three semi-independent districts and later into two entirely separate commands. Ugarte was the victim of an experimentalist policy that was characteristic of the late-eighteenth century, but neither his age nor his temperament would permit him the flexibility necessary to take the changes in good grace. When he entered upon his general command in April of 1786, he was in his upper sixties and as stubborn as ever.

By his royal appointment of October 6, 1785, Ugarte was vested with all of the power and authority held by his regular predecessors, Croix and Neve, with the lone exception that dur-

64

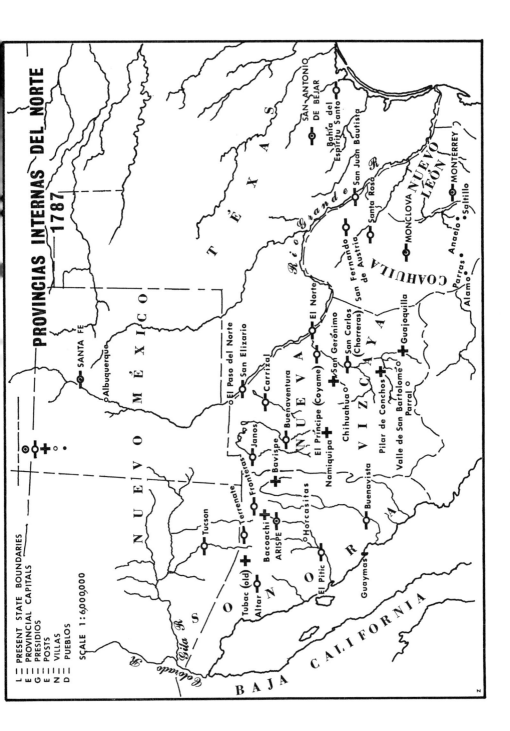

PROVINCIAS INTERNAS DEL NORTE
1787

PRESENT STATE BOUNDARIES
PROVINCIAL CAPITALS
PRESIDIOS
POSTS
VILLAS
PUEBLOS

SCALE 1:6,000,000

NUEVO MÉXICO

SANTA FE
Albuquerque

El Paso del Norte
San Elizario

NUEVA VIZCAYA

Carrizal
Buenaventura
El Príncipe (Coyame)
El Norte
San Gerónimo
San Carlos (Chorreras)
Chihuahua
Namiquipa
Pilar de Conchos
Valle de San Bartolomé
Parral
Guajoquilla

San Fernando
de Austria
San Juan Bautista
San Antonio
de Béjar
Bahía del
Espíritu Santo
Santa Rosa

COAHUILA

MONCLOVA
NUEVO LEÓN
MONTERREY
Anaelo
Saltillo
Parras
Alamo

TÉXAS

Rio Grande

SONORA

Tucson
Tubac (old)
Altar
Terrenate
Fronteras
Janos
Bavispe
Bacoachi
ARISPE
El Pitic
Horcasitas
Buenavista
Guaymas

Gila R.
Colorado R.

BAJA CALIFORNIA

N

ing the viceregal administration of the Conde de Gálvez, he was to be under the instructions and orders of that office in all military, political, and economic matters.[1] At first this was only a slight inconvenience to Ugarte. Gálvez had been a frontier soldier like himself; Ugarte had even served under him for a short time, from 1769 to 1772, when Gálvez was the *comandante de armas* of the Provincias Internas. More important, both the Viceroy and the *Comandante General* had full confidence in each other. When Ugarte arrived in Mexico City to be sworn in by the Viceroy, he stayed on for several days to consult with Gálvez on frontier policy. As he later reported, he and Gálvez saw eye to eye on the problems and measures for their solution. Thus, when Ugarte received his formal instructions from the Viceroy on November 14, 1786, he was able to report that he had already been pursuing the policies outlined for the seven months since he had arrived in his command. And even after his independence from viceregal authority was automatically established when Gálvez died, on November 30, 1786, he departed only slightly from these detailed instructions.[2] Something of the confidence that Gálvez had placed in Ugarte is indicated by the final article of his formal *Instrucción* of August 26, 1786. This stated that Ugarte was not bound inextricably to this set of directives, but could suspend temporarily any which he considered inexpedient, having only to explain to Gálvez the reasons for so doing. Gálvez would then either modify or reassert the provision, as he saw fit.[3] However, by the time Ugarte's mod-

[1] Real cédula, San Ildefonso, October 6, 1785 (cert. copy), AGN, PI 15, Expediente 7.

[2] Ugarte to Antonio Valdés (minister of the Indies), San Bartolomé, October 6, 1788, AGN, PI 77, Expediente 11; Conde de Gálvez to the Marqués de Sonora, No. 891, México, September 25, 1786, AGN, CV 140 (no pagination).

[3] Article 216, *Instrucción formada en virtud de Real Orden de S.M., que se dirige al Señor Comandante General de Provincias internas Don Jacobo Ugarte y Loyola para gobierno y puntal observancia de este Superior Gefe de sus inmediatos subalternos*, August 26, 1786, AGN, PI 129, Expediente 4. Hereinafter cited as Gálvez, Instrucción of 1786. For an English translation accompanied by the original text, see Donald E. Worcester (ed.), *Instructions for Governing the Interior Provinces of New Spain, 1786, by Bernardo de Gálvez*.

Presidio of Tucson, about 1790. Artist's conception by Cal N. Peters.

Arizona Pioneers' Historical Society Collection

Los Chisos Mountains.

From Emory's *Report on the . . . Mexican Boundary Survey*

est reservations and objections to certain articles of the *Instrucción* of 1786 reached Mexico City, Gálvez was dead. Thus, when King Charles III shortly approved the *Instrucción* and gave it the force of a royal ordinance, it was without the amendments that Ugarte proposed.[4]

Although Gálvez's death had left Ugarte temporarily independent of viceregal authority, the *Instrucción* of 1786 remained in force, along with the *Reglamento de 1772*, as a written constitution for the Provincias Internas. In its preamble Gálvez called attention to the well-recognized unhappy state of the northern frontier. In spite of royal efforts since 1723 to improve its condition by reinforcing its troops, realigning its presidios, regulating their operation, allocating millions of pesos from the royal treasury, and even raising private contributions, the frontier provinces were prostrated by the rigors of war, pestilence, and hunger. Although the problems involved in pacifying the region were now more difficult than ever before, Gálvez was convinced that its peace, health, and prosperity would eventually be restored.[5] Of the *Instrucción*'s 216 articles, the first 23 specified the modifications the Viceroy was making in the military administration of the frontier command.

Under this reorganization, Ugarte, as *comandante general*, was still free to exercise the ample powers conceded to his predecessors in this office, but in his subordination to Gálvez he was obliged to direct his reports and requests for assistance to the office of the Viceroy rather than, as in the past, to the minister of the Indies in Spain. Moreover, he was now required to devote his full attention to military affairs and was to delegate all legal and patronage matters to the intendants and political governors. Although he might still issue warrants for military, missionary, secretarial, and auditing expenses, and review the accounts of the treasury officers for the purpose of recommending more efficient procedures, he was expressly prohibited from exercising

---

[4] Ugarte to the Marqués de Sonora, Chihuahua, December 28, 1786 (copy), AGN, PI 254, Expediente 6; Real orden, El Pardo, February 27, 1787 (copy), AGN, PI 77, Expediente 8.

[5] Gálvez, Instrucción of 1786, *loc. cit.*

any real control over treasury business.[6] Thus the *Comandante General* was stripped of most of his political and economic responsibilities and was left as fundamentally a military administrator.

Ugarte's secretarial staff was also reduced. Originally the commandancy-general was assigned a secretary, four clerks, and three scribes to carry on the voluminous correspondence, make appropriate certified copies, enumerate and index letters, and maintain full records in the office's archives. Before long, however, Ugarte lost his secretary, and his staff was reduced to two clerks, one of whom assumed the secretarial duties, and only one scribe.[7]

Next in rank under Ugarte was Commandant-Inspector Colonel Joseph Antonio Rengel, who had full authority over the inspection of the troops in all the provinces. Rengel was aided by two adjutant inspectors, Lieutenant Colonel Roque de Medina in Sonora and Lieutenant Colonel Diego de Borica in Nueva Vizcaya. In New Mexico Governor Juan Bautista de Anza served in the same capacity, and in the provinces of Texas, Coahuila, Nuevo León, and Nuevo Santander, Colonel Juan de Ugalde, the *comandante de armas*, was the assistant inspector. The Commandant-Inspector was to channel all his correspondence dealing with the inspection of the troops through Ugarte.[8]

[6] *Ibid.*, Articles 1–6.

[7] The regular secretary, Pedro Garrido y Durán, was soon detached to serve temporarily as intendant of Sonora; the first clerk, Manuel Merino, was added to the viceregal secretariat; the second clerk, Bartolomé Sáenz de la Fuente, was stationed permanently at Arispe as curator of the archives of the commandancy-general there; and the fourth clerk, Francisco Matamoras, was allowed to go to Mexico City to recover from an illness. This left Juan Gasiot y Miralles, the third clerk, to accompany Ugarte on all of his trips over the Provincias Internas and to handle the secretarial and clerical work previously divided among five men. Ugarte was unable to fill the vacancies because of the scarcity of literate personnel on the frontier. Ugarte to Viceroy Manuel Antonio Flores, San Bartolomé, December 29, 1788 (cert. copy), and to Valdés, Chihuahua, June 9, 1789, AGN, PI 183, Expediente 7, and PI 77, Expediente 2.

[8] For Nuevo León and Nuevo Santander, Ugalde was subordinate to the Viceroy's own inspector-general rather than to Rengel, for these two provinces were not properly within the jurisdiction of the commandancy-general. Gálvez, *Instrucción* of 1786, *loc. cit.*, Articles 15–17, 19; Ugarte, Plan que demuestra el Estado Mayor de las Provincias Internas, Arispe, December 15, 1787, AGN, PI 254, Expediente 2, hereafter cited as Ugarte, Estado Mayor of 1787.

The Commandancy-General

For all military matters involving the expenditure of royal funds, the *Comandante General* was required to consult with and rely on the opinions of the *asesor y auditor de guerra* of the Provincias Internas. During Ugarte's administration this office was filled first by Pedro Galindo Navarro and then by Joseph Matamoros. The remaining general employees of the commandancy-general were a chaplain, Fray Ignacio Ballenilla, and two surgeons, Antonio Comadurán and Gregorio Arriola.[9]

Since the *Comandante General's* primary duty was now to provide for the defense and tranquillity of the frontier provinces and since these embraced a territory so vast that he could neither visit all of its important districts as frequently as was desirable nor expedite orders from any headquarters promptly enough to deal with the changing military situation, Gálvez decided to divide the general command into three semi-independent districts. He therefore assigned two officers of lesser rank to share Ugarte's military responsibilities.[10]

Ugarte himself was to be responsible personally for the western division, which embraced the provinces of Sonora and the two Californias; Colonel Rengel was to have charge of the central division, made up of Nueva Vizcaya and New Mexico; and Colonel Ugalde was to command the eastern division, which now included not only Texas and Coahuila, but also Nuevo León and Nuevo Santander. Ugalde was also given control over the districts of Parras and Saltillo, which were now transferred from the jurisdiction of Nueva Vizcaya to that of Coahuila. For his administration of Nuevo León and Nuevo Santander, which were not properly within the commandancy-general, Ugalde was responsible to the viceroy rather than to Ugarte. To further complicate matters in this reorganization, both Rengel and Ugalde, although subordinate to Ugarte, were permitted to maintain direct correspondence with the viceroy and to operate freely in their respective commandancies for the purpose of waging war on or concluding peace with the hostile Indians. Yet they were to obey

[9] Ugarte, Estado Mayor of 1787, *loc. cit.*
[10] Gálvez, Instrucción of 1786, *loc. cit.*, Articles 7–8.

Ugarte's orders as long as these did not conflict with those which the viceroy issued to them. The theory was that the commandants of the separate divisions needed more freedom in their military operations so as to control more effectively the activities of hostile tribes. It was also assumed that the viceroy, with his direct communication with the king, was in a better position than Ugarte to obtain prompt royal approval for unanticipated expenditures and departures from established procedures.[11] Unfortunately, as it worked out in practice, the entire chain of command became hopelessly ensnarled, and there was much less co-ordination in the efforts to pacify the hostile tribes than there was under the united command.

The general deterioration that followed was due not only to the ill-defined chain of command specified in the *Instrucción* of 1786, but also to the total inability of Ugarte and Ugalde to get along with each other. Juan de Ugalde had become a cadet in 1737 at the tender age of eight, five years after Ugarte had enrolled with similar dispensation for his youth. He had served in fourteen European and African campaigns, spent eight years as governor and military commandant in Peru, and six years as such in the province of Coahuila. As Ugarte's successor in Coahuila, Ugalde had distinguished himself as an indefatigable campaigner against the Apaches. Teodoro de Croix, however, had complained that Ugalde was as hard on his own troops and their horses as he was on the enemy, that while he was in the field he left the settlers exposed to murderous Apache raids, and that he was intemperately insubordinate. In 1783 Croix had summarily discharged him. In an investigation that followed, however, Ugalde was cleared of all serious charges, and in 1786 Viceroy Gálvez elevated him to the position of *comandante de armas* for the eastern division of the Provincias Internas.[12] By this time Brigadier Ugarte may well have become jealous of Colonel Ugalde's more vigorous health and his dashing success as an Indian fighter, but

[11] *Ibid.*, Articles 9–13.
[12] For a sympathetic account of Ugalde's career, see Nelson, "Juan de Ugalde and the Rio Grande Frontier, 1777–1790" (unpublished Ph.D. dissertation, University of California, 1936).

he resented even more having to yield military authority to this younger officer of inferior rank and having to put up with his characteristic insubordination. Apparently Ugarte did not appreciate a trait in others that so distinguished himself. On the other hand, Ugarte was able to work in complete harmony with Colonel Rengel, the commandant of the new central division.

As he later recalled, Ugarte would have requested certain changes in the *Instrucción* of 1786 had Gálvez lived long enough to have entertained his suggestions. Articles 1, 5, 6, 82, and 83 had assured him that he was to retain the same full powers and broad jurisdiction in matters relating to both war and peace that previous commandant-generals had held. Articles 7 and 12 had subordinated the commandant-inspector and the *comandante de armas* to his authority. Unfortunately, however, these provisions had given these two officers an independence in their military operations that was subject only to the viceroy. Ugarte had meant to ask Gálvez to substitute the word "liberty" for "independence" in this connection, just as it was used in Article 13. This would have implied more clearly their subordinate relationship to the commandant-general. Without this change, one of the division commanders, either capriciously or intentionally, might gravely prejudice the commandant-general's over-all policy. Furthermore, Article 18 and 19, requiring the commandant-general to send all proposals for the employment or retirement of officers to the viceroy for his determination, was an infringement on Ugarte's powers as delineated in his royal appointment and in the first articles of the *Instrucción* itself. Ugarte believed that the king had delegated authority over the Provincias Internas to Viceroy Gálvez for the purpose of providing the commandant-general with viceregal assistance, guidance, and expedition, and that it had not been the royal intent to alter the relationship of their authority to one another. Only the inopportune death of Gálvez had prevented Ugarte from making these representations officially.[13]

13 Ugarte to the King, Chihuahua, May 8, 1789, Paragraphs 9–15, AGN, PI 77, Expediente 1.

From the death of the Conde de Gálvez on November 30, 1786, until the arrival at Mexico City of his appointed successor, Manuel Antonio Flores, in August of 1787, viceregal authority was vested in the president of the audiencia of México, Archbishop Alonso Núñez de Haro.[14] During this nine-month interim Ugarte enjoyed the same independent authority over the Provincias Internas that Croix had held, but events moved rapidly to subordinate his office once more to viceregal control. On February 27, 1787, the king formally approved and gave force as a royal ordinance to the *Instrucción* of 1786.[15] Then, on March 20, 1787, still five months before Flores arrived at Mexico City, the king cloaked him with the same powers over the Provincias Internas that Gálvez had enjoyed and declared that his name be interpretated for that of Gálvez throughout the *Instrucción*.[16] Ugarte acknowledged receipt of the latter order on September 17, a month after Flores inaugurated his administration.[17] However, when Ugarte addressed the new Viceroy two weeks later and pledged obedience to him, he promised to recommend a number of modifications, which he considered essential, in the *Instrucción* of 1786 as its own Article 216 authorized him to do.[18]

Manuel Antonio Flores[19] brought to the viceroyalty of New Spain the benefits and shortcomings of a distinguished but turbulent administrative experience. He had previously served the king at Buenos Aires and had more recently completed a six-year term as viceroy of Nueva Granada (1776–82). In the latter realm he had achieved considerable success in promoting economic development, organizing a colonial militia, introducing a public printing press, and opening the royal library at Bogotá to the

[14] *Ibid.*, Paragraph 28. Núñez de Haro was confirmed as acting viceroy on February 25, 1787, but he did not begin signing his correspondence as such until May of that year. See the archival notation in the index, AGN, CV 140.

[15] Real orden, El Pardo, February 27, 1787 (copy), *loc. cit.*

[16] Real orden, El Pardo, March 20, 1787 (copy), AGN, PI 77, Expediente 9.

[17] Ugarte to the Marqués de Sonora, Arispe, September 17, 1787, AGI, Guadalajara 287.

[18] Ugarte to Flores, Arispe, October 1, 1787, AGN, PI 112, Expediente 1.

[19] The new viceroy actually signed his name as "Flórez" instead of "Flores" just as Bucareli signed his "Bucarely," but the other spelling of both names is more prevalent both in contemporary records and in formal histories.

72

citizenry. However, his efforts to raise emergency revenues for the war with England, which broke out in 1779, were not only disapproved by the king and taken over by a special royal investigator, but also seized upon by the citizenry as justification for rebellion. Flores managed to suppress the celebrated Comunero Revolt of 1780–81 in that realm, but his methods were so ruthless that he was forced to resign from his office in 1782. Nevertheless, he somehow retained royal favor and in 1787 was not only appointed to the more important viceroyalty of New Spain, but also awarded the title of Conde. Flores also held the rank of lieutenant general of the Royal Armada when he arrived at Mexico City.[20]

A military and administrative officer of great experience, even in Indian warfare, Flores saw no distinction between the Apache problem on the northern frontier of New Spain and that of the hostiles he had faced in Nueva Granada and the Río de la Plata.[21] He was quick to reach decisions and reluctant to accept criticism, but he was not above modifying his policies on the basis of his own further study and reflection. Ugarte was soon to learn that Flores was not as amenable to reconsidering his orders as Gálvez had been and also that he had less respect for Ugarte's administrative ability and long experience on the frontier. Rather, Flores was more impressed with Ugarte's advanced age and poor health, which rendered him unable to campaign personally against the hostile tribes. On the other hand, Flores was filled with admiration for the vigorous—though sometimes impetuous—military activity of Juan de Ugalde, and this worthy appeared to be ardently interested in displacing the *Comandante General.*

Not satisfied with the military organization of the Provincias Internas as provided by Gálvez's *Instrucción* of 1786, Flores asked the king to increase his own powers so that he might reshuffle the organization to his own liking.[22] He then wrote Ugarte

[20] Alonso Núñez de Haro to the Marqués de Sonora, México, July 7, 1787, No. 132, AGN, CV 142, Foja 37. See also Jesús María Henao and Gerardo Arrubla, *History of Colombia,* 159–61, 171.
[21] Flores to Antonio Valdés, No. 11, México, October 23, 1787, AGN, CV 142, Fojas 138–44.
[22] *Ibid.*

that from his study of the maps, reports, and other documents at his disposal, he had come to the conclusion that it was no longer feasible for a single *comandante general* to direct the war against the hostiles in the Provincias Internas. After the "most serious, prudent, and mature" consideration of the matter, he had decided to divide the Provincias Internas into two separate commandancies-general, as Croix had proposed in his time, and that this "indispensable and useful" division would go into effect on a provisional basis, pending royal approval, as soon as Ugarte received specific orders to that effect by the next mail. By the terms of this impending order Ugarte would continue to exercise his authority in the four provinces of California, Sonora, Nueva Vizcaya, and New Mexico, and he would continue to be assisted by the commandant-inspector, the two adjutant-inspectors, the assessor and auditor of war, and the secretarial staff. Flores believed that this would please Ugarte, for it would unburden him of his most distant duties and responsibilities, facilitate the discharge of his thorny and protracted command, and would bring about more rapidly the ultimate pacification of the Provincias Internas.[23]

Ugarte was noticeably shaken by the announcement. In a confidential letter of December 24, he complained that the imminent division was an affront to his honor, that it would gravely disrupt his general strategy for the pacification of the hostiles, and that it would undermine public respect for his measures. Flores then assured him of his complete satisfaction with Ugarte's zeal and competence. He had, he said, given the matter due consideration. He was adding the provinces of Nuevo León and Nuevo Santander to the Provincias Internas, and rather than burden Ugarte with their administration, he had decided to create a separate command that would be responsible for these and for Coahuila and Texas, which were too distant and scantily populated for efficient control by Ugarte. He was leaving Ugarte in command of the largest and most problem-ridden portion of the

[23] Flores to Ugarte, México, November 21, 1787 (draft), AGN, PI 112, Expediente 1.

frontier, and since he had already reduced hostile attacks in Sonora and New Mexico, and since California still enjoyed complete peace, he now had only to achieve this happy state of affairs in Nueva Vizcaya. Juan de Ugalde was being placed in command of the eastern division of the frontier, and Ugarte was urged to begin as soon as possible to reach an accord with him for combined military operations against, or peace negotiations with, hostiles in Nueva Vizcaya and Coahuila. He would find Ugalde most sincerely amicable and co-operative.[24]

In requesting royal approval for the division of the commandancy-general, Flores went into a much fuller and more intimate explanation. The general command had been created in the first place, in 1776, in order to alleviate the vast duties, cares, and obligations of the viceroy and also to establish a more efficient government for the vast dominions of New Spain. It was for these reasons that it was made independent of the viceroy. However, as soon as Teodoro de Croix had taken possession of the commandancy-general and had made a personal inspection of a large portion of the frontier, he had complained to the king in confidential letters of June 3 and June 29, 1778, of the great difficulties he faced in exercising his authority over such an enormous extent of territory and proposed that it be divided between two commandants-general. Croix had recommended that he be responsible for the provinces of California, Sonora, Nueva Vizcaya, and New Mexico and that another, preferably Colonel Bernardo de Gálvez (then governor of Louisiana) be appointed commandant-general for Coahuila, Texas, Nuevo Santander, and Nuevo León. As Flores understood it, these recommendations had been well received at court, as was another letter dated April 23, 1780, but no action was taken. This might have been because the king's attention was absorbed by the war with England, because the additional staff required would increase expenses, or, perhaps, because neither Croix nor his successor

[24] Ugarte's confidential letter of December 24, 1787, is not in the file, but is summarized in the Viceroy's reply. Flores to Ugarte, México, February 13, 1788 (cert. copy), AGN, PI 77, Expediente 3.

75

brought the proposal to the king's attention again. When Ugarte was appointed *Comandante General*, the king had subjected him to the immediate authority of Viceroy Gálvez, and in Gálvez's *Instrucción* of 1786 to Ugarte, Croix's well-founded concept was revived, but with the division of the command into three rather than two jurisdictions, each independent in purely military matters. Even though Gálvez had subordinated the other two commandants to Ugarte, Flores believed that this was merely nominal and temporary and that it was specified only to placate the ruffled feelings of Ugarte. The powers of the two supposedly subordinate commandants were soon amplified, and their subordination to the *Comandante General* was reduced to rendering reports to him on their military operations and on other developments within their respective commands. Gálvez had realized that the new arrangement would produce frequent disagreeable problems of protocol, ill-feeling, complaints, and appeals—all of which were prejudicial to the royal service—but Flores believed that Gálvez had been guided by the maxim of acting purposefully to overcome all obstacles to the pacification of the frontier, and that his policy had been undermined only by his own illness and death, which restored the commandancy-general to its original independence. Flores was also persuaded that this independence rendered the most essential articles of the *Instrucción* of 1786 unenforceable and therefore left the Provincias Internas in a worse condition than before.[25]

When Gálvez died, Flores noted, Ugarte was in Sonora making peace with the Chiricahua Apaches and prosecuting the war against the other, more hostile tribes of that nation. However, although he had soon achieved the virtual pacification of Sonora, the situation in Nueva Vizcaya had deteriorated. Thus, since the *Comandante General* was unable to reside in all of the provinces at one time, the most important province was without a supreme commander, and the lesser commandants were operating without concerted direction. While Ugalde was campaigning

[25] Flores to Valdés, No. 32, México, November 23, 1787, AGN, CV 142, Fojas 179–88.

against the Apaches in Coahuila, these same Indians were admitted to peace and protection in Nueva Vizcaya.[26]

It was because of the changing situations along the 2,300-mile frontier and the inability of Ugarte to attend to each emergency as it arose that Flores found it necessary and urgent to divide the general command. The great distances involved not only delayed the circulation of and compliance with orders, but also gave free rein to negligent, inept, capricious, and insubordinate field commanders to evade the orders of their superior officers. Moreover, the superior officers were unable to distinguish readily between involuntary and malicious disobedience. The three divisions organized by Gálvez had been meant to remedy these evils, but in specifying the responsibilities and obligations of the two subaltern commandants, the articles of the *Instrucción* of 1786 had produced unfortunate results in Nueva Vizcaya and had undermined Ugalde's military operations in Coahuila.[27]

In dividing the commandancy-general, Flores was also reducing the jurisdiction of Rengel as commandant-inspector to the four western provinces under Ugarte's command. Ugalde, as *Comandante General* of the eastern provinces, was to assume the powers of general inspector in that division. The Aguanaval River was to be the boundary between the two commandancies-general. Flores noted that none of these provisional changes would add to the expense of the royal treasury. On the contrary, they would provide for some justified economies, which he would explain at another time. He admitted that Ugarte's burdens would be more arduous than Ugalde's, for the territories of the western division embraced two-thirds of the entire frontier, were wealthier and more populous than the eastern provinces, were more frequently attacked by the Apaches, and were more isolated from each other by distance and stretches of desert. But Ugarte's difficulties had been even greater before his command was divided, for the provinces of Coahuila and Texas were nearly 1,800 miles from his headquarters in Sonora. Therefore, Flores main-

26 *Ibid.*
27 *Ibid.*

tained, the division would assure that measures for the defense of his provinces would be taken more promptly and that the general pacification of the frontier would be realized sooner. It would also simplify the administration of the troops and their provisioning. The division would in no way violate the *Reglamento de 1772* or the *Instrucción* of 1786. And, finally, it would save expenses.[28]

Offering much the same justification but with considerably more brevity, Flores informed Ugarte that the division of the command was to go into effect on January 1, 1788. Thereafter Ugarte was to have no other duties than the conduct of military operations and peace negotiations with the Indians and the administration of the troops in the four provinces of California, Sonora, Nueva Vizcaya, and New Mexico. He and Ugalde were to maintain continuous and frequent correspondence with each other, exchange information on all developments in their respective territories, co-ordinate their operations against and negotiations with the hostile tribes, and render each other full military assistance. They were to transfer not only troops from one commandancy-general to the other, but even themselves when necessary. Flores expected that harmony, amity, and good faith would prevail between the two commandant-generals.[29] It was expecting too much.

Although grateful for the Viceroy's favors and professing his own complete submission, Ugarte insisted on arguing one essential point. The king had conferred on him the command of all the frontier territories with the same powers that his predecessors had exercised except for his subjection in military, political, and economic matters to Gálvez while he was the viceroy. Ugarte's appointment had been made on Gálvez's request and without any solicitation on his own part. The untimely death of Gálvez had prevented him from effecting any changes in the *Instrucción* of 1786, and thus it had been approved by the king without the

[28] *Ibid.*
[29] Flores to Ugarte, México, December 3, 1787 (cert. copy), AGN, PI 77, Expediente 3.

benefit of this criticism and with some of its articles in conflict with the king's original intentions. Therefore, Ugarte insisted, Flores should re-examine his decision. When Croix had proposed the division of the commandancy-general, each province required all of the attention of one superior officer. Now, however, conditions were much improved. Ugarte could not stand by silently while the appointment of Ugalde cut into his own authority, nor could he understand how his honor could be so discredited by this diminution of his powers after he had put these dominions on such an advantageous footing. Notwithstanding the continued hostilities in Nueva Vizcaya, which he would suppress as easily as he had those in Sonora, the situation was better now than it had ever been in the past. Therefore, Flores should examine the royal decree that appointed him *Comandante General* and suspend judgment until he had studied Ugarte's own reports on conditions along the frontier.[30]

Flores, however, would not reconsider. His reply attempted only to soothe Ugarte's injured dignity. He had assumed authority over the Provincias Internas and divided the commandancy-general—not with the intention of infringing on Ugarte's honor, he said—only to carry out the king's will. He appreciated Ugarte's person, distinguished service, and zeal and would continue to report to the king favorably on his effective measures in pacifying Nueva Vizcaya.[31]

The die was cast. The king had already empowered Flores to reorganize the Provincias Internas as he saw fit,[32] and two months later, on May 15, 1788, he specifically approved the division of the frontier into two separate commands. The royal decree also suppressed the office of commandant-inspector. Rengel was transferred for the time being to Sonora, where he would operate as military commandant of that province until the king could find

[30] Ugarte to Flores (confidential), Arispe, January 6, 1788 (signed copy), AGN, PI 77, Expediente 11.

[31] Flores to Ugarte, México, March 14, 1788 (cert. copy), AGN, PI 77, Expediente 3.

[32] Real orden of March 11, 1788, quoted in Flores to Ugarte, México, June 17, 1788 (cert. copy), AGN, PI 77, Expediente 10.

other employment for him, and Ugarte and Ugalde themselves were to assume the general inspection in their respective commandancies-general.[33]

In the face of royal confirmation of Flores' decision, the matter was determined. Ugarte, however, had not subsided. Still smarting from his subjection to the Viceroy, his loss of authority over the eastern provinces, and the refusal of Flores to reconsider his decision, Ugarte now appealed directly to the king. In a lengthy memorial recounting his past services, the recent erosion of his powers, and his mounting personal debts, Ugarte asked not only that he be restored to his full command, but that he also be promoted to the rank of *mariscal de campo*. Arming his representation with impressive statistics on the number of Apaches his troops had killed, captured, and forced to sue for peace during his two and one-half years in office, he declared that he had expected to witness the complete pacification of the frontier during his own time. Now, however, all was lost. Flores, either influenced by persons of little prudence and less intelligence, or erring gravely in his own judgment, had undermined his efforts by innovations that violated the policies of his predecessors, which had been established by long experienced and royal approval. Flores, whose zeal, rectitude, and talent were well known, was not to blame. Lacking adequate knowledge of the frontier problems, however, he had been deluded by reports which were vitiated by personal motive. He was especially influenced by reports from Ugalde, who, motivated by the same spirit of independence and insubordination that had brought about his removal from the governorship of Coahuila by Croix, had begun to operate against Ugarte's orders immediately after his appointment as military commandant of the eastern provinces. When Flores arrived in Mexico City, Ugarte had written him of Ugalde's disruptive operations, but the new Viceroy had already received Ugalde's report and was so impressed with his military achievements that he immediately decided to elevate him to the commandancy-

[33] Real cédula of May 15, 1788, quoted in Flores to Ugarte, México, August 11, 1788 (cert. copy), AGN, PI 77, Expediente 3.

general of the eastern division. Ugarte had protested at once, calling attention to his own achievements under the united command, but his protests were to no avail. Instead of reproving or correcting Ugalde for his insubordination, Flores had elevated him beyond Ugarte's authority. As a result of Ugalde's intemperate operations, hostilities had increased in both Nueva Vizcaya and Coahuila just as Ugarte had predicted.[34]

By this time Flores himself was having some second thoughts on his division of the commandancy-general, although he did not admit it to Ugarte. In a confidential letter to the king's minister in August of 1788, the Viceroy not only reappraised the situation on the frontier, but also expressed his true evaluation of Ugarte.[35] He was convinced that Ugarte, owing to his advanced age and weariness, could no longer endure the fatigues of military campaigns and was unfit for active command in the Indian wars. However, on the basis of his age, distinguished service, honorable character, and unselfish conduct, he was deserving of the king's reward. Flores had no position for him in New Spain that was suitable to his rank and experience, and he understood that Ugarte could not pay his own way back to Spain because of his personal debts, which now amounted to 60,000 pesos. He would therefore retain him as commandant-general and inspector of the western division of the frontier, even though inept for that duty, until the king could find other employment for him, and he would continue to provide him with the exceptionally high salary of 20,000 pesos, even though this and other expenses of Ugarte's command should be reduced. Flores thought that 8,000 pesos was a sufficient salary for each of the two commandant-generals since they were now subordinate to the viceroy and exercised only military authority.[36]

After reviewing the duties and expenses of the two commandancies and suggesting economies, Flores traced the history of

[34] Ugarte to Valdés, San Bartolomé, October 6, 1788, AGN, PI 77, Expediente 11.
[35] Flores to Valdés, No. 536 (confidential), México, August 26, 1788, AGN, CV 19 (Second series), Fojas 61–96.
[36] *Ibid.*, Paragraphs 4–10.

viceregal control over the Provincias Internas, and then confided to the king's minister that he had misjudged the situation. He confessed that he had been unable to formulate a workable policy on the basis of the reports he had received from the frontier provinces, for these almost always disagreed with one another. He was unable either to ascertain the facts or rely on the recommendations expressed in these messages, for they were colored by passion, caprice, and personal motivation. After reviewing the problems pertaining to Indian relations, troop pay and provisioning, and military discipline and operations as represented in these discordant reports, Flores came to the startling conclusion that, after all, the effectiveness of the commandancy-general while independent from viceregal control had never actually been fairly tested. Croix's independent command had lasted only six years; Neve, his successor, had died after less than two years; Rengel, an interim appointment, was in office only a few months; and Ugarte's independence from the viceregency had lasted only a little longer than Rengel's. Altogether the commandancy-general of the Provincias Internas had been free from viceregal control for only nine or ten years, and Flores now thought that this was too short a period in which to expect the solution of the deeply-rooted frontier problems, especially since none of the commandant-generals had felt that they were adequately provided with troops.[37]

Therefore, Flores now recommended that the Provincias Internas be united once more, placed under a single commandant-general, and made independent from viceregal control. Its commanding officer, he felt, should carry the rank of *mariscal de campo* and should succeed automatically to the office of viceroy at the close of his term as commandant-general. Flores proposed that the two existing divisions of the frontier be administered by commandant-inspectors, subordinate to the commandant-general. Ugalde should fill the inspectorship of the eastern division and Colonel Manuel de Flon (formerly military commandant of Nueva Vizcaya and now intendant of Puebla) that of the west-

[37] *Ibid.*, Paragraphs, 11-54.

ern division. In any case, Flores pleaded, Ugarte should be promoted to some other office because of his age and fragile health. As for the obvious contradiction of his previous recommendation that the commandancy-general be divided, Flores explained that the only real difference was that the two division commanders would now be subordinate to a commandant-general vested with the same powers that had been conferred on Flores instead of to the viceroy himself. As it now existed, the viceroy was too involved with other matters and too remote from the frontier theater of war to direct operations there efficiently. Finally, even if this new proposal did contradict his earlier one, Flores now felt that he should change his mind.[38]

There is no indication that Flores revealed his remarkable about-face inclinations to Ugarte. In fact Ugarte was still without knowledge of it nine months later. In May of 1789 he carried his own case to the personal attention of the king in a fifty-three-page memorial accompanied by numerous supporting documents.[39] Reflecting on his own more than fifty-six years in the royal service, his great loss of personal fortune therein, and the damage his honor had suffered from the reorganization of the commandancy-general, and buttressing his argumentative discourse with frequent allusions to the accompanying documents, Ugarte traced at some length the history of the Provincias Internas from 1752, when it was first proposed as a separate commandancy-general, to its subjection to Viceroy Flores in 1788.[40]

The only assistance he needed from Flores, Ugarte told the king, was implementation of his own strategy for pacifying the hostile tribes and viceregal backing in forcing Ugalde to obey orders. Again he alleged that Ugalde's reports had brainwashed the Viceroy, inducing him to divide the frontier command and elevate himself to full authority over the eastern division. At the time Flores had been in office only three months and had made these changes almost in an instant and certainly without con-

[38] *Ibid.*, Paragraphs 56–78.
[39] Ugarte to the King, Chihuahua, May 8, 1789, AGN, PI 77, Expediente 1.
[40] *Ibid.*, Paragraphs 2–24.

sulting the more experienced Ugarte or even heeding his objections. Ugarte was aware of developments that were unknown in Mexico City. This should have induced Flores to suspend his resolution pending a full report from Ugarte, as Ugarte had tried to persuade him to do, but Flores had already circulated his order to the frontier officers and had asked the king for approval of his decisions. This made it difficult for Flores to turn back or to reconsider.[41]

Ugarte had continued to argue for a united command and to suggest that the division was a mistake. Flores' replies had not satisfied him, and so he now felt justified in representing his case directly to the king. Flores had contended that the distance of Coahuila and Texas from Ugarte's headquarters justified the division, but this reasoning was invalid, Ugarte insisted, for those two provinces were even more distant from the Viceroy's headquarters, to which their new commandant-general had to report and look for guidance. Furthermore, the addition of the more populous provinces of Nuevo León and Nuevo Santander to Ugalde's command of Coahuila and Texas was entirely unnecessary, for the Apaches and Comanches, who had previously attacked the latter two, were now at peace; and even if they should resume their hostilities, troops could readily be borrowed by Coahuila and Texas to reinforce their defenses. Ugarte was competent to deal with such problems. The Provincias Internas had been separated from the viceroyalty in the first place only after long and deliberate consideration; Croix's proposal of 1778 for the division of its command was obviously without merit, for the king had not approved it; the present situation on the frontier made division even less advantageous; the appointment of Ugalde to command of the eastern division was even worse because of his insubordination and his sabotage of the recent peace pact with the Mescalero Apaches; and, finally, Flores should have had more confidence in Ugarte's administration.[42]

For all these reasons and so that the losses suffered from the

[41] *Ibid.*, Paragraphs 26–31.
[42] *Ibid.*, Paragraphs 32–38.

change could be recouped, Ugarte begged the king to return the Provincias Internas to its former unified and independent organization. In approving Ugalde's military operations, recommending him for promotion, and conferring on him command of two of Ugarte's provinces, Flores had been unduly influenced by the "fabricated" reports of the eastern commandant. Ugarte had refuted Ugalde's reports, but Flores had been unmoved. He had also objected to the transfer of two patrol companies from his to Ugalde's command and also to Ugalde's free use of the troops of three presidios and another patrol company of Nueva Vizcaya for his operations against the Mescalero Apaches. Finally, Ugarte's own control over finances had been so restricted that he could no longer obtain the bare necessities for conducting war and maintaining peace without the prior approval of the treasury office, and the red tape and delay that repeatedly resulted from this inconvenience were frustrating his efforts to pacify the hostiles. All of this was contrary to Articles 5, 82, and 83 of the *Instrucción* of 1786, which invested him with financial authority for such operations.[43]

In a much shorter dispatch to the minister of the Indies a month later, Ugarte complained again. The division of the commandancy-general had not only destroyed the important peace with the Mescaleros and perverted the general order of affairs in the provinces, he contended, but had also undermined his own strategic plan for their general pacification and was endangering the lives and property of the king's poor vassals. If the commandancy-general were not restored to its former status, he warned, the total ruin of these provinces was inevitable. Nueva Vizcaya had already been especially hard hit since the disruption of the Mescalero peace, and the loss of 1,291 persons to the Apaches during the last three years was casting a dark shadow over the entire frontier.[44] Although Ugarte had no way of knowing it at the time a brighter day was dawning.

If the untimely death of Gálvez in 1786 had been a blow to

---

[43] *Ibid.*, Paragraphs 39–55, 60–66, 72.
[44] Ugarte to Valdés, Chihuahua, June 9, 1789, AGN, PI 77, Expediente 2.

Ugarte, the premature retirement of Flores in 1789 was a blessing. Suffering from ill health, Flores had requested permission to retire and had obtained royal approval before he had completed two years in office.[45] Ugarte seems to have learned of the resignation five months after the king accepted it. He seems also to have learned of the appointment of Flores' successor at least three months before he arrived from Spain to take office.[46] The new viceroy was Juan Vicente Güemes Pacheco de Padilla, better known as the second Conde de Revillagigedo. His father, the first Conde, had been viceroy of New Spain from 1746 to 1755, and the younger Revillagigedo had been born in the New World, at Havana. He had been sent to Spain for his military training and had risen to the rank of lieutenant colonel in Ugarte's old outfit, the Regiment of Spanish Guards.[47] Perhaps the two had mutual acquaintances in high places. At any rate, Revillagigedo favored Ugarte over Ugalde, Gálvez's Indian policy over Flores', and, temporarily at least, the concept of the united over the divided military command.

[45] Flores' resignation was approved by the King on February 22, 1789, but he was ordered to remain in office until his successor arrived, according to his acknowledgment of the order. Flores to Valdés, No. 967, México, May 27, 1789, AGN, CV 151, Foja 1.

[46] Ugarte to the Conde de Revillagigedo (confidential), Chihuahua, November 20, 1789, AGN, PI 159, Expediente 6.

[47] Revillagigedo assumed viceregal authority on October 16, 1789. Niceto de Zamacois, *Historia de México desde sus tiempos mas remotos hasta nuestros días*, V, 670–71.

CHAPTER V

THE FRONTIER ARMY
1786-1790

As commandant-general of the Provincias Internas, Jacobo Ugarte's foremost obligation was the administration of the armed forces of the frontier and the over-all direction of their campaigns against the hostile Indians. The permanent military force of the northern frontier belonged neither to the regular Spanish army nor to the colonial militia, although at times it relied for reinforcements on both. Rather, it was a special service somewhat inferior to the former and superior to the latter in terms of pay and privilege. Its troops were recruited from New Spain itself, as was the militia, and paid by the crown, as was the regular army, but they operated under a special body of military law prescribed by the king, were assigned almost permanently to the northern frontier, were organized into presidial and mobile companies, and were employed almost exclusively against hostile Indians.[1]

From time to time some Spanish regulars, such as the *Voluntarios de Cataluña* or the *Dragones de España,* were sent to the north to bolster defenses. In addition local militias, recruited from the settlers and supported by the merchants and proprietors, could be called up on special occasions. But the most effective reinforcements were friendly Indians. The Indian service was

---

[1] The specifications for the frontier military service appear in the *Reglamento de 1772.* For the text of these articles, see Brinckerhoff and Faulk, *Lancers for the King,* 11–67.

made up of nomadic tribal warriors serving as allies either independently or in concert with the frontier troops, but almost always under their own chieftains. The organized auxiliaries were usually, but not always, drawn on a quota basis for temporary duty from established native towns, and there were a few special garrisons of Indians regularly organized as military companies. Then, too, individual Indians were hired or impressed into temporary service as scouts, guides, spies, and interpreters.[2] Finally, in times of dire emergency the citizens themselves with whatever arms and mounts they could muster were called up by the provincial governors or local *alcaldes*. But the main burden of offensive and defensive duty was borne by the permanent corps of presidial soldiers.

At the close of 1787 the army of the Provincias Internas numbered on paper approximately 3,200 officers and men, although vacancies and infirmities reduced the effective force to approximately 3,000. These were organized into twenty-four presidios, ten *compañías volantes* (light-horse or "flying" companies), and two companies of Spanish regulars. The province of Nueva Vizcaya, perennially the major target of Apache attacks, had the largest assignment of troops with 1,502 allotted to its seven presidios and six light-horse companies. Sonora had the second strongest force with 906 officers and men for its six presidios, three Indian companies, one company of Spanish regulars, and one picket of Spanish dragoons. Then came Coahuila with 372 troops distributed among four presidios; California (Upper and Lower) with 249 in five presidios; Texas with 187 in two presidios; and finally New Mexico with 120 officers and men in its single garrison. In size the companies varied from only 47 troops, as in Lower California's presidio of Loreto, to as many as 154 officers and men, as in some of the "flying" companies of Nueva Vizcaya.[3]

---

[2] For a full discussion of the different forms of Indian enlistments, see Oakah L. Jones, Jr., *Pueblo Warriors and Spanish Conquest*.

[3] The troops of Nueva Vizcaya were stationed at the presidios of Janos (144 officers and men); San Buenaventura, now relocated about 18 miles downstream from Valle de Chavarría (144); San Fernando de Carrizal (73); San Eleazario (73); El Príncipe, now at Coyamé (73); El Norte, formerly called La Junta

El Paso del Norte ○
SAN ELIZARIO

108   106   104

0   50   100
SCALE IN MILES
31

FRONTERAS
(SONORA)   JANOS

CARRIZAL

CASAS GRANDES ●

SAN BUENAVENTURA

CORRAL DE PIEDRAS ●

EL PRÍNCIPE

EL NORTE

Namiquipa ✚   ● ENCINILLAS

29

San Gerónimo ✚
Chihuahua ○   SAN CARLOS

○ Cosiguiriachi

Pilar de Conchos ✚

CIENÉGA DE OLIVOS

Guajoquilla ✚
Parral ○   ○ Valle de San Bartolomé
Santa Bárbara ○   BOLSÓN
DE
MAPIMÍ

27

LA ZARCA ●   ● MAPIMÍ

EL GALLO ●

NUEVA VIZCAYA
1787
Nazas R.

● EL PASAJE   25

L ― PRESENT STATE BOUNDARIES
E ― PROVINICIAL CAPITAL
G ― PRESIDIOS
E ― POSTS
N ― VILLAS AND MINING COMMUNITIES
D ― PUEBLOS AND HACIENDAS

Z

Cuencamé ○

◎
✚
○
●

◎ DURANGO

Río Grande · *Conchos R.*

Since 1729, when the frontier forces amounted to only 734 troops maintained at a cost of just under 284,000 pesos, the crown had repeatedly increased the military budget, raised the troop strength, and shifted the garrisons to supposedly more strategic sites with a view toward warding off the Apache invasions of the settled areas, all without effect. Even the gradual development of a more flexible and realistic Indian policy did not achieve the desired results, for even this presupposed an effective military force. More to the point was the need for a better training of officers and men, an improvement of weapons and equipment, and adequate provisions for the soldiers and their families—all of which were vital to the morale of the troops. A sampling of the reports of periodic garrison inspections indicates the inadequacy of the arms and equipment of the frontier soldier on the eve of Ugarte's administration.

At the presidio of Tucson, a northern outpost of the Sonora frontier, each soldier was supposed to have been armed with a regular musket (escopeta), or with the shorter-barreled carabina, two pistols, a lance, a bullhide shield, and an arrow-proof jacket

---

(106); and San Carlos de Cerrogordo, now at Chorreras (73). The "flying" companies were at Guajoquilla (154), Namiquipa (154), Pilar de Conchos (154), San Gerónimo (154), Alamo (100), and Anaelo (100).

The troops of Sonora were at the presidios of San Carlos de Buenavista (73); San Miguel de Horcasitas, now at El Pitic (73); Santa Gertrudis de Altar (73); San Agustín del Tucson (73); Santa Cruz de Terrenate, temporarily encamped 18 miles west of Las Nutrias (106); and Fronteras de los Apaches, now removed from San Bernardino to its original site (106). There was an Opata Indian company at San Miguel de Bavispe (91), an Opata company at Bacoachi (91), a Pima Indian company of San Rafael de Buenavista, temporarily stationed at old Tubac (84), a company of Voluntarios de Cataluña, temporarily at Arispe (83), and a picket of Spanish dragoons, now divided and added to the presidios of Tucson and Altar (53).

The Coahuila troops were stationed at the presidios of Monclova, now returned from the Río Grande to the villa of that name (93); Aguaverde, now removed from the Río Grande to San Fernando de Austria (93); San Antonio Bucareli de la Babia, now at Valle de Santa Rosa (93); and San Juan Bautista del Río Grande (93).

California's forces were in the presidios of Loreto (47), San Diego (54), Santa Bárbara (61), Monterey (54), and San Francisco (33). Those of Texas were at the presidios of San Antonio de Béjar (94) and Bahía del Espíritu Santo (93). New Mexico's lone presidial company operated out of Santa Fe (120). See Ugarte, Estado Mayor of 1787, AGN, PI 254, Expediente 2.

of heavy leather (*cuera*). However, of the company's sixty-four muskets, nine were of small caliber; several of the carbines were almost worn out; one-half the pistols were too poorly manufactured to be serviceable; there was a shortage of one lance; and there were only twenty-one leather jackets, none of them properly reinforced, for the company of seventy-three men. The presidial horse herd numbered 356 (eighty-two shy of the six-per-man required by the *Reglamento de 1772*), and there were fifty-one mules (twenty-two under the official requirement). Most of the horses were undernourished. The fort itself was armed with four bronze cannon mounted at the corners of the walls and supplied with adequate powder and with seventy-eight four-pound lead balls.[4]

The eighty-three Spanish regulars at Arispe were armed with only thirty-five reconditioned firelocks (*fusiles*) and seventeen carbines, and these were almost useless owing to their fragile firing mechanisms. There was also a shortage of seventeen lances. Although the Arispe company took part in almost every campaign launched from Sonora, it was one of the most poorly equipped. Its troops rode out on campaign in shirt-sleeves instead of full uniform, entered battle dressed entirely in leather, and fought with bows and arrows as well as with firearms.[5]

At Buenavista the company was made up of Indian troops—Pimas and Opatas—who spoke little Spanish, but were sturdy enough to march long distances on foot and were able marksmen with both guns and bows. Not being issued regular uniforms, each man wore what he wished or had available, but for greater freedom of movement they went into battle naked from the waist up. Only twenty-four of the eighty-four officers and men were provided with muskets, most of them old and unserviceable; twenty-three had carbines whose firing devices were undependable, and the rest were armed with bows and arrows. All carried lances. In times past these Indian troops were also issued mache-

[4] Adjutant Inspector Lieutenant Colonel Roque de Medina, Revista del Presidio de Tucson, October 10, 1785, in Extracto de Revista, 1785–1786, AGI, Guadalajara 521.
[5] Medina, Revista del Presidio de Arispe, March 5, 1786, *ibid.*

tes as weapons, but they had proved too cumbersome for infantrymen and had now been abandoned.[6]

The presidio of Bavispe, a company of volunteers and draftees from the Opata nation, was noted for the good disposition, discipline, sturdiness, height, and agility of its soldiers, and for their ability to live off the wild fruits of the desert country. These Indians knew how to operate and care for their guns and were considered better marksmen with both musket and bow than the Spanish soldiers. They, too, dressed individually and discarded both jacket and shirt before going into battle. Fifty-seven of the Opatas were provided with muskets and three with carbines, all of which were regularly cared for and in medium condition, but some were in need of new parts. This company had only thirty mules (sixty-one short of a full complement) and fifteen of these were unable to carry packs.[7]

Detachments from the regular Spanish army that served on the frontier were usually better dressed, but no less adequately equipped than the colonials. The Spanish dragoons garrisoning the *villa* of El Pitic wore regular uniforms consisting of short red jackets with blue cuffs, blue breeches, white shirt, and blue cape. Of the full complement of fifty men, only forty-seven were effectives and only thirty-nine of these were armed with *escopetas* and pistols. Another six carried *fusiles*, but these as well as the pistols were worn out, and there were enough sabers for only twenty-two of the men. The horse herd suffered a shortage of fifty-seven head, and there was a lack of twelve pack mules.[8]

An itemization of equipment lost by a detachment of troops in a particularly hard-fought battle in Nueva Vizcaya is indicative of what the troops carried into combat and how much they ordinarily had to pay for their accouterments. Each horse was valued at thirteen pesos, a saddle at nine pesos, saddle cover at two and one-half pesos, saddle blanket at three pesos, bridle bit at four

[6] Medina, Revista del Presidio de Buenavista, November 26, 1785, *ibid.*
[7] Medina, Revista del Presidio de Bavispe, January 21, 1786, *ibid.*
[8] Medina, Revista del Presidio del Pitic, November 17, 1785, *ibid.*

pesos, spurs at one and one-half pesos, bullhide jacket at twelve pesos, bullhide shield at three pesos, a brace of pistols at twelve pesos, saber at four pesos, common sword at three pesos, hat at four pesos, new uniform at twelve pesos, cape at eighteen pesos, and serape at four pesos. This amounted to more than one hundred pesos and did not include shoes, stockings, shirt, underclothes, cartridges, musket, and other miscellaneous items, which each soldier was required to purchase. The total losses in this particular battle amounted to 2,245 pesos and 7 reales worth of equipment, but owing to the extraordinary valor displayed by the troops under extremely adverse circumstances the royal treasury assumed the cost of replacements instead of docking the soldiers themselves.[9]

The arms for the frontier troops were shipped from Spain and stored at three arsenals behind the frontier presidial line, at Chihuahua, Arispe, and San Luis Potosí. At the beginning of 1788 these armories had only a small number of muskets in reserve and no pistols at all. Since the presidios were suffering severe shortages at that time, Viceroy Flores put in an order for 3,654 muskets and 1,997 pairs of pistols, which were to be sent to the three arsenals from the stores held at the fortress of Perote, near Vera Cruz. These weapons were finally distributed to the presidial troops in 1789 at a cost to them of just under fourteen pesos for each pair of pistols and each musket drawn from the arsenal at Arispe and just under twelve pesos each for those issued at Chihuahua, the cost of transportation being calculated in the price. As this shipment still failed to meet the requirements, Viceroy Revillagigedo requested the king's minister to have 5,000 guns of the type, caliber, and size specified in the latest *reglamento* made in Spain and shipped to Mexico immediately.[10]

Although the *Reglamento de 1772* did not specify artillery for the presidios, several of the frontier forts had cannon mounted

[9] Lt. José Manuel Carrasco, certification, Chihuahua, November 23, 1789, and Flores to Ugarte, México, June 16, 1789 (draft), AGN, PI 127, Expediente 2.
[10] Revillagigedo to Valdés, No. 120, México, November 26, 1789, AGN, CV 154, Fojas 213–15.

on their walls. However, no artillerymen were listed as such in the muster rolls of 1785–86.[11] Nevertheless, no less a veteran frontier soldier than Ugarte himself felt a need for this specialized weapon. In either 1789 or 1790 Ugarte asked the Viceroy for twenty-six cannon of 4-pound caliber with mountings and ammunition for the presidios of Nueva Vizcaya. Since this was the main theater of warfare at the time, Ugarte thought that these weapons would be particularly effective against Indian attacks *en masse* on the presidios themselves. A large number of cannon were available in the arsenals of Veracruz, Perote, and Mexico City, but they weighed from 700 to 750 pounds each, even when unmounted, and since the transportation of such cumbersome pieces over more than 400 leagues of road to the presidios would be inordinately expensive, the Viceroy agreed to send lighter *pedreros*, the customary cannon for small ships, instead. Some of the presidios of Sonora had cannon of 4-pound caliber, and Coahuila and Texas had others, but there was a shortage in Nueva Vizcaya, New Mexico, Nuevo Santander, and Nuevo León. Furthermore, in the absence of carpenters and blacksmiths to repair them, they were generally without mountings. Therefore, Revillagigedo ordered 132 *pedreros* of 3- or 4-pound caliber from Havana and required that each of the manned frontier posts be furnished with four of them.[12]

Of vital importance for patrol, pursuit, and campaign duty were the presidial horse herds. Pastured near the garrisons, the horses were all too often run off in sneak attacks by small bands of hostiles. Replacements were both expensive and difficult to obtain from the distant stock farms of the interior, and presidial troops were sometimes rendered inactive for from three to six months at a time while awaiting the arrival of remounts. For these reasons and also because range-fed horses did not stand up as well on arduous campaigns as those nourished on grain, Commandant-General Croix had proposed the construction of

---

[11] Medina, Extracto de Revista, 1785–1786, *loc. cit.*

[12] Revillagigedo to Valdés, No. 19, México, October 27, 1790, AGN, CV 154, Fojas 26–27.

stables at the presidios. He had recommended that the walls of the fort be extended to form a large enclosure with haylofts and granaries wherein the horse herd would be better fed and protected from Indian raids; that the animals be pastured outside only during daylight hours. Fewer horses so strengthened would be required for campaigns into hostile country; they would thus stir up less dust and therefore be more likely to take the enemy by surprise; and this smaller number could more easily be protected from theft or stampede.[13] Juan de Ugalde, whose reckless campaigns in Coahuila were particularly hard on horseflesh, opposed Croix's conservation proposal and further antagonized the Commandant-General by asking for twenty-six horses for each of his soldiers![14] The presidial troops were assessed for their remounts as well as for their firearms and other equipment, and in 1785, as a result of the losses of horses over the previous years, one company was in debt for more than 4,000 pesos.[15] Another company, being short fifty-seven horses and twelve mules, owed more than 1,000 pesos in the same year. Three pesos a month were being deducted from the pay of each member of the company to retire the debt.[16] In his *Instrucción* of 1786 Viceroy Gálvez had cautioned Ugarte to be especially attentive to the safeguarding of the remount stations. He directed Ugarte to hold the company commandants, rather than the soldiers themselves, personally responsible for all losses.[17]

Ugarte himself was becoming increasingly concerned with the financial plight of the enlisted men. In 1786 he complained of the indebtedness with which they were saddled and the low-pay scale, which Croix had established for both officers and men. Although the soldiers practiced the most stringent economy, their families were poorly dressed and fed and housed even worse, and the effect was demoralizing. If their pay were sufficient for

13 Thomas, *Teodoro de Croix*, 55–57.
14 *Ibid.*, 61.
15 Medina, Revista del Presidio de Tuscon, October 10, 1785, Extracto de Revista, 1785–1786, *loc. cit.*
16 Medina, Revista del Presidio del Pitic, November 17, 1785, *ibid.*
17 Article 22, Gálvez, Instrucción of 1786, AGN, PI 129, Expediente 4.

adequate subsistence, Ugarte felt, they would be stimulated to a more gallant and effective military performance.[18] In 1787 the annual pay scale for common presidial soldiers was 240 pesos a year and for those serving in the *compañías volantes* only 216 pesos. Captains of presidios drew 2,400 pesos a year and the commandants of "flying" companies, 1,200 pesos.[19]

Historically, the presidial soldier was caught up in the same vicious system of debt-servitude that so reduced the *peón* on the hacienda, and his morale—and thus his effectiveness—was similarly eroded away by the hopelessness of his plight. Originally the troops were free men, paid an annual salary in either specie or cashable treasury warrants. With this remuneration they bought what they and their families needed at the best bargains available. By the seventeenth century, however, a practice had developed wherein they were at first paid one-half their salary and eventually all of it in military equipment and the provisions that they and their families consumed. The distribution of these goods against their salary accounts was often fraught with enormous fraud, for provincial governors, presidial captains and paymasters, and local merchants entered into collusion to mark up the prices on what the troops required. The Rivera inspection and resultant *Reglamento de 1729* attempted to reform the pernicious system by establishing maximum-price lists and uniform-pay scales within each presidio and vesting the provisioning of the troops in the company captain, but the abuses continued with these officers reaping the benefits. Rubí's inspection of 1766–68

[18] Ugarte to the Marqués de Sonora, Chihuahua, May 31, 1786 (cert. copy), AGN, PI 78, Expediente 6.

[19] The complete pay scale for ranks (with *compañía volante* officers and men in parentheses) was as follows: captains, 2,400 pesos (1,200); lieutenants, 700 (600); second lieutenants, 600 (500); ensigns, 500 (480); second ensigns, 450 (450); chaplains, 480 (450); sergeants, 324 (264); corporals, 276 (252); carbineers, 252 (240); and soldiers, 240 (216). There were some exceptions. The captains of Tucson, Janos, Carrizal, and Bahía del Espíritu Santo each drew 3,000 pesos; the lieutenants of the Pima and Opata Indian companies of Buenavista and Bavispe, being veterans and commandants of their presidios, received 800 pesos; and both the Indian officers and men of these companies, as well as that of Bacoachi, received only three reales a day, which would amount to 135 pesos a year, regardless of rank. Ugarte, Estado Mayor of 1787, *loc. cit.*

uncovered a host of irregularities that oppressed the troops. Company captains, some of whom were also provincial governors, were barring from the presidios those merchants who offered goods at competitive prices, and were establishing monopolistic company stores, marking up prices to ensure themselves a comfortable profit, allowing their men to become heavily in debt, and even withholding their men from hazardous duty so as to protect the mortgages on their salaries. Although the soldiers now received pay ranging from 380 to 420 pesos a year, depending upon the distance of their garrisons from Mexico City, the markup in prices sometimes reduced this to 100 pesos in real purchasing power, and it was not uncommon for them to end up with debts of 400 pesos in a single year. The new *Reglamento de 1772* deprived the presidial captains of their lucrative monopoly, placed elected non-commissioned officers in charge of both the pay and provisioning of the troops, and allowed these paymasters a markup of only 2 per cent on their purchases, which was considered sufficient to cover their expenses. In anticipation of a considerable saving to the soldiers, however, troop pay was reduced to an annual rate of from 290 to 300 pesos.[20]

The *Reglamento de 1772* failed to solve the problem. The elected paymasters began to delegate their purchasing responsibilities to private individuals or to buy exclusively from a single merchant instead of shopping for the best bargains. Furthermore, several of them incurred costs in excess of the fixed prices and thereby went into bankruptcy. When this happened the troops were left short of food, clothing, and equipment. Croix's inspection of 1777 discovered that five presidial paymasters had gone into debt, one to the extent of 15,000 pesos; that they seldom kept the company funds in properly-locked chests, or kept clear records of their accounts, or distributed the provisions with any formality, or held regular audits. Deficits continued, troop pay

[20] Max L. Moorhead, "The Private Contract System of Presidio Supply in Northern New Spain," *Hispanic American Historical Review*, Vol. XLI (February, 1961), 31–54, and "The Presidio Supply Problem of New Mexico in the Eighteenth Century," *New Mexico Historical Review*, Vol. XXXVI (July, 1961), 210–29.

fell into arrears, and equipment deteriorated. Sometimes the pay-masters gambled away the company's funds.[21]

Beginning experimentally in 1781 and regularly in 1783, the provisioning of the troops was granted under contract to private merchants, each supplying one or two presidios. But this also proved unsatisfactory. Complaining that they could not profit adequately without charging the troops more than their salaries would cover, one merchant after another refused to renew his contract. This was the situation that Ugarte faced when he became *comandante general*. Far more responsive to the plight of the soldier than he had been as governor of Coahuila (and consequently captain of the presidio of Monclova), Ugarte now let a series of general five-year contracts wherein single private merchants provisioned the several presidios and posts of one or two entire provinces. This offered some improvement, but complaints continued from both the contractors and the troops. One of the general contracts was revoked in 1790, three years before it was scheduled to expire, when it was found that the contractor had failed to live up to some of his guarantees. A guild of merchants was then awarded a similar contract, but there is no evidence that the troops were materially benefited.[22]

The presidial soldier was not only expected to maintain himself, his family, and his military equipment, on his meager pay, but he was also to perform the hazardous duty for which he was stationed at an exposed frontier outpost. He might be called upon to ride through hostile country with an official dispatch to the commandant of another post, to serve with an escort for the mule trains carrying military provisions and supplies, or to stand guard over the presidial horses, which the wily Apache coveted above all else that the white man possessed. But the main purpose of the garrison was to patrol the vast stretches between frontier posts, and especially the mountain passes, to rise to the defense of the neighboring settlements by intercepting the marauders or pursuing them into their mountain retreats to retrieve their plun-

[21] *Ibid.*
[22] *Ibid.*

der and to join with one or more other companies in a general campaign into enemy territory for the purpose of exterminating or, at least, intimidating the relentless foe. The life of the presidial was neither easy nor drab. In order to maintain an incessant watch for either a massive invasion or a small raid, regulations called for one-third of each presidial company to be out on patrol at all times. Therefore almost every soldier spent at least ten days in his saddle each month.[23] Often he spent much more.

The effectiveness of presidial operations was the subject of a running debate between the military and civilian authorities. In Nueva Vizcaya, which bore the brunt of the Apache raids, military operations during the summer of 1788, when the province was particularly hard hit, came under particularly sharp attack from Felipe Díaz de Ortega, the intendant of Durango. Local magistrates and district subdelegates of the intendancy reported not only on the damage inflicted by the Apaches but also on the relative effectiveness of the punitive operations, and the Intendant compiled this information for his weekly reports to the viceroy. Since the authority of the Intendant was newly established and included jurisdiction over much that formerly had been the responsibility of the *Comandante General*, a bitter rivalry developed between Díaz de Ortega and Ugarte, and the reports of both to Mexico City were frequently colored with understandable resentment. Nevertheless, the true picture of Nueva Vizcaya's defenses was not a pretty one.

According to the Intendant, the ferocity of the Apache attacks threatened Nueva Vizcaya with complete ruin. On June 19, a large number of hostiles had invaded the district of Cosiguiriachi, killing an Indian of one of the pueblos that day, a white man the next, and two more whites three days later. On July 2, one settler had been killed at a farm only ten miles from the town of Santa Bárbara and four more at its very gates. On July 3, the raiders stole twenty-two mules and horses from another pueblo in the Cosiguiriachi district and attacked other settlements nearby. Two days later all the inhabitants of two haciendas in the

23 Ugarte, Estado Mayor of 1787, *loc. cit.*

Santa Bárbara district were robbed by a band of Apaches, and the same hostiles then attacked a pack train on its way to Parral. Five of the fifteen muleteers were wounded, twenty loaded mules were driven off, and the remainder of the goods was destroyed. When this was reported to the district commander, Captain Domingo Díaz, he sent only thirty-nine troops. These arrived two days later under a mere sergeant, ascertained the whereabouts of the attackers, and then retired the following day. The Intendant believed that the sergeant and his troops were afraid to pursue the hostiles and felt that they constituted an excessive number for a mere reconnaissance. He also thought that Captain Díaz should have come in person to direct the operation. Díaz had sent sixteen other troops from a nearby detachment to track the enemy, but these had returned without having made contact. Summarizing the situation, the Intendant declared that the province of Nueva Vizcaya was being progressively destroyed by the Apaches and that there was no available military force capable of preventing it.[24]

Apache raids continued in the Santa Bárbara district, and seven days after the subdelegate of the intendancy appealed to Captain Díaz for assistance, ninety-six troops arrived under Captain Manuel Casanova. These began a reconnaissance of the adjacent sierras, but, on receiving a report from Parral that Indians had made off with some horses and mules there, they set off to relieve that mining community. The citizenry of Parral breathed more easily when the troops arrived, but when Captain Casanova led them off into the mountains to pursue the enemy, the inhabitants were once more thrown into consternation and threatened to abandon the town. On July 22, the Indians drove off the horses and mules of the hacienda of Corral de Piedras. Pursued by troops, they abandoned most of the animals, killed one soldier, wounded another and a civilian, and escaped. For their own efforts, the troops managed only to recover 7 horses and 6 saddles, to scalp one Indian, and to relieve another of his ears. The Inten-

[24] Felipe Díaz de Ortega to Viceroy Flores, Durango, July 23, 1788, AGN, PI 127, Expediente 4.

dant thought this a small accomplishment for ninety-six well-mounted and well-equipped troops. On August 2, seventy-three hostiles in four raids within thirteen miles of Santa Bárbara killed eight persons, injured ten, stole more than 200 horses, and menacingly remained encamped in the nearby mountains. The Intendant felt that the troops were competent to protect the civilians, but that Captain Casanova merely antagonized them. The district of Santa Bárbara was so terrorized that every stampede of the livestock was attributed to hostile Indians. The Intendant suggested that although Ugarte doubtlessly believed that the troops were pursuing the enemy incessantly and that nothing had been left undone to defend the province, the facts were other than Ugarte supposed. Even the presidios themselves were under attack.[25]

In his next weekly report the Intendant declared that the rapid incursions of the barbarous enemy were continuing with the greatest tenacity all over Nueva Vizcaya, that they were committing numerous murders and robberies in spite of repeated clamors for relief. This was borne out in reports from the districts of Chihuahua, Conchos, Guajoquilla, the Valle de San Bartolomé, and San Pedro del Gallo, which detailed the murder of eighteen men, the wounding of two others, the temporary capture of five others, and the loss of more than 200 head of livestock in nineteen separate and previously unreported raids between June 10 and July 27. Worse, the hostiles (now identified as Gila Apaches) remained in the nearby mountains ready to strike again. The vast province of Nueva Vizcaya, even with its large population and wealth, could not protect itself, especially while the troops were pursuing the Indians into their own lands. Feigning flight and seeing the settlements again undefended, the Indians were returning by other routes, wiping out what little property remained, and causing the surviving inhabitants to abandon their estates.[26]

25 Díaz de Ortega to Flores, Durango, August 5, 1788, AGN, PI 127, Expediente 4.
26 Díaz de Ortega to Flores, Durango, August 12, 1788, AGN, PI 127, Expediente 4.

A week later the report was that the Apaches had attacked the district of Ciénega de los Olivos, from which several families had previously fled. Others now planned to abandon their homes as soon as they could harvest their crops. On July 23, hostile Indians captured fifty horses from a hacienda and out-distanced the pursuing troops. On July 27, five other Apaches killed a village woman, carried off ten mules and horses, and eluded seven soldiers and a number of settlers who pursued them into the mountains. On July 19, they attacked a number of ranches, killed a man and a boy, captured another child, and also escaped pursuit.[27]

In August of 1788 Viceroy Flores sent Ugarte copies of the Intendant's weekly reports on the Indian attacks. These reports alleged the ineptitude of Captains Domingo Díaz and Manuel Casanova, the general ineffectiveness of the field commanders, the widespread disconsolation of the settlers, and the dire necessity for an improvement in military operations. Flores instructed Ugarte to respond to each of these allegations and to report immediately and in secret on the capability of the presidial and "flying" companies for waging a victorious war against the Apaches. Although the inhabitants of the towns and owners of haciendas and ranchos were supposed to defend themselves, Flores explained, the troops had the obligation to aid them as fully as possible without interrupting their punitive expeditions and offensive campaigns in the Apache country. Flores also admonished Ugarte, as he had done in a previous letter of July 23, to maintain the best harmony and sincerest accord with the Intendant.[28]

On September 22 Ugarte admitted that the Intendant's reports of Apache raids were substantially correct. He had reported these himself on August 25. But the charges that the troops were operating inefficaciously, that their field officers and division commandant were inept, and that Captain Casanova had retired without making every effort to punish the marauders (as reported to the Intendant by the local magistrates) were grossly

[27] Díaz de Ortega to Flores, Durango, August 19, 1788, AGN, PI 127, Expediente 4.
[28] Flores to Ugarte, México, August 20, 1788 (draft), AGN, PI 127, Expediente 4.

unjust. Had these charges been true, he argued, the Indians would have continued to attack in the districts to which the troops had been sent. The fact was that there had been no further attacks in those places during the last month. Ugarte felt deeply the misfortunes from which the interior of the province suffered, and he was ever watchful to remedy these evils, but neither his benevolent desire nor the extraordinary efforts of the troops were sufficient to defend the inhabitants and punish the enemy. Hostilities had been incomparably reduced, but the companies responsible for protecting the interior, even when at full strength, had too much to do, rendering aid the year around to the places attacked, pursuing the enemy, escorting packtrains, and guarding their own horse herds. Moreover, he challenged, who knew of the caution and vigilance that the Apaches exercised in their invasions, the different and distant places they attacked at the same time, the damages they could inflict before the troops arrived, the rapidity with which they fled when pursued, the advantages the mountains offered them in eluding their pursuers, the facility with which they dispersed and hid, the fatigue of the troops from chasing them over the broken terrain, and the many other circumstances that made the punishment of these wild men so difficult? If the Intendant were informed of the nature of Apache warfare, the vastness of the interior of Nueva Vizcaya, the responsibilities of the companies that defended it, and the way the enemy retreated after committing their murders and thefts, he would have done more justice to the officers and men.[29]

Everyone experienced in Indian fighting agreed that it was more difficult and risky to pursue the enemy after he had performed his raids than beforehand, owing to the caution with which he could then frustrate the troops. On the average the troops were able to overtake and punish the raiders only three times in twenty attempts. Even when the troops knew where to seek them, the Indians had such a head start that they could almost always escape, and the best the troops could do was to force

[29] Ugarte to Flores, San Bartolomé, September 22, 1788, AGN, PI 127, Expediente 4.

them to abandon their stolen goods or kill the livestock they had taken in order to flee more rapidly. Nevertheless, Ugarte insisted, these punitive operations were necessary for the consolation and relief of the settlers and for the dispersal and intimidation of the enemy.[30]

As to the Intendant's criticism of offensive operations, Ugarte maintained that these conformed to Title 10, Article 1, of the *Reglamento de 1772*, which required that the troops wage incessant war on the hostiles, attacking them whenever possible in their own camps. These operations also conformed to the plan dictated by the late Brigadier Felipe de Neve, to Paragraph 20 and others of Gálvez's *Instrucción* of 1786, and to the various orders issued by Flores himself, which also required an uninterrupted war on the hostile tribes. This, Ugarte maintained, was the only way to intimidate the Apaches, contain their advance, and achieve a victory.[31]

In reply to the Intendant's charge that Captains Díaz and Casanova, as well as Sergeant Juan Reyes Trujillo, had proceeded improperly in response to the attacks in the districts of Santa Bárbara, Parral, San Bartolomé, and Ciénega de los Olivos in July, Ugarte had already ordered Lieutenant Colonel Diego de Borica, the adjutant-inspector, to prepare charges against them. These charges had been dissolved, however, when the facts became known. Captain Díaz had not taken personal charge of the troops sent to relieve the attacked communities for a very good reason. He was suffering at the time from gonorrhea and was unable to mount a horse, as the surgeon attending him at Guajoquilla would certify. Moreover, the only other officers available were the company paymaster and a lieutenant who had just returned from an all-night ride. Sergeant Reyes Trujillo felt that his thirty-nine men were insufficient to achieve any success against an enemy lodged in the steep and precipitous terrain, especially since the pursuit would have had to be undertaken on foot and some of the men would have had to remain behind to guard the horses. The Ser-

[30] *Ibid.*
[31] *Ibid.*

geant did attack the enemy later at Agua Zarca, where he killed one, wounded another, and recaptured the stolen goods at the cost of one of his own soldiers. Captain Casanova and his command had been unable to make contact with the Sergeant, but reconnoitered the adjacent mountains thoroughly and assured himself that the hostiles were no longer in the vicinity of Parral and Santa Bárbara before he retired on July 28, as the enclosed reports would verify.[32]

The officers and troops, Ugarte continued, were operating with the utmost ardor in their continuous campaigns. Having witnessed their operations himself and having known the officers personally, he could not discover the ineptitude of which the Intendant accused them. There were, to be sure, some who were too broken in health by advanced age or weariness to continue in this fatiguing service, but the Viceroy was aware that Ugarte had petitioned for their retirements. Flores should inform the Intendant that he was not Ugarte's judge nor that of his military subordinates. Nor should the local magistrates pass judgment on the effectiveness of army officers. Ugarte realized that he had been ordered to maintain harmony with the Intendant, but Díaz de Ortega's reports had repeatedly insulted him and his officers and had offered none of the harmony, urbanity, and accord that the Viceroy had so recommended, nor the consideration that a political governor of a province owed to the commandant-general. The troops were serving well, Ugarte maintained, and they had been operating more effectively since he took over the commandancy-general than they had in the past. During the two and one-half years of his administration thus far, they had reduced the enemy Apache strength by 919 persons, a number which included those killed or captured and those rescued from their captivity. This, Ugarte declared, should refute the Intendant's charges that the troops were achieving no results.[33]

If some of the officers and men of the frontier army were less vigorous in the performance than they should have been, others were

[32] *Ibid.*
[33] *Ibid.*

earning special commendation. In August of 1788 three soldiers from the presidio of Janos, returning from a dispatch-carrying mission to Sonora, were fallen upon by twenty-five Apache warriors. Notwithstanding the odds against them, they stood off the assailants for five hours, until darkness and their own stout resistance induced the Indians to retire. One of the three soldiers died in action, another was wounded, and three of their horses were captured, but they had managed to kill one Apache, whose ears they sent to Ugarte as proof, and to wound another.[34] On Ugarte's recommendation, Viceroy Flores ordered the treasurer at Chihuahua to reward the two survivors and the heirs of the slain soldier with a bonus of fifty pesos each.[35] In another such instance a corporal and twenty soldiers, escorting two mule trains laden with grain for the presidio of Janos, were attacked by an unusually large band of Apaches, at least sixty on horseback and an uncounted number on foot. Hopelessly outmanned, the escort suffered four soldiers killed and three injured while managing to kill only two Apache warriors. Four muleteers and two women passengers were also killed, another man and woman were injured, and all the horses and mules were taken by the enemy, but the corporal and the thirteen soldiers who escaped injury immediately joined a punitive expedition, which was sent out from the presidio of San Buenaventura. For their courage in the face of adversity and their determination to return to action without rest, each was granted, on Ugarte's recommendation, an increase in pay of one peso per month.[36] In March of 1788, Lieutenant José Manuel Carrasco with forty-four men from the presidio of San Buenaventura encountered an Apache band four times the size of his own command in the rugged heights of a nearby mountain. In a valiant but futile effort to dislodge the enemy, Car-

[34] Ugarte to Flores, San Bartolomé, September 22, 1788, and Captain Antonio Cordero to Ugarte, Janos, August 24, 1788, AGN, PI 127, Expediente 4.

[35] Flores to Ugarte, México, October 14, 1788 (draft), AGN, PI 127, Expediente 4.

[36] Lt. José Manuel Carrasco to Ugarte, San Buenaventura, May 21, 1788, and Ugarte to Flores, Chihuahua, June 5, 1788, AGN, PI 127, Expediente 3; Flores to Valdés, México, October 25, 1788, and Valdés to Flores, Madrid, March 6, 1789 (copy), AGN, CV 147, Fojas 220, 296.

rasco's detachment fired a total of 1,761 rounds, few of which seem to have found their mark, for only five warriors were killed (although a large number were wounded). The troops were fortunate to retire from the action with only one soldier dead, ten wounded, and more than 2,000 pesos worth of equipment, including seventy-three horses, lost to the enemy. On Ugarte's recommendation the troops were not charged personally for the horses and equipment they had lost, and Lieutenant Carrasco was promoted to the rank of captain.[37] In all such actions the soldiers seem to have been rewarded more for valor than for victory. Such was the intensity of the Apache invasions of Nueva Vizcaya in the spring and summer of 1788.

Ugarte admitted that it was impossible to prevent the Apaches from murdering civilians in and around the settlements of Nueva Vizcaya. The country people insisted upon going out to their daily chores without arms, in small numbers, and in the blindest confidence in their own security, only to become panic-stricken when fallen upon by the savages. Unable to offer military protection to all of the inhabitants everywhere, Ugarte tried to provide for the safety of some. He ordered that woodcutters in the province could go out from the settlements only on Monday of each week, on which day they would be escorted by a squad of soldiers.[38]

Viceroy Flores invited both Ugarte and the Intendant of Durango to submit recommendations for more effective military operations in Nueva Vizcaya and a more advantageous placement of the presidios.[39] Díaz de Ortega responded by reiterating his charges that the troops were not protecting the people, which was their only real purpose, and that in their present positions the presidios were neither preventing hostile invasions nor allow-

[37] Cordero, Diario . . . de las operaciones de guerra, Chihuahua, April 28, 1788; Carrasco to Ugarte, San Buenaventura, May 21, 1788; Flores to Ugarte, México, June 16, 1789 (draft), AGN, PI 127, Expediente 2 and Expediente 3; Flores to Valdés, No. 627, México, October 25, 1788, AGN, CV 147, Foja 218.
[38] Ugarte to Flores, San Bartolomé, September 29, 1788, AGN, PI 128, Expediente 3.
[39] Flores to Ugarte, México, August 20, 1788 (draft), AGN, PI 127, Expediente 4.

ing for the pursuit of the marauders and recovery of their plunder. As a result, he said, the troops were merely squandering the king's money. The presidios were situated too far from one another. The seven presidios of the province were from 65 to 208 miles apart, and they were also far removed from the centers of population they were supposed to protect. Furthermore, during most of the year many of the presidial troops were either occupied in domestic duties for their own support or were away on campaigns in enemy territory and thus unable to protect the territory in their immediate vicinities. The only settlers at the frontier posts were a few chronically ailing and retired soldiers. He recommended withdrawing the presidios to positions closer to the settlements, where the inhabitants could assume the domestic duties that the troops now performed and free them for full-time military service. In order that the royal treasury might not be burdened by the expense of removing the presidios, he recommended that the faithful but destitute vassals of the king be forced to contribute whatever was required.[40] He did not explain what effect this would have on offensive campaigns into enemy territory.

Ugarte, although not willing to concede that the present military operations were ineffective, agreed that several of the presidios were situated too far out toward the Apache country and that they should be pulled back for better protection of the settlements. He admitted that there were many openings in the presidial line through which the Apaches were able to penetrate, but he felt that the outlying presidios were able to accomplish a great deal by co-ordinating their operations with the interior mobile companies at Namiquipa, San Gerónimo, Guajoquilla, and Pilar de Conchos. There was a particularly large gap between Guajoquilla and the Pueblo of El Alamo, through which the Mescalero Apaches sometimes invaded and attacked El Gallo, Ma-

[40] Specifically, the Intendant recommended that the presidios and patrol companies be positioned at Janos, Valle de San Buenaventura, Carrizal, either Bachimba or some other place in the Ciénega de los Olivas district, Pueblo de San Francisco de Conchos, Guajoquilla, Cerro Gordo, El Gallo, El Pasage, and Mapimí. Díaz de Ortega to Flores, Durango, September 9, 1788, AGN, PI 127, Expediente 4.

pimí, Río de Nazas, Cuencamé, and the haciendas of those districts without meeting any resistance. His recommendation was that the garrison at San Buenaventura be moved to Casas Grandes, which could support a regular settlement, and those of El Norte, El Príncipe, and San Carlos de Cerrogordo to positions nearer to the interior settlements and to the Bolsón de Mapimí, which was still a favorite sanctuary of the hostile invaders. In his selection of new presidial sites Ugarte was most especially concerned with the immediate availability of adequate grass, wood, and water.[41]

Wherever the presidios were placed, the interior settlements of the frontier provinces had always been vulnerable whenever the Apaches took the offensive. The best protection, therefore, was a continuous series of offensive operations, which would carry the war into enemy territory and keep them on the defensive. Ugarte was a firm believer in this maxim. Measured only in terms of casualties inflicted on the enemy, organized campaigns into Apache territory seem hardly to have been worth the immense effort involved, but they did impress the hostiles with the hardiness of the frontier troops and the determination of the Spaniards to punish any Indians who wantonly committed murder and robbery. In the end these campaigns induced many Apache bands to sue for peace.

The *Instrucción* of 1786 warned Ugarte that campaigns involving a large number of troops operating in a single body would usually produce unsatisfactory results, for the movement of such formidable armies was slothful, unorganized and noisy. These cumbersome movements alerted the Indians and allowed them to retire into the deserts, where pursuing soldiers and horses were in danger of perishing from thirst and hunger, or into rugged mountains, where there was the risk of ambush. Viceroy Gálvez was convinced that the most fruitful campaigns were those involving detachments of no more than from 140 to 200 troops. This seemed to him a respectable number in itself and one that

---

[41] Ugarte to Flores, San Bartolomé, September 17, 1788, AGN, PI 127, Expediente 4.

could be divided for effective smaller operations. Such detachments, with a reduced number of horses and mules, could more readily find adequate pasture and water, avoid leaving broad trails or raising great clouds of dust, and proceed without forewarning the Indians. Surprise being the greatest advantage in frontier warfare, Gálvez thought it a waste of time to make regularly-scheduled patrols of the same terrain or to pursue the Indians once they were aware that troops were approaching. Ugarte was also instructed to allow detachment commandants complete freedom of action while on campaign and to judge their conduct only by the results they achieved. On the Nueva Vizcaya frontier company commanders were to order frequent operations against the enemy without awaiting precise orders from the over-all command, but they were to report regularly to their superiors and combine their operations with those of Coahuila.[42]

The operational procedure for the presidios called for one-half the force to be employed almost continuously in offensive campaigns, leaving one-half to escort supply trains, guard the post's horse herds, and perform other routine garrison chores. On their return from a campaign, which usually lasted several weeks, the troops so employed took over the routine duty, while those previously so engaged went out on patrol or joined in another campaign.[43] In terms of men, horses, and ammunition expended, the offensive campaigns were expensive operations.

A typical campaign was that undertaken by Captain Antonio de Cordero, of the presidio of Janos, in the spring of 1788. In the previous winter Ugarte had launched a three-pronged campaign, with armies from New Mexico, Sonora, and Nueva Vizcaya, which had converged on the Apache haunts of the Gila River region, but large numbers of the enemy had eluded the pincer movement and were pouring into Nueva Vizcaya to wreak revenge. Cordero's spring campaign was designed to intercept these hostiles before they could reach the interior of the province.

---

[42] Gálvez, Instrucción of 1786, *loc. cit.*, Articles 23, 124, 202–204, 206, 208–209.
[43] Ugarte to Flores, Chihuahua, July 24, 1788, AGN, PI 128, Expediente 3.

For this purpose Ugarte had mobilized 217 troops from four presidios, one light-horse company of Nueva Vizcaya, and the Opata Indian company of Bavispe, Sonora. Although the total force did not assemble at the appointed rendezvous until April 7, the campaign began officially on March 15, when Cordero and his presidials left Janos. It lasted forty-three days.[44]

On the day of his departure Cordero learned that a band of Apaches had killed a dispatch rider from the presidio of San Buenaventura and had seriously wounded his companion. It was then that Lieutenant Carrasco and his 44 valiants from San Buenaventura went out and took on a force of Apaches four times greater than his own, killed 5 warriors, and wounded a large number of others, with a loss to his own command of 1 soldier killed, 10 wounded, and 73 horses captured. Carrasco returned to the locale with reinforcements the next day, but found that the Apaches had moved elsewhere. With this news Captain Cordero sent a lieutenant and 85 men to reconnoiter the adjacent mountains, and on March 20 this detachment found and attacked 150 of the same hostile party. In the course of a three-hour battle this contingent fired 477 shots, but managed to kill only a warrior, a squaw, and a boy, to retrieve 9 horses, and to capture some Apache belongings. The only loss to the troops was a Chiricahua Apache scout, who was killed. When this detachment returned, it was reinforced and sent back into battle, but again the Apaches had departed the scene. On March 29, Captain Cordero sent an ensign with 100 men to pick up the Apaches' trail, and when this officer reported back that the enemy had divided into two parties and that one was moving into the interior to attack the settlements, Ugarte sent Cordero himself to pursue them with 80 men.[45]

After picking up the trail, Cordero captured an Apache brave, a squaw, and a girl who were traveling eastward with a mule towards the Sierra de Encinillas. Interrogated, the warrior at first provided Cordero with a false lead, but eventually guided

44 Cordero, Diario . . . de las operaciones de guerra, Chihuahua, April 28, 1788, *loc. cit.*
45 *Ibid.*

him to an Apache camp in the Sierra de la Mula. By the time
Cordero and his force reached the camp, however, the Apaches
had moved on. Following their trail through that range and the
sierras of El Gallego and Barrigón, Cordero surprised them in
another camp on April 10, in the heights of the Sierra de los
Aparejos, where he captured a squaw, three boys, a horse, and
a considerable amount of loot. Most of the braves were off hunting mustangs, and in pursuing them Cordero was able to capture
only three of their horses. On April 15 he sent out an ensign and
fifty men on foot to reconnoiter, and the next day this party reported that a large band of Apaches was encamped in an almost
impregnable position. Cordero then sent a detachment of fifty
men on foot under another ensign and took fifty mounted troops,
under his personal command, to attack the camp on the seventeenth. After sending their families to safety through a hidden
defile, the Apache warriors put up a stout defense for a time, but
they were eventually dispersed with the loss of at least two warriors. One squaw was also killed, three braves were thought to
have been mortally wounded, and two squaws and one baby
were taken alive. Cordero's losses were only an ensign and an
Opata soldier, both only slightly injured.[46]

On the twenty-second the scouts of the expedition found three
large Apache camps in the Sierra de los Arados, but they fled
before the troops arrived. Pursuing, the troops managed to capture two small children and two mules laden with hides. Then,
after reconnoitering the remainder of that range and the Sierra
Colorada, the troops reassembled on the twenty-fifth of April at
the original rendezvous point, where Ugarte called an end to the
campaign.[47]

Ugarte considered the services of Captain Cordero and his
troops particularly meritorious. The effective results of the campaign only amounted to eight warriors, two squaws, and a boy
killed; one warrior, four squaws, and seven children captured;
and several horses taken. However, Ugarte reported, the prin-

[46] *Ibid.*　　　　　　　　　　　　[47] *Ibid.*

cipal utility of the campaign was the prompt dissipation of the menacing cloud that had hung over Nueva Vizcaya.[48]

If Cordero's 217 men were able to deprive the enemy of only 22 persons, killed and captured, in a six-weeks campaign, that of Governor Fernando de la Concha of New Mexico was able to achieve slightly greater success with one-half that number of troops, but with the support of several armed settlers and Indian auxiliaries. Setting out in August of 1788 from the Río Grande settlements, De la Concha marched into the rugged mountains of southwestern New Mexico with 64 presidials from Santa Fe, an undisclosed number of settlers, and 39 Indian auxiliaries (mainly Navaho, but some Jicarilla Apaches, Utes, and Comanches). En route to the Sierra de la Gila, on the border between New Mexico and Sonora, De la Concha reconnoitered successively the Oscura, Ladrón, Magdalena, San Mateo, Tecolote, Piñón, Mimbres, and Cobre Mountains, but managed to encounter hostile Apaches only twice. In these engagements his forces killed a total of 20 warriors and captured 5 other Apaches, some of whom were women and children. But the achievement, he felt, was greater than the statistics indicated. First and foremost, by sending Navaho warriors against the Gila Apaches he had created a serious breach in the relations between these former allies; second he had put the fear of Spanish arms in the Gileños by invading their own terrain; and, finally, he had discovered the water holes and other essential landmarks of the western ranges, which were necessary for future campaigns. Unfortunately he could not place these on a map, for the only chart of the area had been borrowed the year before by Colonel Rengel for his unsuccessful campaign into that country, and it had not been returned.[49]

It was all too evident that an army of 3,000 was entirely inadequate to defend such a vast frontier. It was also apparent that

[48] Ugarte to Flores, Chihuahua, April 30, 1788, AGN, PI 127, Expediente 2.
[49] Gov. Fernando de la Concha to Flores, Santa Fe, November 15, 1788, AGN, PI 127, Expediente 2.

113

the king and viceroy could never provide reinforcements sufficient for the purpose. Too few in numbers, poorly armed and
equipped, and demoralized by high prices and low pay, the frontier soldiers performed a heroic but ineffective service. The best
that they could do was make the enemy pay dearly for his vic-
tories. How they held their thin line against the Apache invasions
and achieved some measure of respite for the harried settlers can
be better explained in diplomatic than in purely military terms.
Force having failed, the Spaniards resorted to stratagem.

CHAPTER VI

THE INDIAN POLICY
1786-1790

Without doubt the most severe handicap under which Ugarte's frontier army operated was the absence of a well-defined Indian policy. For almost twenty years pronouncements from on high had attempted to formulate a uniform purpose and procedure in dealing with the hostile tribes of the north, but each successive official statement varied from its predecessor and each viceroy interpreted the policy differently. The most remarkable aspect of Ugarte's administration as commandant-general of the Provincias Internas was that he came as close as he did to achieving the complete pacification of the northern frontier amid such confusion of official thought and pronouncement.

A formula for dealing with the hostiles had been evolving from the very beginning. The crown had early made a distinction between the perennially hostile nomadic tribes and the normally peaceful and sedentary Indians, and it had even come to recognize nations that were essentially neutral. But any consistent policy for dealing with them, either separately or collectively, rested on shifting sands. The king himself was caught between the conflicting dictates of moral obligation and practical necessity, and even when humanitarian zeal did not collide with either imperial need or international commitment, there was always the embarrassment of budgetary consideration. The result was inaction or equivocation at the highest level. Moreover, provincial governors and garrison commandants had long acted in the interests of particular rather than general welfare, and so they had achieved little more in their independent military operations than the driving of the common enemy from one refuge to another and the gaining of an only temporary and local respite from the ravages of the marauding tribes.

Ugarte, as the supposed co-ordinator of these operations, was bound to some extent by at least half a dozen mutually inconsistent official guidelines. The first of these was the celebrated *Dictamen,* or recommendation, submitted in 1768 by the Marqués de Rubí.[1] On returning from his inspection of the frontier presidios and consultation with the local commandants and provincial governors, Rubí had proposed basic changes in the heretofore haphazard strategy. In the past the frontier officials had attempted to attract the amorphous and predatory Apache bands to the tranquility of mission life. This, Rubí believed, had been a mistake. The Apaches had proved treacherous to all Spanish offers of peace and protection. Moreover, much more powerful Indian nations to the north of Texas were pressing down upon the missions and presidios of that province and driving the Apaches before them. These so-called Nations of the North were, along with the formidable Comanches, bitter enemies of the Apache bands, and their own attacks on missions and presidios stemmed not from any natural hostility toward the white man, but from resentment of the shelter that the Spaniards had given their historic foe. It had already been demonstrated that the Nations of the North and the Comanches could honor a peace treaty and enter into amicable trade relations—the former with Louisiana and the latter with New Mexico—whereas the Apaches had proved totally undependable. Therefore, Rubí felt, the Spaniards must pursue a more realistic policy. Harsh as it might appear, they must expel the Apaches from every mission, presidio, and settlement along the entire outer frontier and throw them back to their merciless enemies in the north. They should then attempt to cultivate and conciliate those more powerful nations, induce them to join in a combined offensive against the

[1] Rubí, Dictamen, Tacubaya, April 10, 1768, AGI, Guadalajara 511.

Apaches, and, crushing these perfidious marauders between vise-like pressures from both north and south, bring about their total destruction. Without respite or refuge, Rubí believed, the Apaches would be forced to choose between extermination and unconditional surrender. If the latter, they should be admitted to peace and protection only in the widely-dispersed missions of the remote interior of New Spain, for it was only there that they might be Christianized, civilized, and assimilated among the already well-pacified tribes. Then, and only then, according to Rubí, would peace on the northern frontier be assured.[2]

Although Rubí's opinions were not fully endorsed by the king, they did influence the thinking of some administrators. Ugarte, however, was more charitable toward the Apaches. Somewhat more to his liking, but still not completely palatable, was the *Reglamento de 1772*, which was based on Rubí's recommendations but tempered with the king's more humanitarian sentiments. Principally, the *Reglamento* redefined the duties of officers and troops and ordered the establishment of a new, outer line of presidios to ward off the invasions of hostile tribes, but one of its fourteen sections stated the king's Indian policy in rather definite terms.[3]

In the first place, the *Reglamento* declared, the general objective of military operations on the frontier was peace, and the king's main concerns were for the welfare and conversion of the pagan tribes and for the tranquility of the northern provinces. Therefore, while the troops must wage an active and incessant war on the avowedly hostile tribes, carrying it even to their own lands, they were to observe good faith and gentle treatment toward those whom they conquered. Captured warriors were not to be abused (the death penalty would be imposed on anyone killing such a prisoner in cold blood). Rather, these captives were to be provided with rations and sent to Mexico City, there

---

[2] *Ibid.*
[3] Título Décimo, "Tratado con los Indios enemigos ó indiferentes," *Reglamento e instrucción para los presidios que se han de formar en la línea de frontera de la Nueva España, resuelto por el Rey Nuestro Señor en cédula de 10 de Setiembre de 1772,* in Brinckerhoff and Faulk, *Lancers for the King,* 11–66.

to be dealt with by the viceroy as he saw fit. Women and infants taken would be similarly well treated, but an attempt would also be made to convert and educate them.[4]

Although kindness and good treatment of individual prisoners were to be encouraged, such were not to be guaranteed for entire nations, and most especially not for the Apaches. Under a variety of names, groups of these hostile savages had professed a desire for peace or submission whenever they were confronted with superior forces. But, interpreting Spanish clemency as weakness, they had abused the concessions at the first opportunity. Therefore, the Apaches were not to be admitted to peace except when they chose to subject themselves to the king's domination or when they offered strict guarantees and evidence that they intended to keep it; and even then the peace was to be provisional, merely a suspension of hostilities pending approval of the terms by the viceroy.[5] In order to preserve life on both sides and possibly to arouse in the barbarous nations a humanitarian sentiment, the first condition for a truce was to be an exchange of prisoners, and in carrying out this stipulation good faith was to be required at all times. Whenever there was a well-founded expectation of achieving such an exchange, the troops were not to send their captives to Mexico City, but to intern them securely near the presidios.[6]

As for the peaceful or neutral tribes, the best relations were to be maintained. The Spaniards were to overlook some of their faults and lesser offenses and endeavor by good example and persuasion to induce them to receive missionaries and to submit to the king's authority. If, as was their custom, these Indians should steal horses or commit other crimes that could not be overlooked, and if they should refuse to make restitution, force might be used, but only with the least possible injury inflicted on them. No bodily punishment was to be administered either in the field or after their apprehension, and in no case might those arrested be sent into servitude as had been illegally done in the

[4] Título 10, *Artículo* 1, *ibid.*
[5] Título 10, *Artículo* 2, *ibid.*

past. Rather, they were to be treated in the same manner pre-scribed for prisoners of war, and any women or children taken were to be restored to their families so that all might recognize that the arrests had been made in the interests of law and justice rather than of hatred or selfishness.[7]

Thus, the *Reglamento de 1772*, while recognizing the Apaches as unworthy of a general amnesty, ordering a vigorous war against them, and providing for the deportation of captured war-riors to the interior, also insisted on humane treatment for those taken prisoner and left the door open for coexistence under treaties of peace whenever the enemy should enter into them with apparent sincerity. Meanwhile, all friendly and neutral nations were to be courted without reservation.

The next important royal pronouncement of Indian policy ap-peared in the king's instructions of 1776 to the first commandant-general of the now autonomous Provincias Internas.[8] Croix was admonished to give his primary attention to the reduction of the numerous pagan tribes to Christianity and allegiance to the king, for this was uppermost in the royal mind when he established the independent command. To this end Croix was to avail him-self of the gentle and efficacious means required by the laws of the Indies; that is, cajolery, good treatment, peaceful persuasion, gifts, and genuine offers of the king's sovereign protection.[9] And in all, the articles of the *Reglamento de 1772* were to be strictly observed.[10]

The pious intentions of the king were never totally disregarded, but Indian policy was also influenced by the recommendations of hard-bitten troop commanders on the frontier, who saw the problem in a colder light. Croix was guided during his early years in office as much by the resolutions adopted by his councils of war at Monclova, San Antonio, and Chihuahua as by royal policy. As these advisory juntas were made up of governors and military

[6] Título 10, *Artículo* 3, *ibid.*
[7] Título 10, *Artículo* 6, *ibid.*
[8] Real Instrucción dada a dn. Teodoro de Croix, San Yldefonso, August 22, 1776, AGN, PI 77, Expediente 4.
[9] Paragraph 12, *ibid.*   [10] Paragraph 23, *ibid.*

commanders, practical officers such as those whom Rubí had interviewed, they readily endorsed the harsh recommendations of that inspector. They again singled out the Apaches as the only truly implacable enemy, urged Croix to wage a war of extermination against them, and called for the enlistment of the Nations of the North to assist in this bloody project. As a refinement of their own they also recommended dividing the Apache tribes themselves and pitting them against each other. They especially urged Croix to cultivate the Mescaleros and turn them against the Lipanes, their rival kinsmen.[11] By following this advice Croix managed to turn the tide in the Apache war. All that was lacking for the achievement of total victory, he reported, was the arrival of the additional troops he had requested. Instead of reinforcements, however, he received an order from the king requiring him to curb his offensive operations.[12] Spain was about to go to war with England.

The royal order of February 20, 1779, was something more than a stopgap measure requiring stringent economies on the domestic scene in order to prosecute an expensive war abroad. It was also a reassertion of and an enlargement on a consistent royal policy of conciliating the hostile Indians and treating them as human beings. Although its reversal of the aggressive policy recommended by Rubí, the *Reglamento de 1772*, and Croix's councils of war was only temporary, its insistence on peaceful persuasion was neither new nor transitory. In short, the royal order of 1779, ostensibly born of economic and strategic necessity, was consistent with traditional royal attitude and would be basic to subsequent crown policy.

As the minister of the Indies expressed it, the king would prefer lesser conquests by gentle means to more formidable ones with bloodshed; he would rather be remembered as a humanitarian than as a conqueror.[13] The royal order went on to explain

[11] Bolton, *Athanase de Mézières*, II, 152–70; Thomas, *Plains Indians and New Mexico*, 190–213; Thomas, *Teodoro de Croix*, 36–38.

[12] Thomas, *Teodoro de Croix*, 43–44.

[13] José de Gálvez to Teodoro de Croix, El Pardo, February 20, 1779 (cert. copy), AGN, PI 170, Expediente 5.

that the kind of military campaigns that had been successful in European wars would never pacify, let alone exterminate, the kind of enemy that infested the northern frontier of New Spain. The numerousness of these hostiles, their dispersion over a vast area, the little they had to lose by attacking, and the facility with which they took refuge in the rugged terrain all had become unhappily apparent in the offensives already waged against them. Their own terrain, their agility, their very poverty and nakedness, and even their cowardice and lawlessness had given them an advantage over the troops; and the military operations, far from reducing their raids, had elevated the enemy from petty thieves to astute warriors. Worse, their numbers were increasing, not only beyond the frontier, but well within it, for they were now being joined by previously friendly Indians, even those who had been converted to Christianity and subjected to civilized life in towns. The enemy, like shot, now threatened to pierce the Spanish defenses in a thousand places, to wear down and annihilate the soldiers, to impede the advance of the settlements, and even to force the Spaniards to give up lands they already held.[14] Apparently the king was not impressed by Croix's reports that victory was in sight.

To remedy the unhappy situation Croix was instructed to abandon his plans for a great offensive thrust against the Apache and confine his operations to purely defensive action. He was to concentrate on protecting the towns, ranches, and other settlements. By maintaining his troops under rigid discipline and accustoming them to the kind of fighting required to ward off Indian attacks, he was to present a firm and powerful resistance. He was authorized to launch punitive expeditions, however, for it was hoped that these would dishearten the hostiles and persuade them either to withdraw from the frontier or seek peace and friendship.[15]

Those hostiles who might surrender and aspire to live in peace were to be treated with gentleness, humanity, charity, and good

[14] *Ibid.*
[15] *Ibid.*

faith. Croix was not to force them to settle in the Spanish towns or even to form permanent villages of their own, but was to leave them in their just and natural liberty. According to the official reasoning, if these Indians were not oppressed, injured, or forced to serve the Spaniards, they could be converted from enemies to friends, and they would then see for themselves the advantages of the rational life of the white man and the aid that organized society could offer them.[16]

To encourage this Croix was to provide such Indians with gifts, not only articles they normally desired, but also others, which would offer them new comforts, and which could be obtained only from the Spaniards. In this way they would little by little come to prefer Spanish commodities to their own. They would then begin to imitate the Spaniards in agriculture and handicraft, lose their own natural aversion to manual labor, and convert their camps into more permanent settlements. If some of the tribesmen could be induced to come into the Spanish towns voluntarily, others would follow, especially when they saw the piety and justice of law and order. Thus, without their realizing it, those still hostile would diminish in number and those friendly would increase. In time they would abandon their rude customs and insensate attitudes and would even cover their nakedness with regular clothing.[17]

Having quietly inspired the savages to seek the comforts and luxuries of civilization, Croix was to encourage them to use Spanish firearms for their hunting and defense. It was hoped that they would thereby forget how to use or even manufacture their native arms.[18] This, of course, was a reversal of past policy, which generally attempted to keep guns out of Indian hands.

It was hoped that by introducing Spanish food, clothing, and even firearms to the unconquered tribes, they could be made dependent upon the Spaniards. Provided with these necessities and treated humanely, the Indians would then desire to become Span-

[16] *Ibid.*
[17] *Ibid.*
[18] *Ibid.*

ish vassals. Croix was to redouble his vigilance to see that they were not treated as slaves, as they had commonly been up to that time, for the king wished them to be cared for as children. The final step in their pacification would be their conversion to Christianity by the peaceful persuasion of the clergy, and Croix was to assist in these efforts.[19]

Such was the reasoning of the royal order of 1779. For the present it merely frustrated Croix's plans for an all-out war on the Apaches, but in time it would be basic to the remarkably successful strategy of Jacobo Ugarte y Loyola. Initially, Ugarte was bound by the royal policy enunciated in both the *Reglamento de 1772* and the royal order of 1779, but shortly both of these pronouncements were superseded by the celebrated *Instrucción* of 1786.

The *Instrucción* of 1786 did not introduce drastic changes in the Indian policy, as some historians have intimated.[20] Almost its only innovation was a synthesis of the policies of the past, principally Rubí's recommendations of 1768, the *Reglamento de 1772*, the instructions to Croix of 1776, the resolutions of the councils of war at Monclova, San Antonio, and Chihuahua of 1777–78, and the royal order of 1779. To anyone fully acquainted with these pronouncements the articles of Viceroy Gálvez's instructions to *Comandante General* Ugarte should have a familiar ring. Although revolutionary in some few details, the *Instrucción* of 1786 was extraordinary mainly in its clarity of statement and detail in specification. Now, for the first time, a policy was stated in its entirety, given the force of a royal ordinance, and (thanks to Gálvez's previous frontier experience) accepted generally by the presidial commanders as a practical rather than ideal prescription for the ills of the Provincias Internas. Along with the *Reglamento de 1772* it remained fundamental policy throughout the remainder of the Spanish period. In 60 of the first 116 paragraphs of his instructions to Ugarte,

[19] *Ibid.*
[20] See, for instance, Hubert H. Bancroft, *History of the North Mexican States and Texas*, I, 648–49, and Park, "Spanish Indian Policy in Northern Mexico, 1765–1810," *loc. cit.*

Gálvez spelled out the basic procedure for dealing with the *indios bárbaros* of the northern frontier.[21]

In justifying his approach to the problem, the Viceroy recognized that the nomadic tribesmen of the north were warriors by profession; that they were skilled not only in the use of their native weapons, but of firearms as well; that they were better horsemen than the Spaniards themselves; that they fought with agility, cunning, and valor; that they seldom struck unless certain of victory; and that, when pursued, they could always find refuge in the fastness of the rugged mountains.[22] Gálvez was convinced that since they were unable to supply their own primary needs from hunting and gathering and since their own surplus of seeds, wild fruit, and peltries was seldom sufficient to trade for the Spanish horses, guns, ammunition, and ornaments that they craved, they had either to plunder or perish. He recognized that they sometimes made peace in order to obtain these commodities, either as presents or in trade for their own goods. But he also realized that their love of liberty and idleness together with their hunger, or greed, often led them to break these pacts. Sometimes, leaving their families in perfect safety where they still kept the peace, they would go off to raid where they had no such agreement; and they saw nothing wrong in this.[23]

To deal with such an enemy Gálvez provided Ugarte with a vigorous plan for pacification. It was brutal and deceptive in the main, but temperate and just in some important respects, a finely-drawn compromise between the war of extermination recommended by Rubí and the peace by persuasion ordered by the king. As had others before him, Gálvez recognized that the several Apache tribes constituted the most implacable enemies on the northern frontier. But, owing to the widely varying estimates reported from that quarter, he was unable to determine the total number of their warriors.[24] He was sure that they would never submit to Spanish rule voluntarily, but he felt that they

[21] Gálvez, Instrucción of 1786, cited fully in Chapter IV, n. 3.
[22] Paragraphs 27 and 33, *ibid.*
[23] Paragraphs 39–41, 44–46, *ibid.*
[24] Paragraphs 51, 198–99, *ibid.*

could be weakened by division and induced to destroy themselves.[25] Accordingly, Ugarte was to exploit the existing discord between the Apaches and the Nations of the North and that among the separate Apache tribes themselves, reviving especially the bloody conflict that formerly existed between the Mescaleros and the Lipanes.[26]

Ugarte was not only to divide and conquer; he was also to display alternately the feathers of the hawk and the dove. On the one hand he was to wage an incessant war on the heathen marauders, attacking them in all of the provinces, in their own lands, at all seasons of the year, and without respite. But, on the other hand, he was to accept their overtures for an armistice whenever offered, even without sincerity. In view of the inadequacy of the military forces on the frontier, a bad peace, as Gálvez put it, was better than a good war.[27] He recognized that the northern tribes were fickle and often made peace only in bad faith, but, he pointed out, the Spaniards were guilty of the same insincerity. Moreover, even though the Indians might break the peace many times, they would seek it again whenever confronted by the renewal of a vigorous war. Ugarte must require the Spaniards to observe scrupulously the terms of each peace and compel the Indians to do likewise, punishing the latter for their serious breaches of the terms but overlooking their trifling violations. By waging a vigorous and incessant offensive against tribes that openly broke the peace, Ugarte would subject them to a constant pressure and deprive them of the advantages they had enjoyed under the terms. This, in turn, would incline them to seek peace again and make it more lasting.[28]

In order to satisfy the requirements and desires of the savages, improve their way of life, and also reduce them economically to Spanish vassalage, Ugarte was to promote trade with those who made peace. Although such concessions were admittedly deceptive, Gálvez felt that they would be more fruitful than open war-

25 Paragraphs 29, 52–53, *ibid.*
26 Paragraphs, 50, 53–54, *ibid.*
27 Paragraphs 20, 29, *ibid.*
28 Paragraphs 36, 48–49, 55, *ibid.*

fare in achieving pacification.[29] So that the Indians might not be cheated in the exchange of goods and thereby become antagonized, Ugarte was to provide strict regulations for such trade.[30] Moreover, he was to expect losses rather than profits at first, for the Indians had little of value to offer. In the long run, however, this would reduce the number of hostiles, for the one-sided benefits of the exchange would provide the Indians with their needs and desires and eliminate the necessity for their plundering of Spanish settlements. The Spaniards would then be able to reduce their expenditures on military forces and eventually realize incomparable gains from such economizing. The savings thus effected, however, should be invested in presents for the peaceful tribes. Outright gifts were essential, Gálvez thought, because whatever the Indians could obtain in barter for their paltry trade goods was wholly inadequate to supply their needs and thus keep them at peace. Thus, whenever a band of Indians concluded an armistice, the local commandant was to reward the petty chief with from fifteen to twenty pesos worth of goods and provisions and issue each of the warriors one or two pesos worth of such supplies for himself and his family.[31]

Even the implacable Apaches, once they were weakened by the internal dissension that Ugarte was to promote, could gradually be made dependent by accustoming them to Spanish foods, drinks, clothing, and arms issued as gifts or exchanged in trade. Perhaps they would even become greedy for the possession of land. It would not be easy to establish trade with the Apaches, Gálvez admitted, except for the Lipán tribe. The Lipanes had valuable furs to offer, and they had a craving for dried meat, raw sugar, maize, tobacco, brandy, guns, ammunition, knives, cloth, clothing, vermillion, mirrors, glass beads, and especially horses, mules, and cattle. If the Lipán Apaches could be induced to maintain abundant herds of their own, Gálvez thought, they would be less inclined to make raids on Spanish livestock.[32]

[29] Paragraphs 38, 42–43, *ibid.*
[30] Paragraph 84, *ibid.*
[31] Paragraphs 18, 79, *ibid.*
[32] Paragraphs 52–54, 57–58, 62–63, *ibid.*

The Indian Policy

In the past there had been a serious attempt to keep intoxicating liquor from the Indians, especially the hostiles, but Gálvez now reversed this policy. The French had introduced the liquor trade into Louisiana, and while he was governor of that province, he had seen it work to the advantage of the white man. He now believed that it could be practiced with the same effect in the northern provinces of New Spain. By encouraging the Indians to develop a taste for spirituous beverages, he reasoned, the Spaniards could gain and maintain their good will by supplying it to them. Furthermore, liberal indulgence in this new delight would induce them to divulge their secrets, forget about raiding, and, as habit made a necessity of this luxury, even become more dependent on the Spaniards.[33]

Firearms had also been traditionally withheld from the Indians, except for a few presents to friendly chieftains and for those issued temporarily to auxiliaries and allies for campaigns against the hostiles. The royal order of 1779 had endorsed a freer dissemination of these weapons, but Gálvez now attacked the entire notion that they were more effective to the Indians as weapons than were bows and arrows. An Indian bow, he insisted, could discharge an arrow with force enough to pierce either a bullhide shield or the heaviest quilted leather jacket. While it was true that an arrow's range was less than a bullet's, the hostile Indians regularly kept well beyond gunshot distance whenever they were outnumbered, and when they had a numerical advantage they closed in for hand-to-hand combat. Furthermore, for each musket shot fired at them they were able to return many arrows with telling effect; and when their bowstrings became loose, they could tighten them more quickly than they could repair or even reload a musket. Thus, if the Indians could be induced to abandon the bow for the gun, Gálvez reasoned, they would be at a decided disadvantage. Guns were more difficult to obtain, repair, and operate effectively than bows, and so the Spaniards should be more liberal in trading muskets, powder, and ball to the Indians. However, he cautioned, the muskets should be long ones.

[33] Paragraphs 64–67, *ibid.*

These would be awkward for an Indian to use while on horseback. They should also have weakened barrels, stocks, and bolts, making them easily damaged and in continuous need of readjustment, repair, and replacement by skilled Spanish gunsmiths. Having accepted firearms, the Indians would abandon their native weapons, lose their skill with them, and become dependent upon the Spaniards for both the supply and maintenance of their new ones.[34] For one reason or another, probably because of the short supply of firearms for the troops and settlers themselves, this intriguing recommendation seems never to have been carried into full effect, at least during Ugarte's administration.

Having laid down these general guidelines, Gálvez got down to the specific problems of the individual provinces and the procedures that Ugarte should follow in resolving them.

The province of Sonora, beleaguered by the Gila Apaches from the north, was in a precarious situation. It was necessary to reduce the Seris and Tiburones, who were again in rebellion. However, Ugarte was instructed to wage no campaign against them unless he was certain of its success, for on the first signs of Spanish weakness the Gileño invasions from the north would deluge the province. The Sobaipuris and Piatos should be kept at peace and, along with the Opatas and Upper Pimas, used in campaigns against the hostiles. The Yaquis, Mayos, and Indians on the Río Fuerte, who were now living in mission towns, should be attracted to work in the mines. This would keep them busy and out of trouble, and it would also replace the workers who had abandoned the mines because of Apache attacks. The Yumas, near the confluence of the Gila and Colorado Rivers, were to be left alone, notwithstanding their treacherous massacre of Spanish settlers there in 1781. No action was to be undertaken against them until after the Seris, Tiburones, and Gileños had been conquered. When the Gila Apaches had been defeated, or at least chastised, Gálvez was confident that the other hostiles would fall more easily.[35]

[34] Paragraphs 70–74, 77–78, *ibid.*
[35] Paragraphs 106–14, *ibid.*

The Californias, isolated from the barbarous tribes by the high sierras and the Gulf of California, presented no such problems. Most of the Indians there were living at peace, either in their own communities or in mission towns. Ugarte was to see only that they remained at peace, that they not be allowed to use horses, and that their innocence be preserved.[36]

Nueva Vizcaya, being immediately to the east of Sonora, was of major concern. This extensive province was frequently invaded —from the northwest by the Gila Apaches and from the northeast by both the Mescaleros and Lipanes. Although the Lipanes were supposedly at peace, they occasionally perpetrated robberies and attributed these violations to the Mescaleros. Gálvez, however, was especially apprehensive over the Tarahumaras, an interior nation that had long been reduced to mission towns. Although these Indians had not revolted openly since 1728, their loyalty had long been suspect, and Gálvez feared that the continuing Apache invasions would incite them to a general uprising. Many Tarahumaras had already fled their missions and reverted to heathenism, and some had gone over to the Apaches. Ugarte was to exercise great prudence to prevent further defection. Other Tarahumaras were being driven to despair by an all-too-vigorous prosecution for their alleged transgressions. Ugarte was to bring an end to this harassment, offer the Tarahumara renegades a general amnesty, provide those already imprisoned with an immediate trial, send those convicted to Mexico City without delay, remove all vagrants of other nations from their villages, and allow the magistrates, priests, and missionaries to handle all Tarahumara criminal cases locally and without notoriety. Some of the Tarahumaras had become acquainted with Gálvez when he was a military commandant in Nueva Vizcaya. Should any of these wish to present their grievances to him personally, Ugarte was to provide them with military escort and allow them to come to the viceregal capital to do so.[37]

In New Mexico Ugarte was to maintain the long-standing

[36] Paragraph 116, *ibid.*
[37] Paragraphs 125–35, *ibid.*

peace with the Utes in the north and employ them against the Comanches to the northeast and the Navahos to the west whenever the latter two should become hostile. He was also to keep the peace with the Jicarilla Apaches in the northeast and court favor with the Comanches by conceding to both whatever they requested at the annual trading fair at Taos. He was to attract the Navahos by gifts and trade concessions and vigorously encourage the recent rift between them and their former allies, the Gila Apaches. He might allow the Apaches to the south (Faraones, Mimbreños, and Mogollons) to come to El Paso for trade, but he must keep these under skillful surveillance so as to prevent their raiding the settlements of Nueva Vizcaya. Finally, Ugarte was to keep Gálvez promptly informed on developments in the still apostate Moqui (Hopi) towns in the west.[38]

Since the eastern provinces—Texas, Coahuila, Nuevo León, and Nuevo Santander—were being separated from Ugarte's command, the details for their administration were addressed to Colonel Juan de Ugalde. As *comandante de armas* of this division, Ugalde was to be subordinate to Ugarte, but he was also vested with authority to act first and report afterwards. Ugalde was to wage incessant war on the Mescalero Apaches, who were the only openly hostile tribe in the eastern provinces, and these campaigns were to be conducted at his own discretion. However, whenever the Mescaleros should sue for peace, they were to be granted it under prescribed terms.[39] Although the Comanches, Nations of the North, and the Lipán Apaches all continued to keep the peace they had signed in Texas and Coahuila, they were not to be trusted. Yet, their friendship was to be maintained at all costs, for their employment against the hostile tribes was vital to Gálvez's over-all strategy.[40] While the ancient and irreconcilable hatred between the Lipanes on the one hand and the Comanches and Nations of the North on the other was to be skillfully and discreetly promoted, Gálvez would hold Ugalde or any

[38] Paragraphs 163–70, *ibid.*
[39] Paragraph 175, *ibid.*
[40] Paragraphs 176–78, *ibid.*

Spanish Weapons.

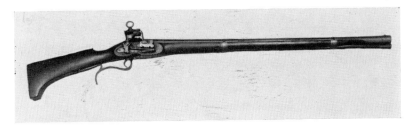

Escopeta.

Photograph by Bruce D. Lindsay

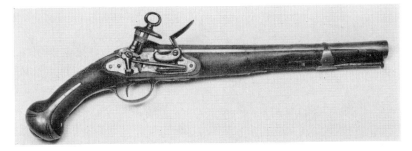

Enlisted man's cavalry pistol, miguelet lock.

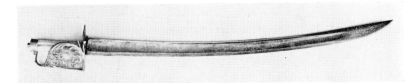

Officer's sword, late eighteenth century, found in Mexico,
now at Tubac Presidio State Park.

Courtesy of Sidney B. Brinckerhoff

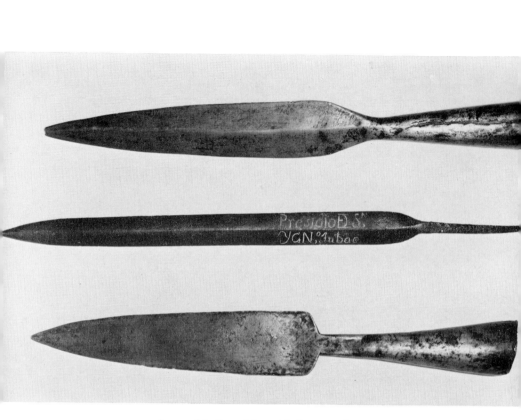

Lance blades of Spanish frontier design.

Photograph by Bruce D. Lindsay
Courtesy of Sidney B. Brinckerhoff

other officer involved strictly responsible for any unprovoked act that might result in war with either of these groups. Gálvez himself would reserve the right to determine whether or not war, even under provocation, might be declared.[41] Ugalde was to exploit the enmity between the Mescalero and Lipán Apaches and keep them divided by any means he could devise, but he was to prevent the Lipanes from attacking the Nations of the North or the Mescaleros, and the Nations of the North and the Comanches from attacking the Spanish settlements.[42] Finally, Ugalde was to report regularly on the activities of the Borrados, or Chichimecos, in Nuevo Santander and recommend means to reduce these nomads, whose treason and bloody thievery had continued in spite of their armistices.[43]

Summarizing his lengthy instructions for the conduct of Indian affairs, the Viceroy considered it possible to drive the openly hostile tribes from the frontier settlements or force them to make peace by means of incessant military operations; to attract those who sued for peace to a tranquil life and a dependence on the Spaniards by making trade concessions and presenting them with gifts; to induce those who broke the peace to seek it again by renewing the war against them; and to weaken those who remained hostile by exploiting their intertribal rivalries and baser instincts. In short, Gálvez was especially interested in promoting the self-destruction of the Apaches, since they were the avowed enemy of the Spaniards along the entire frontier.[44]

In order to give lasting force to his comprehensive instructions to Ugarte, the Viceroy submitted them to the king's minister of the Indies for royal approval. In so doing he admitted that the detailed statement actually deserved more time than he was able to devote to it, especially for informing himself more fully on the true state of conditions in the frontier provinces. He had been obliged to dictate the instructions in the brief moments of respite that his illness and his infinite other duties allowed. He had drawn

[41] Paragraphs 179–80, *ibid.*
[42] Paragraphs 181, 183, *ibid.*
[43] Paragraphs 188–91, *ibid.*
[44] Paragraphs 195–99, *ibid.*

on his long experience in the Indian wars and on the advice of competent authorities whom he had convened for the purpose. The result was a formula, which established a basic system for the conduct of Indian affairs—one which linked the rigors of incessant war with both the benevolence of peace and the friendly ties of reciprocal commerce. Admittedly these pronouncements would not in themselves remedy the difficult problems of the frontier provinces, but they would open the way for other, more solid measures, which in time could bring nearer the longed-for general pacification.[45] The king's approval of the *Instrucción* of 1786, giving it the force of a royal ordinance, was communicated to Ugarte on February 27, 1787.[46]

Another commandant-general might have found himself unduly restricted by Gálvez's detailed instructions, but not Ugarte. As governor of Coahuila he had stubbornly resented and vociferously restricted the directives of Viceroy Bucareli, and as *Comandante General* he was soon to challenge those of Gálvez's successor. But he found little to criticize in the *Instrucción* of 1786. Here was a systematic plan based on practical experience and long-accepted principles, propounded by a soldier who had been directing campaigns against the northern tribes even before Ugarte himself confronted them, who had thus faced these problems personally, and who had enriched his experience in Indian affairs while governing Louisiana. Finally, Gálvez had called the veteran Ugarte himself to Mexico City and had consulted with him at length before drafting the instructions and sending him off to his new command. Whether the Viceroy drew on Ugarte's own, more recent knowledge on this occasion, or whether he merely briefed him orally, is not clear. But a profitable exchange of views seems to have occurred. At any rate Ugarte was, as he later asserted, in such complete agreement with Gálvez's Indian policy that by the time he received the *Instrucción* of 1786 he

[45] Gálvez to the Marqués de Sonora, No. 891, México, September 25, 1786, AGN, CV 140 (no pagination).
[46] Marqués de Sonora to Ugarte, El Pardo, February 27, 1787 (copy), AGN, PI 77, Expediente 8.

had already been following its main tenets for seven months.[47] The facts bear this out.

Ugarte assumed active command of the Provincias Internas in April of 1786. The *Instrucción* of 1786, issued on August 26, reached him on November 14 of the same year. Meanwhile, on October 5, 1786, Ugarte had provided the governor of New Mexico with detailed instructions for solidifying a peace with both the Comanches and the Navahos, which anticipated both the aims and procedures outlined in the *Instrucción*.[48] When he entered into negotiations with the Mescalero and Mimbres Apaches in Nueva Vizcaya and the Chiricahua Apaches in Sonora, he dictated similar terms for their capitulation, and during the same period he was prosecuting a hard war on the recalcitrant Gileños.[49]

The practicality of the *Instrucción* of 1786 together with the unusual harmony which existed between the Viceroy and *Comandante General* might well have achieved the complete pacification of the northern frontier had not a series of unfortunate circumstances cut short Ugarte's early successes, momentarily altered the official policy, and destroyed the harmonious relationship between the two principal administrative officers. First, the *Instrucción* itself, by endorsing both the prosecution of a rigorous war and the acceptance of an insecure peace, contradicted the articles of the *Reglamento de 1772*, which remained in force. Second, the inopportune death of Gálvez on November 30, 1786, only sixteen days after Ugarte received the *Instrucción*, eliminated all opportunity for a determination of his true intent. And finally, the succession of Manuel Antonio Flores to the viceregal office brought to power a superior officer of quite different experience and therefore contrary views.

For some few months Ugarte was free to operate without viceregal supervision, for the control of that office over the com-

[47] Ugarte to Antonio Valdés, San Bartolomé, October 6, 1788, and to the King, Chihuahua, May 8, 1789, Paragraph 16, AGN, PI 77, Expediente 1 and Expediente 11.
[48] See below, Chapters VII and VIII.
[49] See below, Chapters VIII and IX.

mandancy-general had been vested only in Gálvez personally, and during this brief period Ugarte was bound in his Indian policy only by the expressed desires of the king. On March 20, 1787, however, the king invested the new viceroy with the same authority that Gálvez had exercised.[50] Still, when Flores arrived at Mexico City to assume office five months later, Ugarte presumed that he would await further and more recent information before venturing to formulate new policy. Indeed, he seemed to believe that the *Instrucción* of 1786 had already established the policy and that the new viceroy would merely support the *Comandante General's* enforcement of it. Certainly there was nothing to indicate the contrary in their early exchanges of correspondence.

Ugarte reported on October 1, 1787, that he had continued to maintain pressure on the hostile Apaches by ordering regularly-scheduled campaigns against them. In the seventeen months since he first assumed his command his forces had killed 294 of the enemy, captured another 305, liberated 15 of their own captives, and induced several bands to sue for peace. Following established practice his military commandants had presented him with the ears of the warriors they had killed in action and had sent to the jails and workhouses those they had captured. According to the reports of these campaigns, most of the hostiles killed were men and most of those taken were women and children, for the troops always tried to spare the latter. Ugarte had just sent 17 Apache warriors in chains to Guadalajara, but retained some others for military scouting service. He had sent the captured children to the Real de los Alamos for distribution in private homes elsewhere with the expectation that accommodating citizens would rear, dress, educate, and Christianize them. In this way Ugarte hoped to civilize a number of the Apaches and thus reduce their over-all hostile strength.[51] Flores replied that he was

[50] Real orden, El Pardo, March 20, 1787, AGN, PI 77, Expediente 9.
[51] Ugarte, Relación del número de enemigos Apaches que han muerto y aprisionado las Armas del Rey y de las cautivas que han libertado en las Provincias Internas, desde 9 de Mayo de 1786 en que tomé el mando general de ellas, Arispe, September 30, 1787, and Ugarte to Flores, Arispe, October 1, 1787, AGN, PI 112, Expediente 1.

pleased with the progress of Ugarte's military operations and handling of the captured Apaches. He would shortly have the prisoners of war sent overseas so that they would never return to ravage the frontier. He would also see that the women taken would be maintained in charity houses and that the captive children would be reared in private homes of the interior.[52]

Meanwhile, however, Flores had taken exception to the basic policy that Gálvez had prescribed. He was in agreement with those principles that identified the Apache as the foremost enemy, and which urged unremitting operations against them by both the troops and friendly Indian nations. But from his own experience with hostile tribes in the Río de la Plata and Nueva Granada he had learned that the Spaniards could place little faith in the armistices and peace pacts of savages. Reports from New Spain's northern frontier indicated that the Apaches were as faithless as those he had dealt with in South America. While he agreed with the basic maxim of placing the enemy under constant pressure to surrender by alternating attack with negotiation, he would always prefer the sword to the olive branch. Peace with these people, he declared, would never be enduring as long as they entered into it voluntarily, but only when they were constrained to seek it by the rigor and terror of incessant military persecution. Only then would they see its advantages and gradually become truly dependent upon the Spaniards.[53] It was in this rejection of purely voluntary peace offers that Flores undermined the flexible Indian policy practiced by Ugarte, endorsed by Gálvez, and confirmed by the king.

By the autumn of 1787 the divergent views of the Viceroy and *Comandante General* had destroyed whatever harmony might have existed between them at the outset. Flores had so altered the precepts of the *Instrucción* of 1786 as to throw the general Indian policy into the same confusion that had reigned before the *Instrucción* was conceived. Ugarte, resentful of the revoca-

[52] Flores to Ugarte, México, November 21, 1787 (draft), AGN, PI 112, Expediente 1.
[53] Flores to Valdés, No. 11, México, October 23, 1787, AGN, CV 142, Fojas 138–44.

tion of his short-lived autonomy, exasperated by the undermining of basic policy, and disdainful of his new and less apprecia-
tive superior, challenged Flores at each turn and employed every
artifice at his disposal to preserve Gálvez's policy. To each new
directive from Mexico City he responded with argument, delay,
and appeal. For a time Ugarte was forced to yield, step by reluctant step, to the demands of his superior, but in the end the
sanguinary policies of Flores were repudiated.

Flores' Indian policy seems to have been well developed by
the summer of 1788, when he elaborated it to the minister of the
Indies. The Apaches, he maintained, had gained an advantage
from both the war and peace offensives that had been waged
against them in the past. Through frequent and friendly contact
with the Spaniards the innocence of their barbarity had been
transformed into a most intelligent maliciousness, and this had
enabled them to elude Spanish patrols and penetrate the presidial line. Their own misery, want, and vengeful spirit in the
face of military persecution had made them stout warriors and
sharp thieves, and the Spaniards had therefore to multiply their
defenses. Taking advantage of what they had learned while
negotiating with the troops, the Apaches were now desolating
the frontier settlements. It was now impossible to pacify them,
but by not admitting them to peace until they were completely
terrorized and forced to surrender with the full realization of the
consequences of bad faith, they could at least be deprived of
their knowledge of the plans and operations of the troops.[54]

Peace with the Apaches based on anything but sheer intimidation was unsound, according to Flores. These savages had too
little to offer for such an arrangement to be based on trade; a
peace subsidized by donations for their support would be too
costly to the royal treasury; and maintaining them in gainful
employment was out of the question because of their deceit, in-
gratitude, perfidy, and bad faith. Against his better judgment
peace now existed with the Lipán and Lipiyán Apaches of

[54] Flores to Valdés, No. 390, México, June 24, 1788, AGN, CV 146, Fojas
442–48.

Coahuila, with the Jicarillas in New Mexico, with the Chiricahuas in Sonora, and, supposedly, with some Mescalero bands in Nueva Vizcaya, although these latter had broken it in Coahuila. Flores was not in favor of the Mescalero peace, and even though he had condescended to that of the others, he was uncertain of its wisdom in view of conflicting reports reaching him. Some authorities on the frontier held with Gálvez's maxim of forcing tribes of the same nation to attack and destroy each other; others favored his preference for a bad peace to a good war. In the present circumstances, at least, Flores had no confidence in this second maxim, and he had ordered that it not be followed. He also had doubts about the effectiveness of the first, for the Apache tribes, by whatever name the Spaniards gave them, were all of one nation, stretching in their temporary encampments from the Gulf of Mexico to that of California. They were all linked together by bonds of kinship, friendship, and a more or less firm alliance. Therefore, as he understood it, if the Spaniards could detach some tribes or bands and induce them to fight the others, many of these would merely enjoy security and copious presents, learn the movements and operations of the troops, and inform their still hostile kinsmen, who would thereby escape the brunt of the Spanish attack. And this would soon result in the loss of the provinces, the lives of many of their inhabitants, and millions of pesos, which the king was spending for the salaries, provisions, and pensions of the officers and men of the presidial companies.[55]

For these reasons Flores was inclined to order that war be made without distinction on the entire Apache nation. However, since he himself was too far removed from the actual scene to appraise the situation adequately and had to rely on the opinions of both Ugarte and Ugalde, he would reserve a final decision until the results of his own policy had become apparent.[56]

Meanwhile, Flores had ordered Ugalde to prosecute a strenuous war against the Mescaleros and to continue it until they were forcibly subjugated or exterminated, availing himself of the

[55] *Ibid.*
[56] *Ibid.*

aid of the Lipán and Lipiyán Apaches who were at peace in Coahuila. He had also ordered Ugarte to wage full-scale war against the Gila Apaches in the west and authorized him to employ troops from both Nueva Vizcaya and Sonora and also the now friendly Chiricahuas for the purpose. Should the Chiricahuas, Lipanes, and Lipiyanes fail to assist in these campaigns, Flores felt that war should be declared on them as well, and that no Indian of the Apache nation should be admitted to peace in Nueva Vizcaya either then or later. This province had always been the major target of their hostilities and must therefore be the theater of war.[57]

Flores thought that there were very strong reasons for preserving at any cost the friendship of the Comanches and Nations of the North in New Mexico and Texas. If these should declare war on the Spaniards, a sizeable increase in troops and expenses, which might not be forthcoming, would be necessary to place the entire realm on the alert and prevent a formidable inundation of barbarians. And if the Nations of the North should reach a reconciliation with the Apaches, the situation would be even worse. With respect to the former Flores would scrupulously follow the *Instrucción* of 1786, preserving their friendship because they had not been primarily destructive and were acquainted only with New Mexico and Texas. They had occasionally attacked settlers of those provinces for encroaching on their lands, but it would be unreasonable and unjust to betray them and make war on them without further provocation. This was especially true since they had served as reliable allies against the Apaches, pressing them from the north while the Spaniards attacked from the south. There were some who thought otherwise of the Indians of the North, but the general attitude was based on the aforementioned reasons and favored peace with them. Experience had proved that their armistice and treaties were more honest and lasting than those of the Apaches, and even if this were not so, their alliance was essential, for without the aid of the Nations of the

[57] *Ibid.*

North the Apaches would never be pacified. Therefore, their confidence and military aid must be encouraged.[58]

By August of 1788 Flores was less certain of the true state of affairs on the frontier than he had been earlier, thanks to the conflicting contentions of Ugarte and Ugalde. He admitted to the royal ministry that some frontier officials had confidence in an alliance and friendship with the Apaches while others clamored against their perfidy and bad faith. Some attributed most of the attacks on Nueva Vizcaya to the mission Tarahumaras and to the villainous castes living among them, while others defended them as being unduly oppressed. In Sonora similar notions were expressed against or in favor of the Seris, Tepocas, Tiburones, and Pimas. There were also accusations of treachery in Coahuila and Nuevo León, and those who believed that the Borrados of Nuevo Santander could easily be subjugated had opponents who branded them as being as warlike and fearful as the Apaches.[59] In all his wavering, however, Flores confided none of his doubts to Ugarte.

Frustrated by the Viceroy's apparent intransigent stand against the flexible policy he had been pursuing, Ugarte finally carried his case to the king in May of 1789. In a lengthy memorial he reviewed the background of the current dilemma, attacked Flores' policy, and defended Gálvez's and his own.[60] He agreed with the *Instrucción* of 1786 in all matters relating to war on the hostile tribes—creating division among them, extending peace to those who sued for it, using friendly tribes as auxiliaries against the hostiles, and cementing friendship with trade and fair treatment. In these points, he argued, the *Instrucción* conformed with previous royal orders.[61] His own campaigns, by creating consternation among them, had forced the hostiles to sue for peace. This was especially true in Sonora, where the Chiricahuas and

[58] *Ibid.*

[59] Flores to Valdés, No. 536 (confidential), México, August 26, 1788, AGN, CV 19 (Second series), Fojas 61–96.

[60] Ugarte to the King, Chihuahua, May 8, 1789, *loc. cit.*

[61] Paragraph 10, *ibid.*

the rebellious Seris were soon reduced to a peace they still honored. The Chiricahuas had also made peace in Nueva Vizcaya, as had the Mimbres Apaches for a time, and almost all of the Mescaleros had been at peace in that province for more than a year. In Texas and New Mexico the Taovayas, Tawakoni, Kichai, Iscani, and lesser factions of the so-called Nations of the North had already made peace, and in his own time an alliance had been perfected with the powerful and warlike Comanches. The Comanches had also been reconciled with the friendly Utes, and a beginning had been made in allying with the Navahos and disuniting them from the Gila Apaches.[62]

Ugarte believed that the new peace with the Comanches and Nations of the North would assure the old peace in Coahuila with the Lipán Apaches, their implacable enemies; that the Lipanes, no longer able to attribute their occult raids to the Mescaleros because of the latter's peaceful establishment far from the camps of the former, would cease committing such hostilities rather than risk war with the Spaniards and their new allies. Then Ugalde's eastern provinces, being free from attack, could send most of their troops to reinforce those of Nueva Vizcaya, and there the two forces together with Mescalero auxiliaries could wage a most severe war on the Gila Apaches and the Mimbreños who had broken their peace. At the same time an offensive could be waged against the Gileños by the armed forces of Sonora with Chiricahua auxiliaries, striking from the southwest, and by those of New Mexico reinforced by Pueblo, Comanche, Ute, and Navaho war parties, attacking from the northeast. In this way the Gila Apaches would shortly find themselves forced to surrender or perish. This, Ugarte contended, was the plan of action he had been preparing since he first assumed the general command.[63]

This grand strategy, however, had been frustrated by Flores' division of the Provincias Internas into two separate commands, by Ugalde's antagonization of the peaceful Mescaleros, and by the Viceroy's preference for Ugalde's rather than his own pol-

[62] Paragraphs 20–21, *ibid.*
[63] Paragraphs 23–24, *ibid.*

icies.[64] Realizing that Flores had been misled by the eastern commander, Ugarte had protested and set the record straight, but Flores had not replied. Instead he had ordered Ugarte to remove the peaceful Mescaleros to Ugalde's dominions and never allow them to return to Nueva Vizcaya. Ugarte had protested again, calling Flores' attention to the grave consequences it would have for both Nueva Vizcaya and Coahuila if the Gila Apaches should invade again. The Mescaleros, if exiled from their present peaceful abodes, would rise up in arms, and the troops would be diverted from their chief task of defending the provinces from the Gileño invasion. Flores had also ignored this argument.[65] So the Mescaleros were expelled from Nueva Vizcaya at the very time they were preparing to join the troops against their rebellious kinsmen in Coahuila, and Ugarte had to witness the sacrifice of the happy effects of his early pacification measures, the shedding of the blood of many innocent vassals, and the abandonment of the good faith of the Spanish nation.[66] Ugarte had reported these sad results to Flores and pleaded for the readmission of the Mescaleros and for their use as auxiliaries against the truly hostile Apaches, but Flores remained adamant. In Nueva Vizcaya the Viceroy would permit peace, if they should offer it, only with the Gileños![67]

Ugarte believed that experience had proved that while one faction lived at peace the whole country gained respite from its attacks, the troops were successful in their operations by having to make fewer campaigns, and the friendly faction provided trained guides, expert spies, and valiant soldiers to array against the remaining enemy. Even if these friends again became enemies, it would be only after they had weakened themselves from fighting as auxiliaries against the hostiles, and if they had been treated justly while at peace, they would seek it again after experiencing the rigors of war. This formed the principal basis of the system of waging peace alternately with war on all the en-

[64] Paragraphs 30, 42–55, *ibid.*
[65] Paragraphs 56–62, *ibid.*
[66] Paragraphs 63–64, *ibid.*
[67] Paragraphs 65–69, *ibid.*

emies without distinction, according to their own situation and inclination.[68]

And so the great debate went on. Finally it was fate rather than reason that resolved the issue. Ill health forced Flores to retire from office in October of 1789, the next viceroy reverted to the policies Ugarte had espoused, and the pure recklessness of Ugalde led to his removal as a rival commandant-general. Ugarte himself remained in office only long enough to see the rehabilitation of his own policies. Important as were the grand designs of kings, viceroys, and commandant-generals, however, Indian policy was primarily determined by the attitude and acts of the Indians themselves. It is therefore essential to examine these realities in their own settings.

[68] Paragraph 70, *ibid.*

CHAPTER VII

THE COMANCHE ALLIANCE

As Ugarte well realized, the pacification of the Apaches depended upon the military assistance of other Indian nations. The so-called Nations of the North had so terrorized the Lipanes that they had sought Spanish protection in Texas and Coahuila. Pressure on the Apaches was increased by the weight of the more powerful Comanches, not only on the Lipanes but on the Llaneros and the Mescaleros, both of whom sued for peace in Nueva Vizcaya. In the west the Gileños and their kinsmen, the Mimbreños, Chiricahuas, and Navahos were beyond the ordinary range of the Comanches, but during Ugarte's administration they were not secure. As a means of cementing their new alliance with the Spaniards, the warriors who had so terrorized the Apaches of the plains now struck out on their own or in company with Spanish troops to harry those in the mountains of the western desert.

The groundwork for the Comanche alliance had been laid by the governors of New Mexico before Ugarte assumed his general command. Governor Tomás Vélez Capuchín (1749–54 and 1762–67) had maintained a casual peace with the marauding Comanches during his two administrations, but it was Governor Juan Bautista de Anza (1777–87) who revived this relationship and then perfected it under Ugarte's wise direction. A veteran presidial commander in Sonora who had opened a land route to Alta California and established a colony at San Francisco, Anza was an exceptionally energetic governor in New Mexico. Having anticipated a heavy raid on his province in 1779, he mobilized a formidable campaign of his own, penetrated hostile territory as far as the front range of the Rockies, and fell on a Comanche encampment numbering 120 tents. In two engagements his forces killed or captured 131 of the enemy, including the principal chief and his heir apparent, took more than 100 muleloads of spoil, and dispersed the remainder of the assembled tribesmen.[1]

During the next few years, while Spanish funds and forces were diverted from the frontier to support the war with England, the Comanches managed to regain the advantage. With the restoration of international peace in 1783, however, Commandant-General Croix and his successor, Neve, reversed the situation by arming the Nations of the North and persuading them to attack the lordly warriors of the plains in force. Harried by the tribes of the Texas frontier and denied trading privileges with the New Mexican pueblos, the Comanches realized the futility of their situation within the next two years. By 1785 more than 400 of them trooped into Taos seeking amnesty in New Mexico, and three of their chiefs arrived at San Antonio to negotiate a similar arrangement in Texas.[2]

As the price for peace, Governor Domingo Cabello of Texas stipulated eight articles of capitulation, and these were accepted tentatively by the Orientales, the eastern Cuchantica branch of the Comanches, in October of 1785. Commandant-Inspector Rengel submitted these terms to Viceroy Gálvez for his approval in January of 1786. The terms were essentially the same as those that Governor Anza demanded of the Comanches in New Mexico: (1) the mutual cessation of all hostilities and the establishment of brotherly relations; (2) the extension of this amity to the king's Indian and Spanish vassals in all the provinces; (3) the release and restoration to their own people of all Spaniards held captive by the Orientales; (4) the exclusion from the eastern Comanche villages of all Europeans except Spaniards; (5) the recognition by the Orientales of the friends and enemies of the

---

[1] Thomas, *Forgotten Frontiers*, 55–71.
[2] *Ibid.*, 71–72.

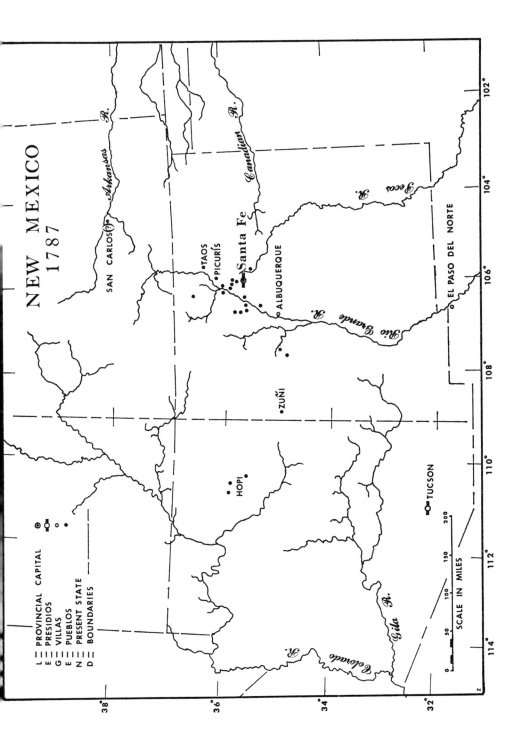

NEW MEXICO
1787

PROVINCIAL CAPITAL
PRESIDIOS
VILLAS
PUEBLOS
PRESENT STATE
BOUNDARIES

SAN CARLOS(?)

Arkansas R.

Canadian R.

TAOS
PICURÍS
Santa Fe
ALBUQUERQUE

Pecos R.

Rio Grande R.

EL PASO DEL NORTE

ZUÑI

HOPI

TUCSON

Gila R.

Colorado R.

SCALE IN MILES
0 50 100 150 200

102°
104°
106°
108°
110°
112°
114°

38°
36°
34°
32°

Spaniards as those of their own; (6) the prosecution of war by the eastern Comanches against the Lipán Apaches and the rendering of full reports on their campaigns to the authorities at San Antonio; (7) the admission of the Orientales into Coahuila for the purpose of attacking the Lipán and Mescalero Apaches only on permission of the governor of Texas; and (8) the annual distribution of presents to the chiefs of the Orientales and principal tribesmen as proof of Spanish good will.[3]

In New Mexico Governor Anza also accepted the overtures of the Comanches, but he refused to offer any guarantee until all branches of the nation were willing to accept the terms in unison. There were then three rather well-defined Comanche groups: the Jupe or Yupe (People of the Timber), the Yamparica (Root-Eaters), and the Cuchantica or Cuchanec (Buffalo-Eaters), the easternmost of which were known as the Orientales. The Jupe ranged from the southern part of present Wyoming southward to the Arkansas River; the Yamparica from what is now northern Colorado southward, among the Jupe, to the Arkansas; and the Cuchantica from the Arkansas River southward to the Red River and eastward to the Taovayas (Wichita) villages on the latter river. In November of 1785 chiefs of the three branches of the Comanche nation were summoned to a council on the Arkansas River, and although some from the northernmost Jupe and easternmost Cuchantica bands were not present, they nevertheless elected a commissioner to negotiate peace with Governor Anza.[4]

[3] These articles are summarized in a report of Ugarte's successor: Pedro de Nava to Viceroy Miguel Joseph de Azanza, Chihuahua, July 23, 1799, AGN, PI 12, Expediente 2. A translation of the report appears in Odie B. Faulk, "Spanish-Comanche Relations and the Treaty of 1785," *Texana*, Vol. II, No. 1 (Spring, 1964), 44–53. See also Faulk's *The Last Years of Spanish Texas, 1778–1821*, 64–66.

[4] Pedro Garrido y Durán, Relación de los sucesos ocurridos en la Provincia de Nuevo-México con motivos de la Paz concedida a la Nación Comanche y su reconciliación con la Yuta desde 17 de Noviembre de 1785 hasta 15 de Julio de 86, Chihuahua, December 21, 1786 (cert. copy), Paragraphs 2–4, AGN, PI 65, Expediente 2. Thomas, *Forgotten Frontiers*, 72–73, erroneously dates the council on the Arkansas River as November of 1786. For a discussion of the more recent groupings of the Comanche nation, see Rupert N. Richardson, *The Comanche Barrier to the South Plains Settlement*, 18–21.

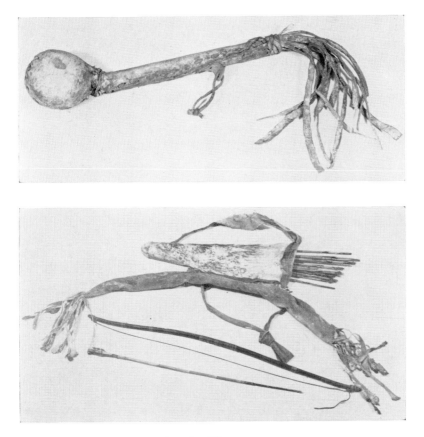

Apache Weapons.

Top, Coyotero Apache war club of rawhide with wrapped stone head; bottom, Apache bow and flint-tipped arrows with reed shaft and hardwood foreshaft, bow case and quiver of antelope hide.

Apache rawhide shield, with cover, nineteen inches in diameter.

The choice of the council fell upon Ecueracapa (Leather Cape), known sometimes as Contatancapara (Warrior Without Equal). Ecueracapa, a chief of the Cuchanticas with a reputation for great wisdom and valor, then sent emissaries to Santa Fe. For a time the success of the negotiations was threatened by the obstructionist tactics of the Utes, who were already in peaceful alliance with the Spaniards, but were historically hostile to the Comanches. However, Governor Anza managed to soothe the ruffled feelings of the Utes and even induced them to enter into deliberations. Then, on February 25, 1786, Ecuercapa himself arrived at Santa Fe and, purportedly speaking for all three branches of the Comanche nation, agreed to the preliminary terms stipulated by Anza. These included the Comanches' formal reconciliation with the Utes and Ecueracapa's own assumption, with Spanish support, of the principal chieftainship of his entire nation. The Ute, Comanche, and Spanish commissioners adjourned to the Pueblo of Pecos, where 200 Comanche braves were also convened, and there on February 28 a provisional peace pact was sealed. On the next day Anza formally opened the annual trade fair at Taos to the Comanches and published a schedule of prices to prevent the Spanish and Pueblo Indian merchants from defrauding their new customers. On the same day, March 1, the Utes and Comanches solemnized their reconciliation, and the representatives of both nations departed for their homelands in peace and good will.[5]

During the next four and one-half months several chiefs and tribesmen of the three branches of the Comanche nation came to Taos and Pecos to trade and to Santa Fe to be recognized by Anza and to assure him of their fidelity. Finally, Ecueracapa and other chiefs proved their desire for a sincere alliance by attacking the Apaches in southern New Mexico.[6] Meanwhile the Governor's commissioner, Francisco Xavier Ortiz, visited eight Comanche villages, extending as far east as the salt plains of the Canadian River and the canyon of the Cimarron. In the smallest

[5] Garrido y Durán, Relación, *loc. cit.*, Paragraphs 5–25.
[6] *Ibid.*, Paragraphs 26–43.

of these encampments Ortiz counted 30 tipis, and in the largest, 175. In all he estimated that there were 700 lodges with three or four warriors and seven or eight women and children in each.[7]

On July 15 Governor Anza submitted a full report on the Comanche negotiations to Ugarte, who had recently succeeded to the commandancy-general.[8] After studying these particulars for several weeks, the new *Comandante General* composed a detailed instruction for Anza's further procedure.[9] It is in this remarkable document that Ugarte best expresses his own views on the proper ways and means of achieving a lasting peace with the nomadic tribes of the frontier. Obviously inspired by the royal order of 1779 and anticipating the more detailed articles of Galvez's *Instrucción* of 1786, which he would receive almost six weeks later, Ugarte's directions to Anza reveal a keen sense of justice, a practical knowledge of Indian psychology, and a humanitarian optimism quite out of character with the stereotype of the colonial Spanish military mind. Seventeen years of administrative experience seem to have converted the old soldier into an ebullient idealist.

Ugarte expressed his approval of and deep gratification for what Anza had accomplished in negotiating a preliminary peace with the Comanches and reconciling them with the friendly Utes. However, he was now calling on Anza to arrange for a second general council of the Comanche nation, one that would be held at a time and place that would permit the attendance of representatives of all its bands. The northernmost Yamparicas, cut off by heavy snows, and the eastern Cuchanticas, already in negotiation with the governor of Texas, had not attended the council held on the banks of the Arkansas in November of the previous year, and Ugarte now insisted that these groups ratify

[7] Francisco Xavier Ortiz to Anza, Santa Fe, May 20, 1786 (cert. copy), AGN, PI 65, Expediente 2.

[8] Garrido y Durán's *Relación* appears to be a summary of Anza's report of July 15 and its supporting documents composed by Ugarte's secretary. A translation appears in Thomas, *Forgotten Frontiers*, 294–321.

[9] Ugarte to Anza, Chihuahua, October 5, 1786 (cert. copy), AGN, PI 65, Expediente 2. This important document is also translated in Thomas, *Forgotten Frontiers*, 332–42.

the articles of peace in unison with the rest of the nation. He also wished to expand the provisions of the preliminary pact.

Most important of all, Ugarte wanted Anza to induce the new council to elect one of its members as superior chief and to cloak him with absolute control over the affairs of the entire nation, especially over those matters pertaining to the terms of peace. He believed that the permanence of the peace depended more than anything else on this election and the acceptance, maintenance, and strengthening of the position of such a potentate. Anza, therefore, should bestow on this principal chief the title of captain general and award him an annual salary of 200 pesos, to be paid in such goods as he might esteem. The election, however, was not to be left to chance. Since the important Cuchantica chief Ecueracapa had already proved himself to be well-behaved, righteous, popular with his nation, and favorably disposed toward the Spaniards, Anza was to see that he was elected to this office. Certain that the Governor could swing the election in that direction, Ugarte enclosed with his instructions a certificate for the title of captain general with Ecueracapa's name already entered.

So that Ecueracapa might better exert his authority over the more remote segments of the nation, Anza was to provide him with a subordinate chieftain who would carry the rank of lieutenant general and reside among the Jupe and Yamparica branches. A certificate for this latter office—carrying a salary of 100 pesos worth of goods each year—was also enclosed, but on it the name was left blank. This title was to be awarded to a chief nominated by the captain general of the Comanches and acceptable to Anza. If the Governor thought a second such officer advisable, he might also appoint one to reside among and govern the easternmost Cuchanticas. Although the latter appointment should be made by the governor of Texas, who was already treating with them, Anza should determine which of the chiefs of the Orientales might be most acceptable to Ecueracapa. Ugarte also wanted Anza to appoint as many as four Spaniards to reside among the Comanches as interpreters, two with the captain general and two with the lieutenant general. Owing to the delicate

nature of their duties, the interpreters were to be carefully selected with a view to their good behavior, acceptability to the
Comanches, proficiency in their language, knowledge of their
customs, and ability to write Spanish. Each interpreter was to receive the pay of a New Mexican presidial soldier. Having gained
the election of the principal officers and acceptance of the interpreters, Anza was to induce the general council to ratify the
terms of peace as Ugarte now extended them.

First, the Comanches must undertake to collect in their encampments all vagrants and dispersed members of their nation
and pursue and destroy those who refused to submit to an orderly
village life. Next, the Comanches must agree to deliver alive to
the Spaniards for a stipulated ransom all the Apaches they had
captured who were under the age of fourteen. However, the
Spaniards were not to rescue adult Apaches of either sex, even
if they faced death at the hands of their captors. In Ugarte's
opinion, the cruelty and stubbornness with which the Apaches
had been assailing the Spaniards, in violation of all the rules of
warfare and laws of humanity, rendered them unworthy of Spanish consideration, either for their liberty or for their preservation.

The Comanches were also obligated to restore to the Spaniards, in this instance without compensation, all captives they had
taken from friendly tribes, such as the Utes, whether the prisoners were Christian or heathen. For the release of those whom
they had purchased rather than captured and who might wish
to return to their own people, the Spanish were obligated to
compensate their owners for the price they had paid.

Ugarte also wished Anza to bind the Spaniards to make like
restitution of such Comanches as they held, even those already
sent to the fortress prison of San Juan de Ulúa, unless they were
already baptized or wished to remain among the Spaniards. This
concession was designed to prove the good faith and equitability
of the Spanish efforts for peace, but Ugarte also felt that it would
have significant political advantage. On returning home from
San Juan de Ulúa, where they were held, some of the Comanche
prisoners would probably spread among their tribesmen an idea

of the power of the Spanish king, the numerousness of his troops and vassals, the orderliness of his government, and whatever else they might have observed in the cities through which they passed on their way home, and these impressions would doubtlessly make their own people look on Spanish officials with timorous respect.

Ugarte thought the Spaniards should undertake to educate such sons of the Comanche chieftains as might wish this advantage. Anza had reported that several chiefs and other members of the nation had expressed a desire to learn the language and customs of the Spaniards, and Ugarte considered this a most felicitous disposition on their part. If Anza should receive similar requests in the future, he was to explain to the Comanches that the long study required would only fatigue the adults without their learning enough to make the effort worthwhile. If they should wish these advantages for their children, however, Anza should make it clear that the king would find it in his pious heart to approve this laudable intention, and he would have them brought to Mexico City and educated there at royal expense. Anza should also explain that some of the kinsmen of these children might accompany them to the viceregal capital, bear witness to their treatment there, and return to reassure their parents. In suggesting this opportunity to the Comanche council, Anza was to reveal no other motive than a desire to serve the best interests of the Comanches themselves. Realizing that some of the youths might eventually succeed to general command over their nation, Anza was to see to it that those who might be selected be not only of proper age to benefit from the instruction but also be of families of the principal chiefs. He was also to point out that when the Comanche youth had been instructed in the dogma of Catholicism, they would not be admitted to that faith immediately but would first be returned to their own people and then allowed to make a free choice of religion. Anza might incorporate this guarantee in the treaty if the Comanches so desired. Ugarte felt that such a training program for the sons of chieftains would not only provide secure hostages for the fidelity of the Comanches but would also eventually spread throughout their entire nation the same principles of religion and civilization with which the youngsters themselves would be inspired. In fact, Anza might do well to encourage this same program among the Utes and Navahos.

The Utes should be invited to send delegates to the general council so as to witness the articles agreed to by the Comanches and thus be dispelled of any suspicions of collusions against their own nation. This would also provide Anza with an occasion to have the Utes and Comanches ratify their recently negotiated reconciliation. Then, too, the Navahos would learn of this unity and would naturally be inspired with its terrifying consequences to them if they should fail to keep the peace, which they had just concluded in New Mexico, or slacken their war effort against the Gila Apaches, who were the mutual enemies of the Utes, Comanches, and Spaniards.

For the newly established trade between the Comanches and Spaniards Anza was authorized to draw up new and more equitable price schedules, establish more favorable sites for the fairs, dictate such other arrangements as would reduce the grievances of the Comanches in their commercial relations, and incorporate these regulations into the final treaty.

As a guarantee for the exact compliances by the Comanches with their stipulated obligations Anza was to see to it that all of their chiefs not only agreed to these at the council but that they also specified in Anza's presence the penalties that they would impose on their tribesmen for each infraction. Anza should impress the chiefs with the absolute necessity of exacting rigorous punishments for breaches of the peace, but he should take no part in stipulating the nature of these penalties. And in no case was he to intervene against the imposition of punishments. Rather, he was to require such of the accused as might have justification to carry his complaint either to the court of Captain General Ecueracapa or to the council of chiefs, which might be established for judging such cases. Experience, Ugarte observed, had proved that while an Indian generally accepted punishment for his crime submissively when it was administered by a superior of his own nation, he resisted and resented condemnation by Spanish judges, even when the latter were more moderate and pious in determining the sentence. Nor should Anza protect or grant immunity to any Indian fugitive merely to avoid the displeasure of the chiefs. He should make it public in the Comanche villages that he would grant no such asylum. If the decisions of a corporate nation, or a single authority, were to be respected, the rigorous administration of justice was absolutely necessary; for, as Ugarte believed, the smooth operation of government depended upon respect for the law. He did realize, however, that a case might arise in which it might be convenient to offer clemency, as when a crime against the Spaniards was committed by an Indian of some importance—the son or relative of some principal chief—in which case inflexibility on Anza's part might noticeably alter good relations. In such an instance prudence required that indulgence was preferable to satisfaction for the injury. This, however, Anza was to employ with such discretion as not to inspire disobedience or insubordination, for upon the slightest carelessness in such a matter, license would quickly develop, and all the fruit of their laborious efforts would be lost in an instant.

Ugarte was willing to allow the Comanches to move their encampments nearer to the New Mexican settlements, as they had requested. In their present positions they could better protect the province from hostile tribes, and their natural addiction to warfare could be employed in the general subjugation of the Apaches, but Ugarte thought it would be better to civilize the Comanches than to exploit their military prowess. If only they could be induced to cultivate the soil, he reasoned, they would gradually and insensibly come to depend upon crops and would give up hunting. Living in fixed villages and developing a high regard for their new possessions would guarantee their permanent tranquility, and in a short time they would become the most useful of the peaceful tribes. For this important attainment Anza was to employ all his wisdom. He was to assure the chieftains that, unlike the fruits of agriculture, the game the Comanches hunted with such fatigue was exhaustible and was even now becoming scarce; that farming was more appropriate to the institutions of man, who was born to live in society; that the peace, which they had accepted, offered them security for dedicating themselves to agriculture, for royal funds would assist them in making a start, and nearby Spanish farmers would serve them as models; that they would not have to abandon the chase immediately but could enjoy the fruits of both hunting and farming and thus provide themselves abundantly with the necessities for a life of tranquility. Sparing no means to make this a reality, Anza was to issue the Comanches whatever assistance they might require. He was not to resort to pressure or coercion in converting them to farming but was to reveal only an interest in their own welfare and allow their own convenience to attract them to the new way of life. However, so as to encourage them to get on with the laying out of fields, building of dams, and opening of irrigation ditches, Anza was to settle Spaniards and Pueblo Indians among them and equip both these and the Comanches with oxen, plows, and other necessary implements.

Although peace had already been negotiated with the eastern Cuchanticas in Texas, Ugarte wanted Anza himself to assume the responsibility in New Mexico for solidifying it with the Comanche nation in general, especially since the chiefs with whom he was dealing had not demanded annual presents as had those in Texas. Apparently the Comanches in Texas had not agreed on a general chief to whom they would be responsible for fulfilling their obligations, and there was some confusion over the identity of the eastern Cuchantica leaders. Ugarte wanted Anza to try to determine whether Ecueracapa, the general peace commissioner and presumably the captain general-elect of the Comanches in New Mexico, was the same as Camisa de Fierro (Iron Shirt), the most prominently mentioned chief of the Orientales in Texas.[10] Anza was also to learn all he could

[10] Anza had identified Ecueracapa as Cota de Malla (Coat of Mail) in his reports of July 15, 1786, as summarized in Garrido y Durán's Relación, loc. cit., Paragraph 5. At the end of the year, however, Ugarte learned from a group of Comanche chieftains, including three sons of Ecueracapa himself, that the sur-

about another Comanche chief, Cabeza Rapada (Shaven Head),
who was killed during the current year, along with many of his
band, in a battle with a large number of Mescalero, Lipán, and
Natagé Apaches.

Ugarte admitted that the measures he was suggesting to Anza
for the establishment of a general and secure peace and alliance
with the Comanches would require additional funds. He had
sent Anza 1,000 pesos, 400 horses, 20 mules, and 2 carbines by
the last caravan from Chihuahua. This, however, would not cover
all the expenses, especially since part of the money was earmarked
to buy presents for the Utes and Navahos. Therefore Ugarte
had decided to raise the annual budget for New Mexico's expenditures for peace and war to 6,000 pesos.

Finally, since Ugarte was unable to foresee all the contin-
gencies that might arise in the course of the negotiations, he was
empowering Anza to take such measures as he might deem fitting
and proper and also to alter Ugarte's own instructions wherever
necessary to serve the best interests of the king.[11]

Accompanying Ugarte's extensive instructions to Anza was his
approval—with specific modifications—of the preliminary pact
that the governor had concluded with Ecueracapa. Article 1,
calling for the immediate cessation of hostilities, was to be accepted with the understanding that it was to pertain not only
to New Mexico but to all the provinces in which the Comanches
ranged. Article 2, allowing the Comanches to encamp under the
king's protection near the Spanish settlements, was to be granted
only with Anza's prior permission, in the number he should
allow, and on the condition that the Comanches kept the peace
with all Indians who were friends of the Spaniards. Article 3,
providing for the free and safe passage of Ecueracapa to Santa
Fe and of the entire nation to Pecos for commercial purposes, was

name Cota de Malla belonged to quite another chief, one who enjoyed equal
rank and influence among the Eastern Comanches who were congregated in
Texas, and that this worthy had recently been killed in battle. Ugarte to the
Marqués de Sonora, Chihuahua, January 4, 1787 (cert. copy), AGN, PI 65,
Expediente 2.

[11] Ugarte to Anza, Chihuahua, October 5, 1786, *loc. cit.*

to be governed by a body of trade regulations, which would be drawn up in consultation with the principal chiefs and on the basis of Ugarte's proposals. Article 4, requiring the Comanches to intensify their attacks on the hostile Apaches in concert with Spanish troops, was to stipulate that the campaigns were to be under the direction of the governors of New Mexico and Texas and that the eastern Comanches and other friendly nations near the Taovayas villages participate. Article 5, providing for some token of Ecueracapa's plenipotentiary office so as to win him the support of all other chiefs, was approved without amendment.[12]

Governor Anza apparently convened a second council of the Cuchantica Comanches in late October or early November of 1786, somewhere in their own territory. There the favored Ecueracapa was duly elected captain general of the nation, one Tosacondata was chosen second-in-command of the Cuchanticas, and the expanded articles of peace were ratified. Anza then sent by the November caravan to Chihuahua the articles of peace for Ugarte's approval. These were escorted by twelve prominent Comanches. Three of these were chieftains: Tosacondata, whom Anza wished Ugarte to decorate with the insignia of his new office; Oxamaguea, who, being the eldest son of Ecueracapa, would deliver the treaty in person; and Encantime, a war chieftain of the Jupe branch of the nation. Two other sons of Ecueracapa (Tomaneguena and Tahuichimpia), five braves, and two of Tosacondata's squaws completed the delegation. Anza asked Ugarte to provide Oxamaguea and Tosacondata with staffs of office and written titles and to send another staff for Ecueracapa.[13]

The Comanche delegation arrived at Chihuahua on December 30, and was received with full honors. Ugarte summoned the

[12] Artículos de Paz concertados y arreglados en la Villa de Santa Fée y Pueblo de Pecos entre el Coronel dn. Juan Bautista de Anza, Governador de la Provincia de Nuevo-México, y el Capitán Comanche Ecueracapa, Diputado General de esta Nación, en los días 25 y 28 de Febrero de 1786 (endorsed with modifications by Anza at Santa Fe on July 14 and by Ugarte at Chihuahua on October 5, 1786) (cert. copy), AGN, PI 65, Expediente 2. A translation appears in Thomas, *Forgotten Frontiers*, 325–32.

[13] Anza to Ugarte, Santa Fe, November 18, 1786 (cert. copy), AGN, PI 65, Expediente 2.

principal officials and dignitaries of the city to their reception, entertained the delegates several times in his own home, and supplied them abundantly with food, clothing, horses, and small gifts. Each of the three chieftains was given a musket in special consideration of his rank, and another gun was provided for delivery to Ecueracapa. Tosacondata was decorated with a medallion somewhat smaller than that previously sent Ecueracapa, and both Oxamaguea and Encantime were presented with others of still lesser size. Having come, as they explained, to greet the *Comandante General* in behalf of Ecueracapa and the Comanche nation under his command and to learn whether Ugarte's intentions regarding the peace conformed to the articles they had signed with Anza, they were very pleased when Ugarte assured them that Anza's measures had emanated from his office. They then resolved to keep the peace inviolably and to assist in bringing the Jupes and Yamparicas under its protection. Ugarte was convinced of their sincerity.[14]

Ugarte was also impressed with their appearance. He noticed that all the Comanche delegates were robust, good-looking, extremely happy, and of a physiognomy that exhibited the warlike, frank, and generous nature that distinguished their nation from the others of the northern frontier. Their dress was simple, fashioned by themselves from buffalo skins. Their faces were painted with red ocher and other earths, and their eyelids were enlivened with vermillion. They were fond of adornments, especially for their hair, which they braided and interwove with imitation gold buttons, colored glass beads, ribbons, and many other shiny articles. In notable contrast to the men, the women were unkempt, had their hair cut short—a sign among them of slavery and abjection—and enjoyed no more esteem than what their masters dispensed in proportion to their services.[15]

Ugarte did not deliver staffs of office to the three chiefs or send one for Ecueracapa, for he had just received a disconcerting

[14] Ugarte to the Marqués de Sonora, Chihuahua, January 4, 1787 (cert. copy), and to Anza, Chihuahua, February 7 and February 8, 1787, AGN, PI 65, Expediente 2 and Expediente 3.
[15] Ugarte to the Marqués de Sonora, Chihuahua, January 4, 1787, *loc. cit.*

report from Texas. From that quarter he had learned of a Comanche superstition, which he felt might also prevail in New Mexico. It was believed that if such an insignia were lost or broken, by whatever accident, it would inevitably presage the immediate and disastrous death of its owner. The eastern Cuchantica chieftains, so persuaded by their oracles, had already returned the staffs that had been presented to them. However, if Anza could assure him that the Comanches of New Mexico were free from any such superstition, Ugarte would have staffs manufactured and sent to them on another occasion.[16]

Nor did Ugarte see fit to expedite titles to the three chieftains. Having already sent one for Ecueracapa and another for a lieutenant general to reside among the Jupes and Yamparicas, he had since received certain information that had given him some second thoughts on the subject. The Jupes and Yamparicas, ranging to the north of the Cuchanticas, had a chief of great popularity who was the father of Encantime, but Ugarte now found it unfeasible to make him a lieutenant general. The independence from the Cuchanticas of these northern tribes might lead them to resent the subordination of their chieftain to Captain General Ecueracapa, he explained, and the salary for the lesser rank, being only half that of the Captain General, might also excite envy and cupidity. Therefore, Ugarte directed, Anza should put these considerations and the consequences to test and make such final arrangements for a firm peace as would give no cause for its interruption. He should be guided only by the spirit of Ugarte's instructions of October 5, 1786, and should make such amendments to them as seemed practical for the achievement of the desired end. If it appeared more convenient to give the Jupes and Yamparicas a superior chief of their own, independent of Ecueracapa and the Cuchanticas, Ugarte would have no objections. And if he found it advisable to reward such a dignitary with special treatment and gifts instead of a fixed salary, that too would be satisfactory.[17]

[16] Ugarte to Anza, Chihuahua, February 8, 1787, *loc. cit.*
[17] *Ibid.*

Finally, should the twelve Comanches returning from Chihuahua spread reports of the good treatment they had experienced there and should others wish to make the same trip, Anza should not prevent it. He should warn them, however, that they must be accompanied by an interpreter and that they would be received only for the purpose of selling their peltries at a more favorable price or in recognition of their having participated in a military campaign against the Apaches. Ugarte had ordered the military commandants to receive Comanche visitors at the presidios and provide them at Chihuahua with the assistance necessary for their return and for operations of war against the Apaches. They were to be courted with *cigarros*, sugar, and such food as they might need, but nothing else. The ample gratifications dispensed to the twelve Comanche delegates was not to serve as a precedent. Anza was to inform them of this so that none for selfish reasons might begin a long trip, which might be frustrated; for if all the Comanches were allowed to come to Chihuahua and be treated as were the first delegates, the cost would be much more than the 6,000 pesos assigned for such purposes.[18]

The final treaty with all three branches of the Comanche nation was concluded at long last on April 21, 1787. Anza had met with the principal Jupe, Yamparica, and Chuchantica chiefs in a general council held in their lands and there had concluded the final agreements.[19] Ecueracapa seems to have been confirmed as captain general of the entire nation along with two lieutenant generals, Tosacondata for the Cuchanticas and a Jupe chief named Paruanarimuca for both his own branch and the Yamparicas.

By this time the Navahos were also attracted to the Spanish cause, and with the Utes, Jicarillas, and now the Comanches as allies and with the Pueblo nations regularly furnishing auxiliaries

[18] *Ibid.*

[19] Ugarte to Governor Fernando de la Concha, Arispe, January 23, 1788 (cert. copy), and to Viceroy Flores, Janos, March 13, 1788, AGN, PI 65, Expediente 2 and Expediente 8. Neither the final articles nor the cover letter of the treaty is in the files examined.

for the presidial troops at Santa Fe, the stage was set for a major offensive against the enemy Apaches. Under Anza's auspices the Comanches had already campaigned on their own as early as April of 1786, and by the next month a remarkable practice had been developed whereby Ecueracapa was reporting the results of the Comanche campaigns in hieroglyphics on a tally sheet furnished by the Governor. On May 19, 1786, Ecueracapa made such a report certifying that he and 4 other chiefs with a total of 347 warriors had killed 6 Apaches, captured 2 others, and recovered 65 horses and 20 mules, with the loss to themselves of only 1 killed and 6 wounded.[20] At the end of July of the next year a similar report was made of 95 Comanches under 1 chief killing 5 Faraón Apaches in the Sierra Blanca and taking 35 prisoners of both sexes along with 16 horses, with the loss of only 1 Comanche killed and 6 wounded.[21]

In accordance with the final treaty articles, the Comanches had agreed to deliver all their Apache prisoners under the age of fourteen to Governor Anza, but Ugarte ordered Anza's successor, Fernando de la Concha, to ransom all Apache prisoners taken by the Comanches and to send them in irons to Nueva Vizcaya along with those taken by the Spanish troops. He agreed with De la Concha's practice of rewarding the Comanches with a horse, a bridle, and two knives for the surrender of each Apache captive of either sex and any age.[22]

Meanwhile, since November of 1786, members of the Lipán Apache tribe, who enjoyed peace with Coahuila and Texas to the south, were filtering into New Mexico and making overtures for a similar arrangement with that province. This disturbed the Comanches, who now begged Anza not to make such a concession. If he did, they declared, the Comanches would then have no enemies on whom to make war and would consequently be-

[20] This curious tally sheet is reproduced and explained in Thomas, *Forgotten Frontiers*, 324–25.
[21] Anza to Ugarte, Santa Fe, October 20, 1787, and Ugarte to De la Concha, Arispe, January 23, 1788 (cert. copy), AGN, PI 65, Expediente 8.
[22] De la Concha to Ugarte, Santa Fe, June 26, 1787, and Ugarte to Flores, Chihuahua, July 31, 1788, AGN, PI 65, Expediente 6.

come effeminate![23] After receiving a number of such reports, Ugarte ordered first Anza and then his successor to maintain peace in New Mexico only with the Comanches, Utes, Navahos, and Jicarilla Apaches, and not even to listen to the propositions of the Lipanes, Lipiyanes, Natagees, Faraones, Mescaleros, Gileños, or Apaches under any other name. Since the granting of trade and protection to the Lipanes would endanger the permanence of the peace conceded to the Comanches, the governors were to dissuade them gracefully from seeking protection in New Mexico, even though they enjoyed it in Texas and Coahuila.[24] Viceroy Flores not only approved Ugarte's position in this matter but vigorously insisted upon it.[25]

One of the fondest hopes of the Spaniards in their epic struggle to pacify the nomadic tribes was that these predators could be induced to settle down in fixed villages and gain their livelihood from farming and trading. As the royal order of 1779 had expressed, this was essential to the establishment of permanent peace on the northern frontier. That the proud Comanches would ever accept the humble life of the sedentary farmer was little short of fantasy according to most of the experienced frontier officials, but Ugarte was forever optimistic of this attainment. It was this confidence that most distinguished him from the other administrators. He was therefore most gratified when Governor Anza reported that one group of the Comanches had spontaneously requested assistance in settling down to such an existence. On July 14, 1787, Anza had notified Ugarte that Lieutenant General Paruanarimuco had come to him and asked for Spanish assistance in establishing fixed villages for the Jupes. On July 25 he had repeated the request, this time with such urgency that Anza had granted it without asking for Ugarte's authorization. Anza had sent the Jupes a supply of tools, building materials, and thirty laborers under a competent foreman. These Paruanarimuco

[23] Anza to Ugarte, Santa Fe, July 14, 1787 (cert. copy), AGN, PI 65, Expediente 8.

[24] Ugarte to Anza, Chihuahua, January 26, 1787, and to De la Concha, Arispe, January 17, 1788 (cert. copies), AGN, PI 65, Expediente 8.

[25] Flores to Ugarte, México, July 23, 1788 (draft), AGN, PI 65, Expediente 3.

received at Taos on August 10 and took to the proposed site of the new settlement, on the banks of the Arkansas River. This village, shortly named San Carlos de los Jupes, was built by the combined labor of Spaniards and Indians, and the first houses were occupied on September 16, 1787. For a short time all work was suspended when the Jupes learned that Anza was to be replaced as governor of New Mexico, and they even tried to return the tools and laborers. Eventually, however, they were assured that their agreement was with the Spanish government and not with Anza personally, and so work was resumed. By October nineteen houses were completed and a still larger number were in various stages of construction.[26]

Ugarte was highly pleased with the accomplishment, and to encourage the Comanches in their inclinations to settle in fixed towns, he urged Governor Fernando de la Concha to furnish them with whatever conveniences they requested. However, everything was to be done on their own initiative, he cautioned, for otherwise they might become suspicious, resentful, or even confident that the Spaniards would do all of the work and pay the full cost. If this latter should occur, it would not only put the royal treasury to considerable expense but would also deprive the Comanches themselves of an appreciation for their new houses, irrigation ditches, and cultivated fields. Then, on the slightest pretext, they would return to their errant ways. De la Concha was to provide everything they could not furnish themselves and to station Spanish farmers nearby for them to emulate, but the Indians were to work their own fields.[27] The Utes, not to be outdone by their new allies and traditional rivals, were also showing an interest in permanent farming communities. This, Ugarte believed, should be encouraged, for it would in-

[26] Anza to Ugarte, Santa Fe, July 14 and October 20, 1787, and De la Concha to Ugarte, Santa Fe, November 10, 1787 (cert. copies), AGN, PI 65, Expediente 1 and Expediente 11. The essential correspondence on this subject is translated in Alfred B. Thomas, "San Carlos, a Comanche Pueblo on the Arkansas, 1787," *Colorado Magazine*, Vol. VI, No. 3 (May, 1939), 79–91.

[27] Ugarte to De la Concha, Arispe, January 22, 1788 (cert. copy), AGN, PI 65, Expediente 11.

finitely further their civilization, vassalage to the crown, and Christianization.[28]

The expenses of the Pueblo of San Carlos to the government involved wages for the workers and foreman, the supply and transportation of seed, grain, flour, sheep, and oxen, and the grinding of cornmeal. According to the Governor's commissioner to the Jupes, the total cost to the treasury was 691 pesos and 7 granos.[29] It was a noble experiment but, at least for immediate results, a bad investment. The Jupes occupied their new houses for only four months, at most, and then abandoned them. As De la Concha reported it, a superstition among them required that they move from their village whenever one of their prominent tribesmen died there and establish a new site at a distant place. In January, 1788, one of Paruanarimuco's favorite squaws died, and immediately all of his people left San Carlos. De la Concha had no hope of their returning and no idea of how to proceed under the circumstances. He thought that nothing short of a divine miracle would ever overcome their rusticity and barbarism, and so he had decided never again to support the establishment of such communities.[30]

Obviously disappointed, Ugarte urged the Governor to try to persuade the Jupes to return to San Carlos and, if possible, to dispel them of the superstitions that had induced them to leave it. If all such attempts should fail, however, Ugarte wanted De la Concha to resettle the town with Spanish families who could sustain themselves with only slight government aid and who might maintain in this outlying position such frequent contact with the northern Comanches as would gradually attract them to a civilized way of life. Then, too, if those Comanches should break the peace, this new community could serve as a fortified

---

28 Ugarte to Flores, Janos, March 13, 1788, AGN, PI 65, Expediente 11.

29 José Maldonado, Cuenta y Razón de los gastos errogados en la Nueva Población de San Carlos para la Havitación de la Nación Comanche en el Río de Napestle, Santa Fe, May 6, 1788, AGN, PI 65, Expediente 11.

30 In this dispatch the Governor referred to the Comanches at San Carlos as Yamparicas rather than Jupes. De la Concha to Ugarte, Santa Fe, June 26, 1788 (cert. copy), AGN, PI 65, Expediente 11.

base of operations for troops, which might be sent against them.[31] In a letter to the Viceroy the *Comandante General* defended his alternate proposal, on the grounds of both strategy and economy, citing three articles of the royal instructions to Croix of August 22, 1776, as further justification.[32]

Viceroy Flores vetoed the entire project. He had never expected the Jupes to take root, he declared, and the recent events now justified his misgivings. The amount spent on San Carlos had been wasted, and if he permitted the site to be reoccupied by Spanish families, this would only require additional expenditures. Moreover, even these might be insufficient to save the unfortunate settlers of so remote a place from the inconstancy and furor of the Comanches in case they should mount a major attack. Ugarte was to spend no more funds for the founding of towns for unchristianized Indians of any nation without the Viceroy's express permission. Repeated experience had shown that such projects resulted only in further burdening the royal treasury, increasing the hostility of the savages, and exposing the provinces to their funestral attacks.[33] Begrudgingly, Ugarte acknowledged this decision, and passed it on to De la Concha.[34]

Meanwhile the Comanche alliance was bolstering Spanish military strength in the eternal war on the Apaches. In the campaign of September, 1787, against the Apaches to the southwest of the Moqui villages, Comanche warriors were actually integrated with the presidial troops, armed settlers, and Pueblo auxiliaries. This force had suffered a stinging defeat, and, worse, the Spaniards had retreated precipitously in full view of their Comanche allies, who for their own part held fast and lost one warrior. Fortunately, the reversal was only temporary. A new expedition was mounted in the following month by the commandant-inspector. Colonel Joseph Antonio Rengel had come

[31] Ugarte to De la Concha, Chihuahua, July 22, 1788, (cert. copy), AGN, PI 65, Expediente 11.

[32] Ugarte to Flores, Chihuahua, July 31, 1788, AGN, PI 65, Expediente 11.

[33] Flores to Ugarte, México, September 16, 1788 (draft), AGN, PI 65, Expediente 11.

[34] Ugarte to Flores, Valle de San Bartolomé, October 13, 1788, AGN, PI 65, Expediente 11.

to New Mexico to make the first inspection in twenty-one years of the troops of that province, but the Apache problems now absorbed his attention. In his expedition of October, 1787, Rengel's troops, militia, Pueblo auxiliaries, and other Indian allies were accompanied by Captain General Ecueracapa and thirty-four Comanche warriors, who made up about 10 per cent of the entire force. But the Commandant-Inspector's diary of the campaign disparaged his Comanche allies at every turn.[35]

The march, he reported, was slowed by the disorder, insubordination, and willfulness of the Comanche warriors. They strayed from the column, maltreated and frequently had to change their horses, allowed them to stray in the Zuñi villages, and even commandeered those of the soldiers. They scattered in disorder, lit fires that gave away their position to the enemy, treated like servants the soldiers who brought them food, and otherwise put a strain on the important peace between their nation and the Spaniards. When less than eight miles from the enemy encampments, fearing that they would be placed in the front ranks as they had been in the previous campaign, the Comanches became dispirited and balky. Rengel then called up Ecueracapa and eight of his war chieftains. He reminded them that they were not really needed at all, that they were volunteers, that the Spaniards would spearhead the attack, and that Rengel himself would lead the charge. With this assurance only five Comanches elected to remain behind with the supply train. The attack, on November 5, scattered the Apaches and, according to Rengel, this time impressed the Comanche allies thoroughly with the intrepidity of the Spanish troops. The Commandant-Inspector was almost equally as critical of the settlers and Pueblo Indians who accompanied the expedition as he was of the Comanches. However, he felt that the Comanches, owing to their conduct, should thereafter attack the Apaches only in campaigns of their own. They should be furnished with Spanish horses,

[35] Rengel, Diario de la Campaña que sale de la Villa de Santa Fée del Nuevo México a last ordenes del Comandante Ynspector don Joseph Antonio Rengel, en 21 de Octubre de 1787, El Paso del Norte, December 4, 1787, AGN, PI 128, Expediente 2.

arms, and ammunition, but they should no longer be integrated with the Spanish forces. The main purpose of integration, he argued, was to impress the enemy with the Spanish-Comanche alliance, and this had already been achieved in previous campaigns throughout southern New Mexico and Texas. Furthermore, the Comanches acting alone were successfully destroying the enemy and making them come in to seek peace, and Ecueracapa himself was amenable to such separate operations as long as the Spaniards furnished the necessary assistance.[36]

Viceroy Flores agreed with the Commandant-Inspector's recommendations, and, accordingly, in the summer of 1788, Ecueracapa with Spanish arms, ammunition, food, and other supplies led 170 Comanche warriors against the Apaches in the Blanca, Organo, Oscura, and Fray Cristóbal Mountains. Meanwhile, the Governor was planning a campaign with regular troops accompanied by a small number of Comanches and Utes. These Indians, however, were to be employed not as auxiliaries but as hostages for the security of the general peace with their respective nations and also as advertisements to the enemy of the new alliances.[37]

Governor De la Concha was more impressed with the Comanches than was Rengel. During his first three months in office he had found that their good faith had been constant, and that their friendship, obedience, military support, and commercial relations had been improving steadily. They had already attended seven trade fairs at Taos, one very large one at Pecos, and still another at Picurís, the first ever held at that pueblo. Although the Picurís Indians and the Comanches, having long been bitter enemies, were suspicious of each other at the outset, no untoward incident had occurred, and troops were no longer needed there to police the exchange of goods. Several Comanche chieftains had already visited De la Concha at Santa Fe to demonstrate their loyalty. Whenever Ecueracapa was summoned, he came immediately; and whenever Rengel called on him for war-

[36] *Ibid.*; Rengel to Ugarte, El Paso, December 29, and to De la Concha, December 28, 1787 (signed copies), AGN, PI 128, Expediente 2.

[37] Flores to Rengel, México, July 21, 1788, and De la Concha to Flores, Santa Fe, n.d. (Summer, 1788), AGN, PI 128, Expediente 2, and PI 254, Expediente 1.

riors, he supplied more than was requested. Gentleness, affec-
tion, and some distribution of presents were keeping the Comanches, even the more obstinate Jupes and Yamparicas, in good
disposition and obedience.[38] After ten months in office the Governor still found the nation in general to be both tranquil and
obedient. Only the Jupes, who were the most perverse of the
three branches, had broken the peace, and this was a minor infraction. Some of them had stolen eighteen horses from a small
party of Spaniards. When called to account for the misdeed, Captain General Ecueracapa was more than 182 miles from Santa Fe
and ready to lead his warriors against the Apaches; yet, in spite
of the protests of several of his impatient chieftains, he came to
the capital at once. Properly contrite and respectful, Ecueracapa
begged for patience. The culprits, he explained, were young men
with little or no judgment or discipline and who had no appreciation of either his own counseling and pleading or those of the
principal men of the nation. Ecueracapa offered to accompany
the Governor's commissioner to the lands of the Jupes to obtain
complete satisfaction, just as soon as he returned from his impending campaign against the Apaches, but De la Concha was
fully satisfied with his explanation, especially since the robbery
had been the only breach of the Comanche peace.[39]

The security of the peace was no doubt bolstered by the relief
that the Spaniards furnished the Comanches whenever they fell
on hard times. In the autumn of 1787, for instance, the buffalo
herds on which they so depended for sustenance had abandoned
their customary range because of a severe drought, and for seven
months the Cuchantica Comanches, being without robes to trade,
stayed away from the Pueblo fairs and suffered intense privation.
Moreover, their necessary search for the buffalo was limiting the
frequency of their attacks on the Apaches. De la Concha had tried
to alleviate their needs by sending them a supply of maize.[40] By
June 15, 1789, the Governor had provided them with 150 bushels

[38] De la Concha to Ugarte, Santa Fe, November 10, 1787 (cert. copy), AGN,
PI 65, Expediente 1.
[39] De la Concha to Ugarte, Santa Fe, June 26, 1788, AGN, PI 65, Expediente 5.
[40] *Ibid.*

of corn, but several of the tribesmen had already perished.[41] Two weeks later Ecueracapa and 180 other Comanches came to Santa Fe to request further assistance, and this time the Governor supplied them with an additional 144 bushels of corn, 64 of which were donated for the purpose by the citizenry of Santa Fe. De la Concha feared that the clamors for such assistance would be even more frequent if the buffalo further delayed their return.[42] Ugarte and the Viceroy both approved the expenditures for the relief of the Comanches.[43]

In addition to such subsistence allotments, the Comanches received other gratifications. Each April and May large numbers of them, along with others of all the friendly Indian nations, gathered at Santa Fe for the arrival from the south of the merchant caravan. It had become a regular practice to distribute presents to them at that time. These gifts, De la Concha felt, were essential for maintaining their good will. The Comanches especially had to be lavished with presents in the spring of 1790, for one of their war parties had been attacked during the previous winter by Mescalero Apaches who were traveling under the escort of Spanish troops from Nueva Vizcaya. The Mescaleros had captured ten Comanches in this unfortunate clash, and these had to be provided with food, clothing, presents, and transportation from Chihuahua to Santa Fe. Added to this expense was that of supplying the allies for their campaigns against the enemy, of ransoming the captives they took, and of entertaining delegations that continued to come to Santa Fe and Chihuahua to pay their respects to the Governor and the *Comandante General*.[44]

In 1789 the Governor asked Ugarte for 4,000 pesos for mili-

[41] De la Concha to Ugarte, Santa Fe, June 15, 1789 (cert. copy), AGN, PI 65, Expediente 14.

[42] Concha to Ugarte, Santa Fe, July 6, 1789 (cert. copy), AGN, PI 65, Expediente 15.

[43] Ugarte to De la Concha, Chihuahua, July 21, 1789 (cert. copy), and Viceroy Conde de Revillagigedo to Ugarte, México, October 24, 1789 (draft), AGN, PI 65, Expediente 15.

[44] De la Concha to Ugarte, Santa Fe, June 15, 1789, and to Revillagigedo, April 20, 1791, and Commandant-General Pedro de Nava to Revillagigedo, Chihuahua, June 24, 1791, AGN, PI 65, Expediente 14 and Expediente 16.

tary and Indian supplies for the next year. This was 1,000 pesos less than his request for the current year. Of the reduced amount, 1,000 pesos were to go for the replacement of horses and mules at the Santa Fe presidio, which had suffered a severe depletion of its stock from the rigors of winter and the ravages of wolves. Another 1,000 pesos would be spent on grain for the campaigns and for the Indians who came to Santa Fe for relief, and the remaining 2,000 pesos, a lesser amount than usual, for presents to be distributed among the allies.[45] The gifts ordered for the friendly Indians were itemized as 700 yards of red cloth, 80 yards of blue cloth for uniforms, 40 blankets, 1 piece of blue Mexican cloth, 12 pieces of light cotton cloth from Puebla, 3 of Pontivy cloth, 1 of blue twisted silk, 6 skeins of agave fiber, 24 gross of brass buttons, 8 dozen lightweight hats, 12 dozen largest-size shoes, 6 pieces of carmine-colored Chinese silk ribbon, 2 boxes of lustrous Barcelona ribbon, 3 pieces of scarlet cloth, 1 piece of blue serge, 2 bags of *mucheguilla* thread, 40 dozen belt knives, 20 dozen mirrors, 20 spans of strung beads (cream and blue enamel), 6 dozen pairs of medium-fine scissors, 3 pounds of small coral, 4 pounds of Chinese vermillion, 4 pounds of carmine, 25 pounds of indigo, 8 pounds of red lead, 500 loaves of brown sugar, 1 load of refined sugar, 600 bars of soap, and 12 high-quality, large, wooden staffs from Michoacan.[46]

The few thousand pesos expended annually in military supplies, assistance in time of need, and outright gifts to the Indian allies of New Mexico was a small price for the service they rendered. It amounted to direct subsidization, but the presents and supplies addicted the nomads to the Spanish cause, attracted them to a more civilized life, and induced their warriors to campaign against the implacable Apaches. Without the military assistance of the Comanches, Ugarte could never have accomplished his remarkable, although temporary, pacification of most of the Apache tribes.

[45] De la Concha to Ugarte, Santa Fe, June 15, 1789, *loc. cit.*
[46] De la Concha, Noticia de los efectos que se necesitan para gratificar a las Naciones Gentiles Amigas y demas gastos de Guerra en la Provincia de Nuevo-México que deben servir para el año de 1790, Santa Fe, July 4, 1789, AGN, PI 65, Expediente 14.

CHAPTER VIII

THE WESTERN APACHES

All of the bands and tribes of the Apache nation which inhabited the lands to the west of the Río Grande in New Mexico and the Camino Real in Nueva Vizcaya were arbitrarily classified by the Spaniards as western Apaches. And within this major division they recognized five principal tribes: the Mimbreños, Gileños, Chiricahuas, Tontos, and Navahos.[1] From time to time they alluded to smaller Apache groups, such as the Mogollons and the Salineros, who seem to have been kinsmen and affiliates of the five well-recognized tribes, but these as well as the major groups were identified only by the mountains and plains through which they ranged. It was a loose classification and a confusing one as well. For instance, the Spanish term "Gileño" was applied specifically to one of the recognized tribes and also, generically, to the entire western division of the nation. The Apaches themselves recognized no national or even tribal government, and the chieftains of mere bands held effective authority only in wartime. Finally, Spanish contact with the Apaches was so tenuous that they were not always able to identify even the bands, especially when these were engaged in hit-and-run raids, and most of the

[1] By Ugarte's time the Spaniards were beginning to set the Navahos apart from the other, more nomadic Apaches and to recognize them as a separate nation. But like their kinsmen, the Navahos spoke a dialect of the Athapaskan language and originally belonged to the Southern Athapaskan culture. Ethnologists do not agree on the classifications or even the origins of the separate Apache groups.

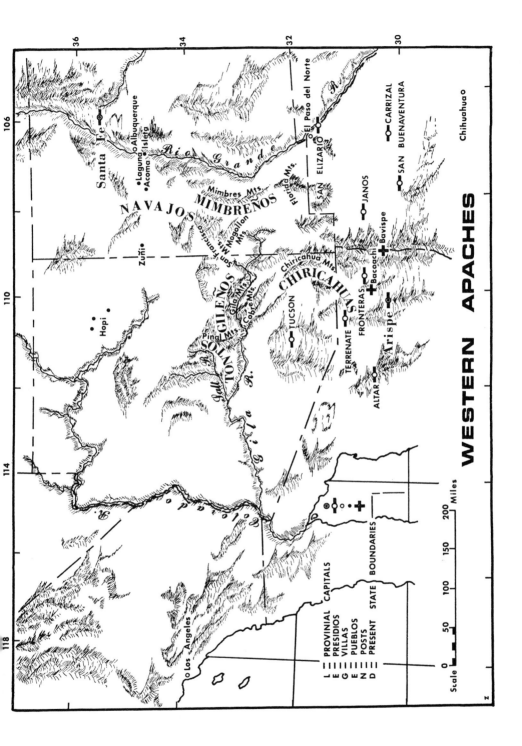

WESTERN APACHES

Scale

0	50	100	150	200

Miles

L ═══ PROVINIAL CAPITALS
E ═══ PRESIDIOS
G ═══ VILLAS
E ═══ PUEBLOS
N ═══ POSTS
D ═══ PRESENT STATE BOUNDARIES

Santa Fe

Laguna ● ○ Albuquerque
Acoma ● ○ Isleta

Zuñi ●

Hopi ●

Rio Grande

Rio Colorado

Gila R.

Salt R.

Los Angeles ○

NAVAJOS

MIMBREÑOS

Mimbres Mts.

Florida Mts.

San Francisco Mts.

Mogollon Mts.

Gila Mts.

Pinal Mts.

Coke Mts.

Chiricahua Mts.

GILEÑOS

TONTOS

CHIRICAHUAS

TUCSON

TERRENATE

FRONTERAS

Arispe

ALTAR

SAN ELIZARIO

El Paso del Norte

R.

SAN

JANOS

Bavispe

Bacoachi

SAN BUENAVENTURA

CARRIZAL

Chihuahua ○

N

military reports attributed the activities of these elusive warriors only to the nation in general. It was only when the Apaches were negotiating for peace that specific identification was possible and useful information obtainable.

The easternmost tribe of the Western Apaches was the *Iccujen-ne*, whom the Spaniards called Mimbreños after the Sierra de los Mimbres, which they frequented in what is now southwestern New Mexico. The Lower Mimbreños, those occupying the eastern slopes of this range, often allied with the Faraones, an Eastern Apache tribe, for raids on the New Mexican settlements while the Upper Mimbreños more often affiliated with the Gileño and Chiricahua tribes to the west and concentrated their hostilities against the communities of Nueva Vizcaya and Sonora.[2] In Ugarte's time the known Mimbreño war chieftains were Inclán (El Zurdo, or The Left-Handed), Yagonglí (Ojos Colorados, or Red Eyes), Tasguienachi (sometimes rendered as Jasquunachi), Esguelnoten, Naguiagoslan, Come-Zacate (He Eats Grass), Nayeyel, Tacolcan, Natanijú, and Mantas Negras (Black Blankets).[3] Some of these, however, may have been Gileños, for they frequently united with those warriors when on the offensive.

To the west of the Mimbreños were the *Tjuiccujen-ne*, or Gileños proper, who occupied the Sierra de la Gila immediately north of the river of the same name in what is now southeastern Arizona. In their raids they ranged into the Moqui (Hopi), Zuñi, and Navaho lands to the north and the settlements of Nueva Vizcaya and Sonora to the south, often in conjunction with bands of Mimbreños and Chiricahuas.[4] In these forays their bands were so confused with those of the latter two tribes that the Spaniards seldom distinguished their chieftains from those of their near neighbors and often referred to all, generically, as Gileños.

---

[2] Matson and Schroeder, "Cordero's Description of the Apache—1796," *loc. cit.*, 335–56.

[3] Ugarte, Extracto de las novedades ocurridas en la paz con los Apaches y su estado en el dia de la fecha, Arispe, July 15, 1787, and Ugarte to the Marqués de Sonora, Arispe, April 16, 1787 (cert. copies), AGN, PI 112, Expediente 1 and Expediente 2.

[4] Matson and Schroeder, "Cordero's Description of the Apache—1796," *loc. cit.*

Ranging to the south of the Gileños proper were the *Segatajen-ne*, or Chiricahuas, inhabiting principally the mountains of that name in the southeastern corner of present Arizona but inhabiting the adjacent ranges as well. For their customary raids into Sonora and Nueva Vizcaya the Chiricahuas frequently allied with the Mimbreños, Gileños, and, until 1786, with their northern kinsmen, the Navahos.[5] During the Ugarte administration the war chieftains known to the Spaniards were Isosé (sometimes given as Aysosé), Chiganstegé (El Chiquito, or The Little One), Asguegoca (a brother of El Chiquito), Echini, Asguenitesy, Chamy, Compá, and El Chacho (The Boy).[6] Again, it is quite possible that some of these chieftains were Gileños rather than Chiricahuas and were merely bound to the latter by ties of kinship or friendship.

Far to the west, in the Pinal Mountain and Tonto Basin regions of the Salt River, north of the Gila and east of present-day Phoenix, Arizona, were the *Vinniettinen-ne*, the Tonto or Coyotero Apaches. They were the westernmost of the Apache nation and also the least known by the Spaniards. Sometimes they joined with the Chiricahuas to raid the Sonora settlements.[7]

The northernmost of the Western Apaches were the *Yutagen-ne*, or Navahos, who lived a semi-sedentary life in present-day northeastern Arizona and northwestern New Mexico, between the Utes on the north, the Gileños and Chiricahuas on the south, the Moquis (Hopis) on the west, and the Spanish settlements of New Mexico on the east. Unlike their Southern Athapaskan kin—the Apaches proper—the Navahos had relatively fixed villages in Ugarte's time, sowed abundant corn and other vegetables, raised livestock (principally sheep), and manufactured coarse cloth, fine blankets, and other woolen goods, which they traded to the Pueblo Indians and at the Spanish settlements while

---

[5] *Ibid.*

[6] Ugarte, Extracto de las novedades, July 15, 1787, *loc. cit.*; Ugarte to the Marqués de Sonora, April 16, 1787, *loc. cit.*; Captain Manuel de Echeagaray to Anza, camp on the Gila River, October 20, 1788 (cert. copy), AGN, PI 128, Expediente 4.

[7] Matson and Schroeder, "Cordero's Description of the Apache—1796," *loc. cit.*

at peace. When hostile, they joined with Gila and Chiricahua Apache raiding parties.[8] The principal Navaho chieftains were known by the Spaniards as Antonio El Pinto (The Spotted One), Don Carlos, Don Joseph Antonio, and Cotón Negro.[9]

For some years the Navahos, with their fixed villages, croplands, and flocks of sheep, had seen fit to maintain a sort of unaligned position in the warfare between the Spaniards and Apaches. But in the spring of 1783, reports reached the governor of New Mexico that they had joined with the Gileños to mount a major attack on the Nueva Vizcaya presidio and settlement at Janos. When this ominous news was relayed to Commandant-General Felipe de Neve, he ordered Governor Anza to exert every effort to break up this coalition.[10] Meanwhile, the military might of the frontier, having been freed from the limitations imposed on it by Spain's war with England, was marshalled in a major offensive against the Western Apaches, particularly the Gileños, in 1784. Five divisions drawn from the presidios of Sonora and Nueva Vizcaya invaded the homelands of these hostiles in April and May of that year, killing sixty-eight Apaches, capturing thirteen, liberating two prisoners, and taking possession of 168 horses and mules, a great spoil of buffalo and antelope skins, and several weapons and implements.[11]

From New Mexico Governor Anza was able to induce the Navahos to treat for peace by a formidable display of the forces under his command—the presidial troops of Santa Fe, a militia of armed settlers, and a host of Pueblo Indian auxiliaries—and a warning that their enemies, the Utes, would be urged into action if they failed to sue for peace. The Navahos agreed to negotiate

[8] *Ibid.*

[9] Pedro Garrido y Durán, Relación de lo practicado en la Provincia del Nuevo-México por el Gobernador dn. Juan Bautista de Anza para romper la coligación secreta que la Nación Navajo mantenía con los Apaches Gileños, haviéndose conseguido su división y la agregación de la primera a nuestro partido, Chihuahua, December 21, 1786 (cert. copy), AGN, PI 65, Expediente 9. This document is translated in Thomas, *Forgotten Frontiers*, 345–51.

[10] By orders dated December 18, 1783, and January 14, 1784, according to the dispatch of Rengel to Anza, Chihuahua, August 27, 1785, translated in Thomas, *Forgotten Frontiers*, 266–68.

[11] Rengel to Gálvez, Fronteras, July 6, 1784, in *ibid.*, 247–50.

and even sent a war party against the Gila Apaches, but Anza found it necessary to post patrols to prevent them from crossing into Gileño territory and joining those Apaches. He also had to prohibit the Navahos from trading with the Pueblo and Spanish communities of New Mexico before they would agree to discuss terms. Under this pressure forty-six Navahos, including seven chiefs, presented themselves to the *alcalde mayor* of Laguna on June 5, 1785, and volunteered to join the next campaign against the Gileños as a demonstration of their good faith. As a result 120 mounted Navaho warriors and another 30 on foot accompanied 94 Pueblo auxiliaries from Laguna that same month, attacked the Gileños, killed more than 40 of them, and, more important, exhibited themselves as enemies to their kinsmen and former allies. On their return Anza rewarded them by reopening their important trade with the New Mexico towns. After participating in two other campaigns against the Gila Apaches, the Navahos sent 14 of their tribesmen, including 2 chiefs, to Santa Fe in order to solidify their new alignment. One of the chiefs was the famous Antonio El Pinto, who had previously exerted a major influence in maintaining the Navaho-Gileño alliance. Now he confessed his past infidelity, begged the Governor for a pardon, and promised to serve faithfully in the future. El Pinto promised to raise more warriors for the monthly campaigns against the Gileños than the Spaniards themselves would furnish. Duly impressed, Anza asked the acting Commandant-General not only for money, horses, muskets, and ammunition for the coming campaigns but also for four silver-tipped canes and medallions as insignia of office and decoration for the principal Navaho leaders. Rengel expressed his complete approval and asked the viceroy for additional troops so that the Gila Apaches might be attacked formidably from both the north and south.[12]

Notwithstanding this favorable beginning, the rupture of the Navaho-Gileño alliance and the realignment of the former with the Spaniards did not materialize immediately. Early in 1786 Rengel reported that recent word from Anza indicated that the

---

[12] Rengel to Viceroy Gálvez, Chihuahua, August 27, 1785, in *ibid.*, 258–62.

Navahos were still in league with their Apache kinsmen although they were divided on the matter. A majority of them, he asserted, wished to preserve their traditional commerce with the Pueblo communities of New Mexico, avoid a major clash with the Spaniards, and thus maintain in security their flocks, horse herds, croplands, and weaving industry. However, a strong faction, led by Antonio El Pinto, notwithstanding his recent promises to Anza, favored continuing their alliance and trade with the Gileños in order to preserve their possessions from attack from that quarter. The dilemma of the Navahos was that they were dependent upon their livestock, land, and the manufacture of woolen blankets—which prospered while they remained where they now lived, but which would suffer if they should remove to the rough and sterile terrain of the Gila Apaches—and that they were surrounded by mutually antagonistic peoples—the kindred Gileños on the south, the hostile Utes and Comanches on the north and northeast, and the Spaniards and Pueblos on the east, who could be either friend or foe but never neutral. Rengel felt that the precarious balance would certainly be tilted in favor of the Spaniards if they presented the Navahos with a respectable body of troops.[13]

The acting Commandant-General had already prescribed a strategy designed to rupture the alliance. This involved inciting the Navahos to engage in enough hostilities against the Gileños to render reconciliation with them impossible, maintaining Spanish friendship with the Utes in order to prevent the Navahos from taking refuge in the north, insuring Ute and Navaho loyalty by protecting their trade with the New Mexican communities, and countering the adverse influence among the Navahos of Antonio El Pinto by promoting a rival faction under Cotón Negro, who favored the Spanish alliance. Rengel ordered Anza to distinguish this latter chief if he could gain superiority over the Navahos, by giving him one of the staffs and medallions which he was sending to Santa Fe. He also instructed Anza to employ one-third of the troops of the Santa Fe company against the Gila Apaches as soon as weather permitted and maintain them in continuous

[13] Rengel to Viceroy Gálvez, Chihuahua, February 4, 1786, in *ibid.*, 263–66.

and determined campaigns reinforced with armed settlers, Pueblo auxiliaries, and a number of Navahos equal to at least the total of the others. Anza was to use the Navaho warriors side by side with the troops until they had proved their fidelity to the Spaniards and established a complete breach with the Gileños. He was also to cut off Navaho trade with the New Mexican towns again but reopen it completely once they had proved their faithfulness to the Spanish cause. Finally, he was to arm the Pueblo Indians at Laguna, on the Navaho frontier, so as either to protect or threaten the Navahos, as their relations with the Gileños required.[14]

These pressures had the desired effect. Late in March, 1786, forty Navaho warriors, including four chiefs, met with Governor Anza on neutral ground and agreed to preliminary terms for peace, trade, and alliance. They agreed to Anza's requirements that they submit to the authority of a principal chief, elected by their nation and loyal to the king and his ministers, accept an interpreter who would reside among and advise them, maintain faithful friendship with the Spaniards and subordination to the crown, serve the governor as military auxiliaries in his campaigns against the Gila Apaches, accept the protection of the Spanish government, and become even more sedentary by planting more extensive crops and building earthen huts. A persuasive influence in their adherence to these terms, Anza felt, were the words of two Comanche warriors who accompanied him and who, after the pact was solemnized, threatened the Navahos with extermination by the Comanche nation should they fail to live up to their promises.[15]

The Navaho delegates, of course, were unable to speak for their entire nation, for they were admittedly still trying to persuade the pro-Gileño faction of the benefits of a Spanish alliance. Nevertheless, during the proceedings they presented two of their number as candidates for the principal chieftainship of the nation,

[14] Rengel to Anza, Chihuahua, August 27, 1785, and January 18, 1786, in *ibid.*, 266–68 and 268–73.

[15] Garrido y Durán, Relación de . . . la Nación Navajo, Chihuahua, December 21, 1786, *loc. cit.*

and Anza appointed one of them, now designated as Don Carlos, for the office of general and the other, whom the Spaniards were to call Don Joseph Antonio, as lieutenant general. The Navaho delegation then elected as their official interpreter one of their own people who had grown up among the Spaniards. Finally, on Anza's instructions, the new officers returned to their own lands to seek the approval of the terms by their entire nation and then return to be formally invested with their offices by the Governor.[16]

On March 30, 1786, Don Carlos and the interpreter arrived in Santa Fe and reported that the Navaho nation had agreed to the terms, accepted the officers selected by Anza, and were already preparing to sow seeds and build houses in keeping with their obligations. Don Joseph Antonio did not come, reportedly because he was chasing four Apaches who had stolen some of his horses. During the next three days Don Carlos was invested with his office of general and the interpreter was confirmed in his, after which they left with instructions from Anza to visit and be recognized in all the Navaho villages. The interpreter was gently persuaded to support the two principal chiefs and bring Anza a report on the number of people, horses, and cattle in the nation.[17]

On June 8, General Don Carlos, Lieutenant General Joseph Antonio, the interpreter, and seven other Navahos came to Santa Fe. Don Carlos reported that he had visited all the villages under his command and had been received and recognized with universal applause, that the articles of the pact were approved by free and common consent throughout the nation, and that the pro-Gileño chief Antonio El Pinto had been deposed without opposition. The interpreter informed Anza that the Navaho nation was comprised of 700 families of about 4 or 5 persons each, living in 5 villages, and that it possessed 1,000 warriors and 500 riding horses. Their other livestock (only the female of the species being counted) included 600 horses (apparently unbroken),

[16] *Ibid.*
[17] *Ibid.*

about 700 sheep, and 40 cows. Many of the people who had never sown crops before were now emulating those who had, but the nation was suffering an epidemic. Don Carlos begged Anza to renew the traditional trade privileges with the New Mexican towns. The Navahos, he said, were in need of leather for shoes and other campaign equipment. Anza immediately condescended and also gave the Navahos permission to display their woven goods at the Comanche fair, which would be held in July or August. Then, on June 10, after discussing further plans for the next campaign against the Gila Apaches, Anza presented the delegation with moderate gifts and sent them home.[18]

It was at this stage that the new *Comandante General* entered into the negotiations. On October 5, 1786, Jacobo Ugarte y Loyola provided Anza with detailed instructions for solidifying the Navaho alliance.[19] It was also on this date that he laid down the procedure for finalizing the Comanche peace pact, and the two sets of instructions were similar in formula and spirit.

Ugarte approved and was fully satisfied with Anza's accomplishments in severing the alliance and promoting hostility between the Navahos and the Gileños. He also approved the election of the general and lieutenant general of the Navahos, and so that the authority and subservience of these to the crown might be fully recognized by that people, he was enclosing the proper certificates and authorizing the salary of 200 pesos for the former and 100 pesos for the latter. In filling out the certificates, however, Anza was to indicate the Navaho names of Don Carlos and Don Joseph Antonio so as to prevent any confusion with others of the nation who might have been similarly christened. Governor Anza was also to keep careful watch on the conduct of other Navaho chiefs, especially Antonio El Pinto. The unruly and

18 *Ibid.* The five Navaho villages mentioned in this census were San Mateo, Cebolleta, Chusca, Hozo, and Chilli. Ten years later Colonel Antonio Cordero listed ten villages: Cebolleta, Chacoli, Guadalupe, Cerro, Cabezón, Agua Salada, Cerro Chato, Chusca, Tunicha, Chelle, and Carrizo. Matson and Schroeder, "Cordero's Description of the Apache—1796," *loc. cit.*

19 Ugarte to Anza, Chihuahua, October 5, 1786 (cert. copy), AGN, PI 65, Expediente 9. This illuminating document is also translated in Thomas, *Forgotten Frontiers*, 351–57.

stormy nature of this deposed leader was such that he might attempt to regain his authority, in which event Anza was to see that he was exiled or destroyed. Otherwise there would be no security for the pacification of that nation. Anza was to see that all the chieftains maintained allegiance to Don Carlos by nipping in the bud any dissention that might arise and by requiring all members of the nation, by force if necessary, to reside in the permanent villages and conform to the provisions of the treaty. The interpreter for the nation, who was to reside within it, was to be added to the roster of the presidial company of Santa Fe, paid eight pesos a month, and furnished with horses and other equipment necessary for his service. Anza was authorized to establish a second interpreter with the same emoluments so that one might remain in the villages while the other accompanied the warriors on their campaigns against the Gileños. The interpreters were to serve both as advisers to the Navaho chiefs and as informants for the Spaniards.[20]

So as to protect the Navahos from attack by their former allies, Anza was to concentrate his own military operations against the Gila Apaches and drive them from the mountains of the Navaho country. Although the Navahos were to be encouraged to carry out forays of their own against the Gileños, Ugarte felt that they should first prove their fidelity by supplying contingents of warriors to the Spanish campaigns. This should continue until groups from each village, serving in rotation, had accompanied from four to six campaigns against the enemy, or until every Navaho capable of bearing arms had fought the Gileños at least once. This would not only test their loyalty but also insure against their reconciliation with the Gila Apaches and thus qualify them for independent operations against that enemy.[21]

Since some bands of Gileños had already sought peace in Sonora, Anza was to direct his campaigns from New Mexico against those in the Sierra de los Mimbres, who were still at war, and drive them against the Spanish forces in Sonora. There they

[20] *Ibid.*
[21] *Ibid.*

too would be forced to seek peace. Ugarte hoped to use the Gileños who surrendered as allies in Sonora just as Anza was employing the Navahos in New Mexico, and so it was necessary to distinguish friendly auxiliaries from the enemy. To avoid any confusion Anza was to issue each Navaho war chieftain a band of colored cloth to be worn while on campaign, and Ugarte was ordering the commanders in Sonora to furnish identical insignia to the pacified Gileños who accompanied their troops.[22]

Ugarte felt that one of the most important guarantees for the permanence of the Navaho peace would be their establishment in formal settlements and their devotion to agriculture. Happily, they were already applying themselves to this purpose, but Anza was to encourage it, furnish assistance where needed, and thus avoid any scarcity of necessities, which might induce them to return to their former nomadic life. He was also to see that the Spaniards acted with fairness and good faith in their commercial and other relations with these people, that all grievances of the Navahos be carried to the constituted authorities, and that prompt and effective justice be rendered. Anza was to consult with the Navaho chiefs in drawing up a schedule of just values for the goods that they might seek to obtain in barter at the Spanish and Pueblo towns, for this would offset the unfair advantage that the more civilized elements of society customarily took of the less sophisticated Indians. Admittedly this constituted an infringement on free enterprise, which elsewhere might tend to retard economic development and create ill feeling, but Ugarte thought that controls in this instance were necessary until such time as the commercial experience of the heathen might overcome their exploitable ignorance. As a final measure for the promotion of a secure peace, Anza was to encourage intermarriage between the Pueblo and Navaho people whenever the latter became instructed and baptized in the Catholic religion.[23]

Governor Anza found himself in almost complete accord with Ugarte's instructions. In regard to remuneration for the Navaho

[22] *Ibid.*
[23] *Ibid.*

general and lieutenant general, however, he felt that it would be wiser to reward them annually according to their demonstrated merit rather than with fixed salaries. He had appointed a second interpreter, arranged for the service of the warriors in rotating companies with the Spanish forces rather than in campaigns of their own, and would concentrate his military operations in the Sierra de los Mimbres in order to remove the danger of a Gileño offensive against the Navahos. In response to a subsequent directive,[24] he was investigating reports that Navaho warriors had accompanied a Gileño party in a raid on Arispe, in Sonora, in July of 1786, but as yet he had found no evidence to verify it. He had personally visited the Navaho nation for six days in May of 1787 and had found its people still residing in fixed villages, building new huts, and sowing crops more extensively than ever before. They had agreed that their generals and the interpreters would inspect the villages twice each month to check on their attendance, and in return Anza had promised to extend them the same trading privileges in the New Mexican town fairs that the Comanches and Utes enjoyed. He had also undertaken to aid them in transporting to the interior markets all the blankets and other textiles that they could manufacture, to facilitate their purchase of dyestuffs, and to provide them with tools and other necessary implements for the establishment of new villages. However, he would not encourage their intermarriage with the Pueblo Indians until they were more securely established in formal towns. Finally, he had found no evidence of conspiracy or treason within the Navaho nation.[25]

The breach of the Navaho-Gileño alliance together with the constant pressure of monthly Spanish campaigns into Apache territory began to produce the desired results within five months after Ugarte assumed command of the northern frontier. The first of the Gila tribes to yield was that of the Chiricahuas, several bands of whom sued for peace in Sonora in September of

[24] Ugarte to Anza, Chihuahua, October 25, 1786 (cert. copy), AGN, PI 65, Expediente 9.
[25] Anza to Ugarte, Santa Fe, July 14, 1787 (cert. copy), AGN, PI 65, Expediente 9.

1786.[26] For the next six months additional groups of this tribe came in voluntarily, and although one band became suspicious and fled to the mountains again, there were still 251 Chiricahuas of both sexes congregated near the presidio of Bacoachi at the end of March, 1787. The infants had been baptized, the most prominent chief among them, Isosé, had exhibited a fidelity and conduct beyond all suspicion, and all were living in peace.[27]

The precipitous flight of the lesser chieftain El Chiquito (Chiganstegé) and his band from the vicinity of Bacoachi on March 9 was reportedly due to their fear of a considerable body of troops, which was approaching from the east. This was a force led by *Comandante General* Ugarte himself, which was actually on its way from Chihuahua to Arispe for employment in reducing the hostiles of Sonora. Ugarte and his troops did not actually reach Bacoachi until two or three weeks after the flight.[28]

Ugarte remained at Bacoachi a few days in order to gain the recognition of the peace-seeking Chiricahuas and dispel them of further mistrust. Many who had remained there asked Ugarte for permission to accompany the troops in pursuit of El Chiquito and even to bring in his head, but the *Comandante General* dissuaded them, for he believed that the renegades had fled because of fear rather than bad faith. El Chiquito was reputedly superstitious to the extreme and "the augury of a pusillanimous spirit," had inspired his followers with a certain veneration for his artifices. On his part, Ugarte wished to impress them with the humaneness of the Spaniards and preferred to use force only against those who were implacably hostile. Accordingly, he sent three Chiricahuas to seek out El Chiquito, advise him of Ugarte's arrival and peaceful intentions, invite him to return, and warn him that war would be waged on him if he did not. But even before these emissaries could establish contact with him, El Chiquito sent two of his daughters to Bacoachi. They arrived on

[26] Pedro Corbalan, Informe General de Sonora, Vera Cruz, March 8, 1788, AGN, PI 254, Expediente 7.

[27] Ugarte to the Marqués de Sonora, Arispe, April 16, 1787 (cert. copy), AGN, PI 112, Expediente 1.

[28] *Ibid.*

183

April 12 with word that he and the rest of his band would follow later.[29]

With this news Ugarte, now at Arispe, was filled with optimism. By this time other Apache tribes were beginning to congregate in peace at the presidios in Nueva Vizcaya—the Mescaleros at El Norte and the Mimbreños at San Buenaventura. In spite of what he called the "fickle and inconstant nature" of this turbulent nation, Ugarte felt that there was good reason to expect that these improvements would be lasting. From what he had observed among the Chiricahuas at Bacoachi, good faith and mutual trust prevailed. Although he expected some of these Apaches to rebel from time to time, he also felt that many would realize the advantages of the new friendship with the Spaniards and would remain devoted to the comforts that they would enjoy under this arrangement. He and Intendant-Governor Pedro Corbalan believed seriously that the Chiricahuas could be established in settlements that would in time become self-sufficient. At first, of course, their maintenance would require some royal expenditures, but the king and the viceroy would soon be pleased to witness the end of the bloody and destructive war and, eventually, the Apaches would be entering upon a rational and sociable life with due recognition of their vassalage and even adherence to the Christian religion.[30]

By the middle of May, 1787, only a few more Chiricahuas had surrendered and joined their tribesmen at Bacoachi, but Ugarte expected a much greater influx as a result of the new measures he was taking. El Chiquito and his band had still not arrived, and a party of troops accompanied by several Chiricahua auxiliaries under Ensign Domingo Vergara had searched for him in vain. However, this contingent did find and parley with another band, under the renegade's brother, Asguegoca, but this chieftain steadfastly refused Vergara's demand for submission. Asguegoca even attempted to cast a spell that would render the firearms of the troops ineffective, but Vergara, under the urging of

29 *Ibid.*
30 *Ibid.*

his Chiricahua auxiliaries, called his bluff and ordered an attack. Six Apache men and women were killed and twenty-one others were captured, but Asguegoca escaped, and, of course, El Chiquito remained at large. Meanwhile Ugarte and Corbalan increased the rations that were being distributed to the Chiricahuas at Bacoachi, provided them with assistance in building adobe houses to shelter their families, and experimented with ways and means to get them to take up farming so they could support themselves.[31]

By June 19 a total of 283 Chiricahuas had been assembled at Bacoachi, and all indications there pointed to a permanent and peaceful Apache community. On June 20, however, 119 of them suddenly took leave and were followed eight days later by another 64. Both flights took place without violence, and the fugitives committed no subsequent hostilities. Under these circumstances, Ugarte could charge their desertion only to what he termed the "natural inconstancy" and "ambulant spirit" of these "barbarians." He also suspected the "perverse influence" of an apostate named Juan Antonio, who had been living among them. He was pleased that those under the immediate chieftainship of Isosé, numbering about one hundred persons, remained faithfully at Bacoachi and that some of these joined the troops in operations against the Mimbres Apaches in Nueva Vizcaya. By July 15, moreover, several formerly hostile Apache bands, including those led by El Chiquito, Asguegoca, Echini, Asguenitesy, and Chamy, had sent emissaries to the presidios of Bacoachi and Tucson, bearing excuses for not having accepted Ugarte's offer of amnesty and begging for an extension of time. However, from time to time these emissaries presented demands that were totally unacceptable, and since Ensign Vergara's force had already killed or captured forty-nine of their tribesmen, including several of their most vaunted warriors, Ugarte suspected that those bands were bent more on revenge than submission.[32]

---

31 Ugarte to the Marqués de Sonora, Arispe, May 14, 1787 (cert. copy), AGN, PI 112, Expediente 2.
32 Ugarte, Extracto de las novedades, July 15, 1787, *loc. cit.*

It may have been merely a coincidence, but in the short span of three months Spanish peace negotiations with three distinct tribes of the Apache nation were frustrated by a succession of flights from three widely-spaced presidio reservations. Unauthorized attacks by Colonel Juan de Ugalde on the Mescalero bands that had surrendered voluntarily at El Norte precipitated the flight of four bands from that quarter in April of 1787. In May all of the several hundred Mimbreños who had settled peacefully at San Buenaventura suddenly revolted and fled their assigned village sites. And in June more than one-half of the Chiricahuas at Bacoachi also unceremoniously deserted. The connection between the last two of these three incidents seems to have been stronger than that between the first two.

The Mimbreño peace was negotiated in March of 1787. Two chiefs of that tribe, suffering no doubt from the invasions of their mountain stronghold by Anza's New Mexican forces and new Navaho allies, presented themselves to Captain Antonio Cordero, of the presidio of Janos. Ugarte, then en route from Chihuahua to Arispe, was able to participate in these negotiations personally. After conferring with El Zurdo (Inclán) and Natanijú, Ugarte commissioned Captain Cordero to complete the arrangements, and on March 22 provided him with the essential stipulations for a permanent treaty. Among other things Ugarte required that all of the Mimbres bands establish their camps near the presidio of San Buenaventura and remain there in peaceful pursuits. Shortly after the *Comandante General's* departure for Bacoachi and Arispe, eight Mimbreño chiefs arrived with their bands and settled at the assigned place. On reaching Bacoachi, Ugarte sent five resident Chiricahuas to aid Cordero in solidifying the Mimbreño peace, and by May 21 the number of Apaches gathered at San Buenaventura was estimated at from eight to nine hundred.[33]

Meanwhile, in the latter part of April, two unfortunate events disturbed the progress of peace at San Buenaventura. First a band of Mimbreños, which was supposedly on its way to San Buenaventura to surrender and join its peaceful tribesmen, was attacked

[33] *Ibid.*

by Opata Indian troops of the presidio of Bavispe who were scouring the mountains between Sonora and Nueva Vizcaya in search of hostiles. Two Mimbreños were killed in the assault and the remainder apparently put to flight, for the Bavispe presidials captured a considerable amount of their goods. On learning of the incident, Captain Cordero restored the captured property, explained away the assault as a mistake, and managed to placate the incensed Mimbreños residing at San Buenaventura. A few days later, however, a second such incident occurred. Ensign Vergara, operating out of the presidio of Bacoachi against those Chiricahuas who remained hostile, attacked one of their errant bands and dealt it a crippling blow. Among the casualties were several near kinsmen of El Chiquito, and among the captives was one of his wives and four of his daughters. More to the point, it was reported to the Mimbreños at San Buenaventura that a number of their own tribesmen who were traveling with the hostile Chiricahuas were also victims. Whether this circumstance was true or not, El Zurdo complained of the attack on May 9, and ten days later Nayeyel, another friendly Mimbreño chief, lodged a similar protest. Finally, as it was subsequently learned from the captured squaws, the wily El Chiquito, fearing the consequences of his own resistance while other Chiricahua chiefs were surrendering at Bacoachi, and bent on revenge for the attack on his kinsmen and allies, had sent agents to infiltrate the peaceful Mimbreños and incite them to revolt.[34]

El Chiquito's agents succeeded in winning over most of the resident Mimbreños to his cause, but El Zurdo and Nataniju, who had both treated personally with Ugarte at Janos and were convinced that the Spaniards were proceeding in good faith, refused to join the conspiracy. According to the captured squaws, El Zurdo managed to delay the uprising for several days, even while threatened with assassination by the plotters. During this crisis, however, Mantas Negras, another Mimbreño chief and reputedly the cruelest and most obstinate enemy of the Spaniards, arrived from the mountains to the east and embraced the seditious

[34] *Ibid.*

187

faction. Some of the ringleaders tried to keep the plot under wraps long enough to assassinate the unsuspecting Captain Cordero and incite another band, which was treating for peace at Bavispe, to rebel simultaneously, but on May 21 they could contain the impatience of the others no longer.[35]

On that day the Mimbreños at San Buenaventura rose, attacked the five Chiricahua auxiliaries whom Ugarte had sent as mediators, the interpreter, and ten soldiers who had just arrived with a consignment of horses for the Indians, and then fled the reservation. During the fracas, the rebel tribesmen killed the interpreter, one of the soldiers, and three Chiricahuas, carrying off another of the latter. Before they were overpowered, the Chiricahuas managed to kill five of the rebel Mimbreños, and one of the auxiliaries managed to escape and report the news. Captain Cordero then took such immediate and effective precautions that no other losses were suffered. He dispatched 300 troops in three detachments to cut off their retreat, but these returned with no other accomplishment than ascertaining the direction of the flight.[36]

When the news of the revolt reached Ugarte at Arispe, his first notion was to take a large body of troops to Janos to reinforce Cordero's command and direct operations against the Mimbreños in person. On reaching Bacoachi, however, he was persuaded by the resident Chiricahuas to abandon this plan. From their knowledge of the terrain and experience with the Mimbres Apaches, the Chiricahuas concluded that a large army could never reach Janos undetected by that enemy. On June 8, therefore, Ugarte sent his orders to Cordero in writing under a smaller and more stealthy escort—thirty Opata troops and four Chiricahua volunteers.[37]

Cordero was to call out all available troops in Nueva Vizcaya and co-ordinate his operations with the forces of New Mexico and Sonora. The over-all strategy was for New Mexican troops

[35] *Ibid.*
[36] *Ibid.*
[37] Ugarte to the Marqués de Sonora, Arispe, July 15, 1787 (cert. copy), AGN, PI 112, Expediente 2.

and armed settlers, reinforced by their Comanche allies, to drive the hostile Apaches south of the Río Grande; for the troops of Nueva Vizcaya, hopefully aided by the newly-reduced Mescalero Apaches, to force them westward; and for the Sonora presidials, with Chiricahua auxiliaries, to close the trap in that quarter. Attacked from front and rear and denied asylum on either side, the hostile Apaches would supposedly have no recourse but to plead for peace more humbly than ever before.[38]

Shortly after dispatching these orders to Cordero and to Colonel Rengel, who was temporarily in over-all command of Nueva Vizcaya, Ugarte sent Ensign Vergara with 40 Spanish regulars, 30 presidials from Fronteras, 50 Opatas from Bacoachi, and 10 Chiricahua auxiliaries to seek out the enemy in their own mountain camps. Vergara's force achieved remarkable success, closing with the hostiles four times and killing or capturing 2 Mimbreño chiefs, 19 warriors, and 81 women and children, many of whom had participated in the rebellious flight from San Buenaventura.[39] Added to the 49 victims of his May campaign, Vergara had now reduced the enemy by 151 persons. For this he was shortly promoted to the rank of captain. Meanwhile Ensign Antonio Guerrero, operating out of El Paso del Norte with Navaho and Comanche allies, killed 9 Mimbreños and captured 11 others before returning to base and reporting to Rengel on July 28. On August 10, Guerrero set out again, this time guided by a captured squaw, to reconnoiter the new and more remote campsites to which the Mimbreños had fled after these stinging defeats. Rengel now urged the governor of New Mexico to attack the enemy with his troops and settlers while they still suffered from these strikes and to incite the Comanches and Navahos to do likewise.[40]

An invasion of the mountain stronghold of the Western Apaches by a New Mexican force of presidials, militia, Pueblo auxiliaries, and Comanche allies in September was forced back in headlong retreat, but in October Rengel organized and led a

[38] *Ibid.*
[39] *Ibid.*
[40] Rengel to Anza, El Paso del Norte, August 10, 1787, Spanish Archives, New Mexico State Records Office, at Santa Fe, Archive 961a.

stronger force, which dispersed an Apache camp on November 5.[41] Ugarte, expecting the enemy to retreat toward the mountains of Nueva Vizcaya and hoping to intercept and destroy them en route, marshaled 200 troops from Sonora and 145 from Nueva Vizcaya in December. The Sonora force—mostly presidials, but some Spanish regulars, a part of the Opata Indian company, and a few recently-pacified Chiricahua Apaches—was placed under the command of the newly-promoted Captain Vergara. The Nueva Vizcayans—from two presidios and a light-horse company —were assigned to Captain Cordero. A third force of 180 men— Sonoran presidials supported by a company of Pima and Opata troops—was given to Captain Manuel de Echeagaray and later sent into the Mimbre, Cobre, and Gila Mountains to intercept the enemy as it fled northward again from the armies of Vergara and Cordero. Ugarte gave the field commanders a free hand in their respective operations.[42]

On December 22, in the mountains near the presidio of San Buenaventura, Cordero's Nueva Vizcayans encountered a band of Mimbreños under Chief Ojos Colorados (Yagonglí), killed five warriors and two squaws, captured one boy and twenty-eight horses, and put the rest of the camp to flight. Then, on January 11, 1788, one of his detachments, under Lieutenant José Manuel Carrasco, overtook seventeen Gileños whom they had tracked far into the interior, and in a five-hour battle on the Conchos River killed six braves and captured sixteen head of cattle and three horses. With these two achievements and the loss of one soldier, Cordero retired to the presidio of Janos. Meanwhile Captain Vergara's Sonorans, operating in the high Sierra Madres, suffered extremely from the snows and cold and found the enemy only in terrain too difficult to assault successfully. He did manage to capture one Mimbreño warrior, who turned out to be the brother of Ojos Colorados, and also to liberate a captive whom the Apaches had taken. The third army, under Captain Eche-

[41] See above, Chapter VII.
[42] Ugarte to Viceroy Flores, Arispe, December 24, 1787, AGN, PI 128, Expediente 3.

agaray, left the Sonoran presidio of Santa Cruz in January to intercept the enemies fleeing northward from Cordero and Vergara, closed with them three times in the region between the Chiricahua Mountains and the El Paso district, killed seven warriors and twenty women and children, captured sixteen others, and took forty-eight horses and mules, all with the loss of only two of his own men. In all, sixty-one Apaches, including twenty-one warriors, were either killed or captured in the combined operation.[43]

Although the ranks of the enemy were slightly reduced by this offensive, it failed miserably in its main purpose. As the jaws of the vise closed on their rugged mountain hideouts, the mercurial warriors slithered out of reach and avoided being totally crushed. Not only did they elude the converging armies of Nueva Vizcaya, Sonora, and New Mexico, but they also filtered through the undermanned frontline posts of Nueva Vizcaya and then ravaged the unprotected interior with devastating effect. Had the Mescalero Apaches kept the peace at El Norte and enlisted as auxiliaries, as Ugarte had hoped, the bloody invasion of Nueva Vizcaya might have been thwarted. But that alliance was frustrated by the complete lack of co-operation from Colonel Ugalde in the eastern provinces and of Viceroy Flores at Mexico City with Ugarte's efforts. As a result the Gila and Mimbres Apaches once more gained the upper hand, terrorized Nueva Vizcaya, and created a general crisis in the spring of 1788.

Even the peaceful Chiricahuas in Sonora became restless. More than one-half of the 283 who had surrendered voluntarily and settled near Bacoachi had fled the congregation on June 20, 1787, and since those who remained had regularly furnished warriors for the expeditions against El Chiquito's renegades, they had every reason to expect retaliation. Several families, in fact, had moved nearer to the Spanish settlement for greater protection. Notwithstanding this precaution, however, they were totally surprised by a hit-and-run raid on the night of February

[43] Ugarte to Flores, Arispe, December 31, 1787, and February 15, 1788, and Janos, March 13, 1788, AGN, PI 128, Expediente 3.

7, 1788. Only four peaceful Chiricahuas were injured in the assault, but one of these was the most loyal chieftain, Isosé, who was attacked while asleep and pierced with a lance. Although he managed to wrest the weapon from his assailant, he died the following noon after receiving baptism. He also managed to identify at least two of the aggressors, El Chiquito and his son Antel. Isosé was certain that the lance that he had taken from his own assailant belonged to Antel.[44]

The Spaniards as well as the faithful Chiricahuas mourned the loss of Chief Isosé, for he had repeatedly resisted the efforts of his hostile kinsmen to incite rebellion among those at peace. His bereaved followers now swore to avenge his death. They elected his young son, Aydiá, to succeed him and implored Ugarte to allow them to go out and kill El Chiquito and Antel. Ugarte confirmed the election of Aydiá, even though he was no more than fourteen years old at most, for it was the Chiricahua custom that sons succeeded their fathers in command. He also permitted a force of their warriors to accompany a party of troops, which he sent out to bring in the culprits, for the wily El Chiquito had already eluded three consecutive military efforts to capture him and had also prevented a large number of Chiricahuas from surrendering voluntarily by intimidating them with his sorceries.[45] But the new expedition also failed. The acting war chief of the Chiricahuas died a few days after the party set out, his replacement became ill, and the titular chief, Aydiá, was adjudged too young for actual command, and so the warriors returned to Bacoachi. The troops continued their search for El Chiquito and Antel but failed to find them.[46]

Meanwhile, Ugarte had decided to transfer himself from Arispe to Chihuahua so as to direct the defense of Nueva Vizcaya from the ravages of the Western Apache invasions. On February 27 he paused at Bacoachi to organize a campaign into the Mogollon and San Francisco Mountains, and other mountains between

---

[44] Ugarte to Flores, Arispe, February 16, 1788, AGN, PI 128, Expediente 3.
[45] *Ibid.*
[46] Ugarte to Flores, Chihuahua, April 30, 1788, AGN, PI 128, Expediente 3.

Sonora and New Mexico. Then, shortly before he reached Chihuahua, he canceled that offensive operation and ordered the troops at Bacoachi to reinforce the undermanned presidios of Nueva Vizcaya.[47] The tide of the Apache war had turned against Ugarte, and so had the Viceroy. On April 15, 1788, Flores had nullified the Mescalero peace in Nueva Vizcaya and ordered Ugarte to wage war in the province on all Apaches of whatever affiliation.[48]

While Ugarte and the reinforced troops of Nueva Vizcaya contended with the hit-and-run attacks of both Eastern and Western Apaches through the spring and summer of 1788, Colonel Anza, whom he had sent to supervise operations in Sonora after his gubernatorial term in New Mexico expired, was preparing a prolonged offensive against the hostiles in the mountain ranges bordering the Gila River. In the late summer Anza dispatched a formidable army of presidials and Indian auxiliaries under Captain Echeagaray to harry the enemy in their own lands. While this expedition was combing the rugged borderlands for El Chiquito and his followers, the friendly Chiricahuas in the Bacoachi settlement were becoming even more skittish than before. Perhaps they resented the Spanish attempt to convert them into farmers, perhaps they feared further retaliation from El Chiquito, perhaps they sensed the general deterioration of Spanish control, or perhaps they were chafing under the new and more drastic policy, which Viceroy Flores had imposed and which Ugarte and Anza were obliged to enforce. According to the new order the field commanders had now to treat all Apaches who surrendered under military circumstances—in battle or even while campaigns against them were in progress—as prisoners of war. They were no longer to admit them to a peace such as those at Bacoachi enjoyed unless they surrendered of their own free will, without any military intimidation. Anza found it necessary to repeat this order to the current campaign commander.[49]

[47] *Ibid.*
[48] Flores to Ugarte, Mexico, April 15, 1788 (draft), AGN, PI 112, Expediente 3.
[49] Anza to Echeagaray, Arispe, October 25, 1788 (copy), AGN, PI 128, Expediente 4.

Whatever the reason for the uneasiness of the peaceful Chiricahua, the congregation at Bacoachi suffered its second incidence of desertion in September of 1788. About thirty braves left and shortly returned to spirit away ten of their women and childen. Before they had made good their escape, they were discovered while encamped, and in resisting arrest a brave and a squaw were killed, and several of the fugitives were wounded. Among those who got away was a warrior named Carlos, who fled to the camp of Captain Echeagaray in the Gila region.[50]

On October 4, Captain Echeagaray dispatched one of his Chiricahua auxiliaries, Atanasio, with a message to the commandant of the presidio of Bacoachi with a warning of further trouble. Carlos and another Chiricahua had deserted his camp on October 1, and his other auxiliaries feared that they meant to persuade their families at Bacoachi to desert. Echeagaray also reported that he had killed one hostile Apache in the Sierra de la Florida, captured six others, and learned that a large camp of the enemy had just moved into that mountain range. However, before he could find and attack it, one of his prisoners escaped and warned the enemy camp, which then fled. He also learned from his captives where El Chiquito and Asguegoca were encamped and that they were gathering a large force of warriors.[51]

Echeagaray's next report to Anza stated that on October 8 he had captured four more Apaches including the squaw of Chief Compá, that Compá then gave up himself and the rest of his family in order to be reunited with his spouse, and that Compá had also informed him of the locations of other Apache camps. Another brave, El Chacho, had surrendered voluntarily, and in the attacks on the newly discovered camps, Echeagaray's forces had killed forty-one Apaches, raising this total to fifty-two and the number surrendering to him to twenty-five. With the vol-

[50] *Ibid.*

[51] Echeagaray to Captain Antonio Denojiane, camp San Marcial, October 4, 1788, AGN, PI 128, Expediente 4. A notation by Anza on this dispatch indicates that it was received at Bacoachi on the afternoon of October 6 and at Arispe on October 7 at 11 A.M.; the Chiricahua courier had thus covered the seventy-five leagues (about 195 miles) by the most direct route in only thirty-six hours.

untary surrender of Compá and El Chacho the auxiliaries were breathing easier.[52] Anza had to remind Echeagaray that on the orders of Ugarte, which he himself had circulated on March 26, all Apaches surrendering while troops were operating against them had to be treated as prisoners of war. However, since this might antagonize the Chiricahua auxiliaries, Echeagaray was to explain to them that this was required only because the Apaches had repeatedly abused the good faith with which they had been received by the Spaniards, as for example the recent desertions from Bacoachi.[53]

On October 23 Echeagaray left the Gila River to reconnoiter the Mogollon and San Francisco Mountains. There he found the track of El Chiquito, followed it for fifteen days, but failed to overtake him. Guided by El Chacho, he also reconnoitered the mountains as far as the passes leading to the pueblos of Zuñi and Acoma. Returning to the Gila, he learned from some of the Apaches who continued to come in to give themselves up of a hostile camp in the Cobre Mountains, which he then attacked. In all of these operations the Chiricahua auxiliaries and those who surrendered to him had performed valuable service.[54]

Finally, late in November, Echeagaray returned from his extended campaign and reported his impressive results. His force had killed 54 Apaches, including 22 warriors, captured 125, including 4 warriors, received 55 voluntary surrenders, and recovered 61 horses and mules. Thus, a loss of 234 persons had been inflicted on the enemy in one campaign.[55] Ugarte was sufficiently impressed to recommend Echeagaray for promotion to lieutenant colonel. He ordered Anza to send Echeagaray's captives to Chihuahua, from whence he would have them taken to the Viceroy at Mexico City. But even in consigning the prisoners of war to

[52] Echeagaray to Anza, camp Gila, October 20, 1788, *loc. cit.*
[53] Anza to Echeagaray, Arispe, October 25, 1788 (copy), AGN, PI 128, Expediente 4.
[54] Echeagaray to Anza, camp San Bernardino, November 5, 1788 (copy), AGN, PI 128, Expediente 4.
[55] Echeagaray to Anza, camp San Bernardino, November 21 and Bacoachi, November 22, and to Ugarte, camp San Bernardino, November 27, 1788, AGN, PI 128, Expediente 4.

a distant internment the *Comandante General* displayed a characteristic concern for their welfare. He cautioned Anza to see that they were not detained en route at San Buenaventura, and especially not at Fronteras, for others in the past had perished from the unhealthy climate of these two presidios. As for Compá and others who had surrendered voluntarily, Ugarte instructed Anza to make an exception to the Viceroy's new policy. Since these warriors and their families were kinsmen or dependent friends of the Chiricahuas at Bacoachi, whom it would be inconvenient to insult, and since they had served usefully and faithfully in Echeagaray's campaign, Anza was not to treat them as prisoners of war. Rather, he was to leave them in complete liberty for as long as they complied with their promises to remain at peace.[56]

Apparently those who gave themselves up voluntarily to Echeagaray as well as others who continued to surrender willingly were added to the Chiricahua settlement at Bacoachi, for the congregation there had risen in number from about one hundred, after the desertions of June, 1787, to more than two hundred a year after Echeagaray returned from his campaign.[57] At the beginning of 1791, when Ugarte was about to retire from his command, the Pueblo of Bacoachi was still in existence, and these formerly hostile Apaches were then reported to be clamoring anxiously for a missionary to instruct them in Christianity.[58] Some Chiricahua bands, such as the followers of El Chiquito, remained at large, as did the Mimbreños and most of the so-called Gileños proper, but the pressures of continuous Spanish campaigns with Opata, Pima, and Chiricahua auxiliaries and the supporting strikes of Comanche and especially Navaho allies had reduced the strength of their raids.

The Navahos continued at peace and in alliance with the Spaniards until 1796, when they temporarily rejoined their Gileño

[56] Ugarte to Anza, Hacienda de San Salvador, December 2, and Valle de San Bartolomé, December 12, 1788 (copies), AGN, PI 128, Expediente 4.

[57] Ugarte to Viceroy Revillagigedo (confidential), Chihuahua, November 20, 1789, AGN, PI 159, Expediente 6.

[58] Ugarte to Revillagigedo, Monclova, January 5, 1791, AGN, PI 159, Expediente 6.

kinsmen in a series of raids, but they had remained loyal throughout Ugarte's administration. For a time there was some fear that
the former chief Antonio El Pinto would regain his ascendancy
and break the good relations established in 1786, but on October
7, 1787, when he and several of his companions appeared at the
New Mexican Pueblo of Isleta to trade, Governor De la Concha
had them arrested. Brought to Santa Fe, the prisoners were assured that Antonio was in no danger and was being held only
temporarily, to atone for his past disloyalties. His companions were
then released. When Don Carlos, the Navaho general, came to
Santa Fe to request Antonio's release, De la Concha explained
that he was being held on Ugarte's orders of October 5, 1786.
There was no written proof against him, only suspicion, which
admittedly might not have been well-founded. Informed of the
shaky evidence against the prisoner, Ugarte left it entirely up to
De la Concha whether to detain or free him, and on April 4,
1788, six months after the arrest, the Governor released Antonio
El Pinto to the custody of his nation.[59]

Governor Anza had considered Antonio El Pinto the most pernicious of the Navaho chieftains and the ringleader of the pro-
Gileño faction, but De la Concha was impressed not only with
his intelligence, valor, and unsurpassed influence over his nation
but also with his appreciation of property rights and loyalty to
the Spanish cause. About ten weeks after his release Antonio
came to Santa Fe to introduce his son to the Governor and to
offer his military service in the next campaign against the Gila
Apaches. De la Concha accepted the offer and placed him in
charge of the twenty Navaho warriors who accompanied his own
expedition in August of 1788. The most important result of this
campaign, according to the Governor, was that it established the
greatest proof of the total breach between the Navaho and Gila
Apaches. Not only did the Gileños who fled one attack recognize
the Navahos among their assailants but several of them also

---

[59] De la Concha to Ugarte, Santa Fe, November 10, 1787; Ugarte to De
la Concha, Arispe, January 14, 1788, and De la Concha to Ugarte, Santa Fe,
June 20 and 26, 1788 (cert. copies), AGN, PI 65, Expediente 5.

hurled challenges at Antonio El Pinto and threatened to wipe out his following.[60]

Ugarte had expected to crush the last of the Western Apache resistance in his own time, a hope he entertained even after the Mimbreños broke their peace at San Buenaventura. With troops converging on the Gila tribes from three provinces, supported by Chiricahua auxiliaries in Sonora, Mescaleros in Nueva Vizcaya, and Navahos in New Mexico, they would have had either to surrender or perish. But when Viceroy Flores divided the commandancy-general, giving the eastern provinces to Colonel Ugalde and nullifying Ugarte's peace with the Mescaleros, the entire strategy was frustrated.[61] Even so, Ugarte made impressive progress toward pacification in the western provinces.

As the defensive war raged on in Nueva Vizcaya, a detachment from the presidio of San Buenaventura attacked a Gileño or Mimbreño camp in the interior mountains on March 18, 1790. The troops managed to kill only one brave and to capture only three squaws, but this may have had an important effect. Three days later, as the troops were preparing to strike the enemy again, the Mimbreño chief Ojos Colorados arrived at the presidio of Janos with nine of his warriors, asked for peace, and traded a Spanish captive for some horses. The commandant, Captain Cordero, at first suspected Ojos Colorados of treachery. That chief had reportedly been a ringleader of the Mimbreño revolt at San Buenaventura, and eight days after his overture for peace a night raid was made on the Janos presidial horse herd. However, it was shortly learned that this adventure had been led by Mantas Negras, a rival chieftain. Then, when Ojos Colorados voluntarily

[60] De la Concha to Ugarte, Santa Fe, June 26, and to Flores, November 12, 1788, AGN, PI 65, Expediente 5, and PI 127, Expediente 2. The Gileños did make good part of their boast in 1793, when they killed Antonio El Pinto in one of their raids on the Navaho villages. Ugarte's successor eulogized the fallen chief as a fine, loyal, and singular leader of his nation. Frank Reeve, "Navajo-Spanish Diplomacy, 1770–1790," New Mexico Historical Review, Vol. XXXV, No. 3 (July, 1960), 200–35.

[61] Ugarte to the King, Chihuahua, May 8, 1789, Paragraphs 20–30, AGN, PI 77, Expediente 1.

provided Cordero with a detailed report on the state of the Apache nation, the Captain's suspicions were dissipated.[62]

Ojos Colorados continued his solicitations for peace at Janos with apparent good faith and was presently joined by another Mimbreño or Gileño chief, Jasquunachi (or Tasguienachi). Both volunteered to fight against their still-hostile kinsmen, and Cordero allowed them to accompany a campaign in order to prove their sincerity. By this time, May of 1790, the western frontier of Nueva Vizcaya was enjoying a complete respite from Apache attacks.[63]

Finally, on May 29 and May 30, Ojos Colorados returned to Janos with his entire band and agreed to the stipulations for a secure peace. The five articles of capitulation involved the familiar guarantees: that the band would establish itself permanently in the environs of the presidio, that it would keep the peace faithfully, that it would not attack the Spaniards in any of the provinces, that it would participate in the persecution of the Apaches still at large, and that it would harbor no malefactors. Ugarte urged Cordero to see that the small expenditure of funds for their peaceful establishment would be profitable.[64]

Seven months later Ugarte was able to report that part of the tribe was still living quietly at peace near the presidio of Janos and that the Gileños, formerly such a menace to the frontier, were little by little learning the advantages of friendship and imitating the Spanish way of life.[65] Just how many of the Gileño and Mimbreño bands had settled down in peace is not clear, but Ugarte's successor later reported that both tribes had been at peace since the middle of 1790.[66]

[62] Ugarte to the Viceroy, Nos. 821 and 826, April 2 and 9, 1790 (extracts), AGN, PI 65, Expediente 1. This intelligence from Ojos Colorados may well have formed the basis of Cordero's detailed report of 1796 on the Apaches.

[63] Ugarte to the Viceroy, No. 862, May 19, 1790 (extract), AGN, PI 65, Expediente 1.

[64] Ugarte to the Viceroy, No. 885, June 11, 1790 (extract), AGN, PI 65, Expediente 1.

[65] Ugarte to Revillagigedo, Monclova, January 5, 1791, *loc. cit.*

[66] Brigadier Pedro de Nava to Revillagigedo, Chihuahua, June 6, 1792, Paragraph 36, AGN, PI 170, Expediente 6.

CHAPTER IX

THE EASTERN APACHES
1779-1787

The Eastern Apaches were those tribes who ranged to the east
of the Río Grande in New Mexico and the caravan route between
El Paso and Chihuahua in Nueva Vizcaya. In Ugarte's time there
were four recognized tribes in this division and a number of
related smaller groups. Like the Western Apaches, they maintained no alliance to a general government nor even to tribal
authority, and the chieftains of mere bands were sovereign only
in wartime.

In the southern mountains of New Mexico, between the Río
Grande and the Pecos River, were the *Yntajen-ne*, whom the
Spaniards called Faraones. Driven southward by the Comanches
during the early part of the eighteenth century, the Faraones had
left a group of their tribesmen behind in the Jicarilla Mountains,
where under Spanish protection from their enemies, they took
up farming and traded with the Pueblo Indians of Taos. The
Jicarilla Apaches remained in peace and alliance with the Spaniards of New Mexico, but the remainder of the Faraones sought
protection only in the southern mountains. They raided the
settlements of New Mexico to the north and those of Nueva
Vizcaya to the south, often in collaboration with the Mescaleros
on the east, with whom they were intimately connected.[1]

To the east of the Faraones ranged the *Sejen-ne*, or Mescaleros,
who inhabited the mountains near the Pecos River and extended

[1] Matson and Schroeder, "Cordero's Description of the Apache—1796," *loc. cit.*

Taos

SANTA FE

36

34

C o m a n c h e s

JICARILLA MTS.

FARAONES

SA. BLANCA

SACRAMENTO MTS.

32

ORGAN MTS.

GUADALUPE MTS.

El Paso del Norte

San Elizario

Pecos R.

Colorado R.

Brazos R.

Rio Grande

Carrizal

MESCALEROS

PAISANO MTS.

LLANEROS

SAN ANTONIO

30

El Príncipe

CIENEGA MTS.

El Norte

CHISOS MTS.

SA. RICA

LIPANES

PIEDRAS NEGRAS

Frio R.

Chihuahua

San Carlos

SA. DEL CARMEN

San Fernando

San Juan
Bautista

Nueces R.

R.

Conchos

Sabinas R.

28

Pilar de Conchos

SA. MOJADA

Santa Rosa

Pajado R.

N

BOLSON
DE
MAPIMI

MONCLOVA

26

EASTERN   APACHES

MONTERREY

0   50   100   200

Parras

Anaelo

Scale in Miles

Alamo

Saltillo

z

107°   106°   105°   104°   103°   102°   101°   100°   99°   98°

northward on both banks of that stream as far as the Comanche range.[2] One of the most ticklish of Ugarte's problems lay in trying to maintain a Spanish peace with the Comanches and Mescalero Apaches at the same time. Like most of the Eastern Apache groups, the Mescaleros had been pushed southward from the buffalo plains of New Mexico by the Comanches and had thus been deprived of their main source of sustenance. Beleaguered from the north by the Comanches, they had been thrust against the settlements of Coahuila and Nueva Vizcaya, where they provided for themselves by raiding the cow, horse, and mule herds of the Spaniards. Unlike the Llaneros, or Plains Apaches, to the east, who were caught in the same dire straits, the Mescaleros began to pitch their camps in the mountains, as did the Faraones, and there they gained more security from the pursuit of both the Comanches and the Spaniards. During Ugarte's administration there were eight main bands of Mescaleros, the chieftains of which were Bigotes El Bermejo (Whiskers, or The Crimson One), Cuerno Verde (Green Horn), Montera Blanca (White Cap), El-lite (El Quemado, or The Burnt One), Daxle Ylchí (Patule El Grande), Quijiequsyá (Zapato Tuerto or Twisted Shoe), Gabié-choché (Alegre or Happy), and Yco-Yndixle (Volante or Ligero, i.e., Rover or Flighty).

The *Cuelcajen-ne*, or Llaneros, were the Apaches occupying the plains and sandy stretches between the Pecos and the Colorado River of Texas. They were bordered by the Mescaleros on the west, the Lipanes on the east, the Spanish settlements of Coahuila on the south, and the Comanches on the north. Actually, three lesser tribes were included under this denomination: the Llaneros proper, the Lipiyanes, and the Natagées. Traditionally at war with the Comanches, they attacked the Spaniards less frequently, and when they did, they were sometimes in association with the Mescaleros and Faraones.[3] The principal war chief of the Llaneros, who also exerted some influence over other eastern tribes, was the great Lipiyán warrior Picax-andé-Instinsle,

2 *Ibid.*
3 *Ibid.*

who was known in Nueva Vizcaya as El Calvo (The Bald One). El Natagée, probably of the tribe of the same name, was also a prominent chief.

The easternmost group of the Apache nation, immediately beyond the Llaneros, was the *Lipajen-ne*, or Lipán tribe. The Lipanes, a numerous people, were divided into two large groups, one occupying the upper and the other the lower banks of the Río Grande. The Upper Lipanes sometimes joined the Mescaleros and Llaneros in forays against Coahuila, while the Lower Lipanes lived apart and largely confined their attacks to the province of Texas. Both were bitter rivals of the Comanches for control of the buffalo of the north. The Lipanes had made peace with the Spaniards in 1774, but were not above raiding Spanish herds and blaming the crime on the Mescaleros. Unlike other Apaches they refrained from eating horse and mule meat, and they were considered by the Spaniards as being both cleaner and more gallant than others of their nation.[4]

In 1777 Commandant-General Croix's councils of war at Monclova and San Antonio recommended that friendship be cultivated with all the Eastern Apaches until sufficient troops were available for an all-out war against them. In the following year, however, the junta at Chihuahua proposed that the Spaniards try to divide the two strongest tribes, the Mescaleros and the Lipanes, allying with the former and continuing a war on the latter.[5] Peace, however, was first renewed with the Lipanes, in 1779. In that year Juan de Ugalde, who had succeeded Ugarte as governor of Coahuila, enticed the Mescaleros to attack the Lipanes in concert with his presidial troops; the Spaniards abandoned offensive operations of their own in favor of a campaign of peace by persuasion; and, probably most important of all, the Comanches descended upon the Lipanes in a murderous assault that sent them fleeing to the Spaniards for protection.[6]

[4] *Ibid.*
[5] Bolton, *Athanase de Mézières*, II, 147–163; Thomas, *Teodoro de Croix*, 35–37.
[6] Croix, "General Report of 1781," in Thomas, *Teodoro de Croix*, 71–243, Paragraphs 46 and 68; Faulk, *The Last Years of Spanish Texas, 1778–1821*, 61–62.

After the Lipanes sued for peace in Coahuila in 1779, Governor Ugalde began using them as auxiliaries against the Mescaleros, who continued to maraud in that province. Croix considered the Mescaleros more perfidious, cruel, and barbarous than the Lipanes and unworthy of an honorable peace, but when they came to the presidio of El Norte humbly and submissively seeking peace and protection from the Lipanes, he felt constrained to accept their offer.[7]

Three bands of Mescaleros, led by Patule El Grande, Alonso, and Juan Tuerto, offered the following terms at El Norte: They would settle down in the abandoned pueblo of San Francisco, near the presidio, if they could be joined there by some of their Julimeño and Suma kinsmen from the missions in Coahuila and the El Paso district, respectively; with assistance and instruction from these more civilized Indians they would build houses, grow crops, and perform other agricultural labors; they would rely on the Spaniards to provide during the first year everything necessary to support the families that settled there and to protect them from their enemies; they would subject themselves to the orders of the presidial commandant, become his vassals, behave faithfully, serve as auxiliaries in his campaigns, and fight not only other Apaches but even those of their own bands who persisted in attacking the Spaniards. Croix accepted the proposals, entertained several of the Mescaleros at Chihuahua, distributed presents among them, and conferred titles on the prominent chiefs. He had Patule and Juan Tuerto named war captains and Alonso named governor of their new pueblo at San Francisco. A fourth band of Mescaleros also came to terms, and Croix made its chief, Domingo Alegre, war captain and governor of a separate pueblo, Nuestra Señora de la Buena Esperanza. Both Indian governors agreed to accept Spanish interpreters who would reside in their new pueblos and communicate with the commandant-general.[8] In ratifying this peace in September, 1779, Croix intimated to Lieutenant Colonel Manuel Muñoz, the commandant of El

[7] Croix, "General Report of 1781," *loc. cit.*, Paragraph 92.
[8] *Ibid.*, Paragraphs 201–207.

Norte, that his own ultimate goal was still destruction of the hostile Apaches.[9]

By May of 1780 Croix had become concerned over the Mescalero peace. On the one hand these Apaches had served faithfully and spiritedly as auxiliaries in Muñoz's campaign against a band of Gileños and had even turned on renegades of their own tribe, killing Juan Tuerto, who had caused many outrages in Nueva Vizcaya and Coahuila. On the other hand, their attitude had changed noticeably, and they were now making demands on the Spaniards. Croix felt there was little hope of their taking root in their pueblos and was fearful that they would not only become reconciled with the Lipanes but equally as treacherous to the peace they had solemnized. They had not settled down as they had promised, and although their houses had been completed at San Francisco and more than eighty Mescaleros were living there, Spaniards and other Indians had to do everything for them. They seemed unable to apply themselves either to building or working in the fields and were not even persuading their children to take up such labors. Rather, they still preferred a vagrant life, and there were well-founded suspicions that they were continuing to rob and murder in several parts of Nueva Vizcaya. It was an established fact that they carried on such hostilities in Coahuila. However, Domingo Alegre and others of his band were apparently acting in good faith, and Croix hoped that the money spent on the Mescaleros thus far would bring some beneficial results.[10]

These hopes soon evaporated, however, for a number of incidents occurred that caused the Mescaleros to flee their pueblos and revert to their old ways.[11] During the winter of 1781–82 Patule El Grande and seven other Mescalero chiefs were at large,

9 *Ibid.,* Paragraph 208.

10 *Ibid.,* Paragraphs 212–13.

11 References to these regrettable incidents appear at a later date but with little explanation. According to Ugarte, it was public knowledge that this peace had been broken because of the poor administration exercised by those responsible for its enforcement. Ugarte to Viceroy Flores, Chihuahua, May 20, 1788, AGN, PI 112, Expediente 2.

operating out of the Bolsón de Mapimí and attacking the Coahuila towns of Parras, Alamo, and Anaelo. In these raids they
killed 80 people, wounded several others, and made off with a
large number of horses. Governor Ugalde, who was seeking out
Mescaleros in the north, returned in a rage and made four
assaults on the marauders. In these operations he killed 5 chieftains and an undetermined number of warriors, captured 45,
seized more than 500 horses and mules, and released 6 Spaniards
from captivity. In utter dismay Patule El Grande then sued for
peace, but when Ugalde's terms proved to be too harsh, he fled
with his band and sought better arrangements at the presidio
of San Carlos. The commandant there interned them. Ugalde,
meanwhile, attacked three more Mescalero encampments in the
Bolsón de Mapimí and drove them from the security of that
desert retreat.[12]

When Ugarte became commandant-general and received his
formal instructions from Viceroy Gálvez, the Lipán Apaches
were still formally at peace in Coahuila but were blaming the
Mescaleros for the raids they occasionally made themselves on
Spanish communities. Ugarte and Ugalde, who was now taking
over the military command of the eastern frontier provinces,
were directed to preserve the friendship of the Lipanes and
prevent their reconciliation with the Mescaleros.[13] In July, 1786,
the Mescaleros had raided deep into the heart of Mexico, wiping
out the settlements of Sabana Grande and Gruñidora and attacking those of Mazapil and Cedros with unexampled cruelty and
barbarity.[14] When Ugalde returned to the frontier in his new
capacity, he launched a seven-months campaign against the
Mescaleros on January 19, 1787. Failing to encounter the enemy
in their favorite retreat, the Bolsón de Mapimí, Ugalde's Coahuila troops finally found them in the Sierra de los Chizos on
March 31, and there inflicted upon them the first of a series of
chastisements.[15]

[12] Nelson, "Juan de Ugalde and the Rio Grande Frontier" (unpublished
Ph.D. dissertation, University of California, 1936), 54–63.
[13] Gálvez, Instrucción of 1786, loc. cit., Paragraphs 178, 181.
[14] Nelson, "Juan de Ugalde and the Rio Grande Frontier," 77.
[15] See below, note 30.

The date of Ugalde's first attack on the Mescaleros is important, for when several bands of this tribe sued for peace in Nueva Vizcaya two months earlier and were presented in the following month with the stipulations for their surrender, Ugalde pretended that their only purpose was to escape the terror of his forces. As a matter of his own record, he was not even operating in their territory at the time. What most likely induced the Mescaleros to seek peace was, as they themselves declared, their desire for protection from the Comanches. Each winter when the Mescaleros migrated northward to hunt buffalo they were in mortal danger of encountering this powerful adversary. Whatever their reason, they exhibited considerable skittishness in making their overtures for peace.

On January 24, 1787, a detachment of troops under Ensign Juan Francisco Granados set out from the presidio of San Carlos to hunt down hostile Apaches on the eastern frontier of Nueva Vizcaya. Coming upon a group of Mescalero hunters, the soldiers trailed them until they were discovered by the Indians and then galloped after them in hot pursuit. On January 30 the chase led to a mesa known as Las Varas, where the detachment found a large aggregation of Mescaleros. As the troops approached, however, the Indians fled to the other side of the mesa, leaving ten horses and six loads of buffalo hides, antelope skins, and other goods behind. When the soldiers followed them to the opposite slope, they stopped and indicated by signs that they wished to parley. Granados asked them to approach, and three of them did, announcing that they wanted to make peace and offering to return the next day with their families.[16]

A rendezvous was arranged, and on January 31, fifty mounted warriors and a considerable number of others on foot arrived at the same site fully armed. The Mescaleros tried to get the troops to come up on the slope to barter with them, but Granados prudently declined and ordered the Indians to come down to the plain for such negotiations as they wished to make. Only those on horseback complied, and even they were visibly suspicious.

[16] Ugarte to Flores, Arispe, October 15, 1787, AGN, PI 112, Expediente 1.

Realizing that he could not attack them successfully where they were and being convinced that their pretensions for peace were in good faith, Granados told them to meet him at a nearby water hole. Then, when they failed to appear at the appointed place, he ordered his troops to withdraw. The detachment marched to a site known as Los Alamos de San Juan, and there on February 7 the troops sighted a lone Indian trailing them at a great distance. Granados sent twenty soldiers back to overtake the brave, and when he fled, they followed him to the main Mescalero camp.[17]

Forty mounted warriors and a large number on foot came out to meet the twenty soldiers and greeted them with signs of peace. Then, when Granados and the remainder of his command arrived, they repeated these demonstrations and explained that their chieftains, recalling what had happened to them some years before at the presidio of El Norte, were too fearful of internment to accompany them. The chieftains had volunteered two of their tribesmen and two squaws as hostages, however, and promised to come to the presidio of El Norte in person if they would be permitted to negotiate for peace there. This Granados accepted. Returning to the presidio with the hostages on February 10, the Ensign submitted the diary of his campaign, detailing the entire affair, and this was forwarded to the commandant-general.[18]

Ugarte received this intelligence at Chihuahua on February 12, and on the same day he appointed Captain Domingo Díaz, who had been inspecting the Tarahumara towns of Nueva Vizcaya, to arrange the negotiations with the assistance of Captain Juan Bautista Elguezabal, the commandant of San Carlos.[19] Ugarte's orders to Captain Díaz reveal his own interpretation of Gálvez's *Instrucción* of 1786. The Viceroy had died on November 30, 1786, leaving Ugarte independent of that office for several months, but he was still bound by the *Instrucción* itself, since

[17] *Ibid.*
[18] *Ibid.*
[19] *Ibid.*

it now carried the king's endorsement. In keeping with its provisions Ugarte provided the peace commissioners with detailed instructions but also with broad latitude.

Díaz and Elguezabal were to report to the presidio of El Norte immediately. Then, as soon as they had conferred with the hostages, they were to send them back to the Mescalero encampment with word that peace terms would be arranged only with the chieftains, that these should come to the presidio immediately, and that they would be scrupulously protected from harm. Should the chieftains come, Díaz was to inquire discreetly into their reasons for seeking peace and then propose eleven articles as a basis for its acceptance: (1) The Mescaleros must immediately deliver all of the Spanish subjects whom they had captured; (2) they must cease attacking the towns, haciendas, and presidios of Nueva Vizcaya and Coahuila at once; (3) they must surrender all Spaniards, Indians, mulattoes, and other castes who might have gone over to their camp to guide or assist them in their forays, and these would face the penalty of death; (4) the bands that sought peace must settle near the presidio of El Norte, where they would be assigned plots of bottom land on the Río Grande and assistance from the Spaniards in planting crops; (5) they must maintain themselves there by farming and stock raising, rather than from Spanish rations, but they might supplement their needs by hunting game and gathering mescal when the commissioner permitted it; (6) they must assemble their camps or establish formal towns near the presidio in order to qualify for Spanish assistance, and unless they should adopt the Spanish religion, they must accept the authority of a principal chief, one of their own tribesmen nominated by themselves but confirmed by the Spanish government; (7) under these conditions and with proof of their good faith they would be allowed to barter their goods in all the presidios and towns, exchanging them without discount for the Spanish articles they might need; (8) Spaniards could enter their towns or camps whenever they saw fit, and the Mescalero chieftains must inform the nearest presidio of any breach of the peace terms so that the agitators might be punished; (9) they must specify whether the entire Mescalero tribe was soliciting peace or only some of its bands, and if the latter, which these were, naming their leaders and giving the number of men, women, and children embraced by each; (10) they must submit their livestock for branding to prevent any confusion over ownership; and (11) if the entire nation should not agree to peace, those who did must induce the others to do so, and if the others refused, those making peace must join the Spanish troops in military operations against them.[20]

Captain Díaz was to see that the Indians understood these articles fully and that the peace was to their own benefit since the Spaniards would destroy them if they did not accept it. If they should not wish to accept the conditions, they might retire immediately, but as long as they held to the stipulations they would be protected from all harm. If they should agree to the peace and then break it, war would be made on them even more vigorously, and they would be attacked wherever they went and until they sued for peace again. Finally, Díaz might change any part of Ugarte's requirements as he saw fit after conferring with the Mescalero chieftains and making the proposals known to them. However, he was not to make any concessions that the Spaniards could not honor or which would prejudice the peace itself, and he was to report to Ugarte promptly on whatever transpired, how many bands were seeking peace, who their chieftains were, and how many tribesmen each contained.[21]

Unfortunately for the progress of the ensuing negotiations, the commandant-general was called away from Nueva Vizcaya on more urgent business and was unable to supervise either the negotiations themselves or to adopt in time the emergency measures required by unforeseen developments that undermined them. When Ugarte issued his instructions to Díaz, he was already preparing to march to Sonora to defend it against renewed invasions by the Gila Apaches and to suppress a general

[20] Ugarte to Captain Domingo Díaz, Chihuahua, February 12, 1787, AGN, PI 112, Expediente 1.
[21] *Ibid.*

revolt of the restless Seri Indians. Then, leaving Nueva Vizcaya in the supposedly competent hands of Commandant-Inspector Rengel, with full instructions for perfecting the pact, he left for Arispe.[22]

Ugarte was gone for over a year, and to make matters worse Rengel was residing at El Paso del Norte, the northernmost outpost of Nueva Vizcaya, and was scheduled to make an inspection of the New Mexican troops before returning to Chihuahua. Thus, the negotiations with the Mescaleros took place without the presence or even the proximity of a major executive officer, and the resulting time lag in passing orders through the chain of command was in part responsible for the disaster that followed. Although Ugarte was justified in removing himself to the more critical theater of Sonora, he was nonetheless responsible for permitting his delegated substitute to remain so far from the important scene in Nueva Vizcaya. Two other unfortunate circumstances also imperiled the negotiations. In the first place, Colonel Ugalde, the commandant of the army of the eastern frontier provinces, in which the Mescaleros also roamed, was invested with almost independent military authority even though technically subordinate to Ugarte. He was also endowed with a jealous, ambitious, and aggressive nature. Ugalde had little respect for Ugarte and no confidence at all in the Mescalero Apaches. In the second place, when Viceroy Flores was granted the same authority over the northern frontier that Gálvez had held, the crisis had already developed, and being inadequately informed of the situation there and admittedly prejudiced against all heathen tribes, Flores almost completely undermined Ugarte's peace efforts.

The prospects for a final reduction of the several Apache tribes were most promising in the early spring of 1787. In addition to the Mescaleros who were negotiating at El Norte, the Mimbreños had asked for peace at the presidio of Janos, at El Paso del Norte, and at the Valle de San Buenaventura. Then,

[22] Ugarte to Rengel, Chihuahua, February 12, 1787, AGN, PI 112, Expediente 1.

too, a large number of Chiricahuas were settling down at the Pueblo of Bacoachi, in Sonora, and the Navahos had made peace in New Mexico.[23] Since the Jicarillas in New Mexico and the Lipanes in Coahuila had long been at peace, this left the Gileños as the only major Apache tribe still completely hostile. And Ugarte expected to crush these holdouts with troops now freed from the campaigns against the formerly hostile tribes and with the active support of the now friendly Comanches, Utes, Navahos, Jicarillas, and other Apache groups. Total victory was well in sight, and Ugarte looked forward to the welcome end of the long and bloody Apache wars.[24]

For a time negotiations with the Mescaleros proceeded according to plan. On March 29, 1787, Captain Díaz was able to report that 8 Mescalero chieftains had arrived at El Norte with their bands numbering 300 families and including 400 warriors. He referred also to two other bands of "Mescaleros," one encamped in a sandy district and the other in the Sierra de Guadalupe, in what is now southeastern New Mexico, and also several scattered families, all of which had been summoned and were expected to arrive shortly.[25] The 8 chieftains at the presidio had understood and accepted the eleven conditions for peace, but Díaz had not yet taken a census of the bands as specified in his instructions from Ugarte. He feared that eliciting from them such information as their exact numerical strength and distribution would arouse their suspicions and perhaps endanger the success of the negotiations. Moreover, owing to the extreme misery from which they were suffering, he had taken the liberty of issuing rations to all who had congregated, even though this had not been promised. He had assured them that their tribesmen who were prisoners of the Spaniards would be exchanged

[23] Ugarte to the Marqués de Sonora, Arispe, April 16, 1787 (cert. copy), AGN, PI 112, Expediente 1.

[24] Ugarte to Flores, Informe General, Arispe, December 10, 1787, AGN, PI 254, Expediente 2; Ugarte to the King, Chihuahua, May 8, 1789, AGN, PI 77, Expediente 1.

[25] It was later learned that the two absent bands were actually Natagees and Lipiyanes, rather than Mescaleros, and that there were only eight main bands of the latter group.

for the captives they held and, so as to end hostilities, he was informing both Ugarte and Ugalde of the truce.[26] When Ugarte received this information at Arispe three weeks later, he approved what Díaz had done and ordered both Rengel and Ugalde to cease hostilities against the Mescaleros who had sought peace and to deliver up the captives of this group, whom they held in both Nueva Vizcaya and Coahuila.[27]

Meanwhile, however, Díaz had made another concession to the Mescaleros at the presidio. The chieftains had beseeched him to allow them to remove their camps to the nearby mountains, where they could provision themselves with game, mescal, and other natural fruits, and Díaz had acceded to the request because provisions at the presidio were insufficient to support such a large number of families. To each chieftain and his band he assigned a specific, detached reservation: Bigotes El Bermejo and his people, around the Aguaje del Cíbolo, about eighteen miles from the presidio; Volante, Cuerno Verde, and Montera Blanca and their bands, on lands near the presidio of San Carlos; Zapato Tuerto's and El Quemado's people, around the Aguaje de las Cruces, on the southern slope of the Sierra Rica; and Alegre's band and those of the lesser chieftain Patule, around the Aguaje del Pabelloncito, near the Hacienda de la Ramada. The two remaining bands, under El Calvo and El Natagée, which were then believed to be Mescaleros, were still hunting buffalo and had not arrived.[28] Although this authorized dispersal of the friendly Mescaleros improved their disposition toward a permanent peace and also relieved the strain on the presidio's larder, it also led to other incidents, which shattered not only this important object but also the entire policy that Ugarte had been so assiduously pursuing for the previous twelve months.

Precisely what happened to wreck these well-laid plans is

[26] Díaz to Ugarte, Presidio of El Norte, March 29, 1787 (cert. copy), AGN, PI 112, Expediente 1.

[27] Ugarte to Rengel and to Ugalde, Arispe, April 19, 1787, AGN, PI 112, Expediente 1.

[28] Díaz to Rengel, Guajoquilla, April 13, 1787 (cert. copy), AGN, PI 112, Expediente 1.

difficult to ascertain from the voluminous files of conflicting reports. The only officially-recorded eye-witness account was that of Colonel Ugalde, but he did not present his version until four and one-half months after the fact. Moreover, this was a desperate defense of his own rather precipitous acts, unsystematically enlarged upon from his diary of the seven-months campaign against the Mescaleros, which he launched on January 19, 1787.[29] According to this version, Ugalde and his forces, having failed to find any hostile Apaches in the Bolsón de Mapimí, crossed to the northern side of the Río Grande, invaded the rugged Sierra de los Chizos, and then at the head of only twelve soldiers, encountered a band of "the Enemy" on March 31. Cutting off all escape, he defeated them with small loss to his own troops, captured all of their goods, redeemed a white captive, and received the voluntary surrender of Chief Quijiequsyá, who gave in as soon as he realized that it was Ugalde who was attacking.[30] As it turned out, this was the Mescalero band under Zapato Tuerto, which had been assigned to the southern slope of the Sierra Rica, but which had apparently strayed across this range and the Río Grande to the Chizos Mountains. Ugalde had been away from his headquarters since January 19, which was before the Mescaleros first sued for peace, and had received no official notification of the truce. Ugarte's order for a cessation of hostilities was not written until April 19, more than two weeks after the attack. Therefore, and because Zapato Tuerto's band was obviously "off limits," this first violation of Spanish good faith might well be charged to poor communications and consequent misunderstanding.

The first news of the event to reach the presidio El Norte was brought in on April 7 by one of Chief Patule's squaws. She identified the band that was attacked as that of Zapato Tuerto but erred in the locale, stating that the assault took place while the band was hunting deer in the Sierra del Carmen. According

[29] Ugalde, Extracto y Sumario de la primera Campaña . . . a los Enemigos comunes y crueles Indios Gentiles Apaches Mescaleros, Santa Rosa, August 15, 1787, AGN, PI 112, Expediente 4.
[30] *Ibid.*

to her report, three Indians had been killed, some were taken prisoner, and the entire horse herd was captured. In order to inform the troops of Coahuila of the truce and prevent the possibility of another assault on the Mescaleros, Captain Elguezabal sent Ensign Granados with an escort of sixteen men to find their commandant, advise him of the armistice, and arrange for the return of the captives, horses, and booty taken from the Mescaleros. It was not then known that the attack had taken place in the Sierra de los Chizos nor that Ugalde himself had been in command.[31]

Bearing a letter from Captain Elguezabal dated April 7, Granados reached Ugalde's camp someplace between the former site of the presidio of San Carlos and the Chizos crossing of the Río Grande. There he learned that Ugalde had led the attack in person and that he would reply to Elguezabal's letter in due time.[32] According to Ugalde's profusely expanded diary, Elguezabal's letter, "whose contents I am refraining from translating so as not to use and besmirch paper with superficial, gratuitous, ignorant, and iniquitous propositions," confirmed what the captured chief had told him, that the Mescaleros had sought peace at the presidio of El Norte only to escape the wrath of Ugalde's forces and that no conditions whatsoever had been exacted of them. Ugalde could still not believe that a truce had been granted his avowed enemies and therefore decided to continue his campaign.[33]

According to Elguezabal, two weeks elapsed without a reply from Ugalde. Moreover, that commandant had gone on to attack the Mescalero bands under Cuerno Verde and other lesser chieftains near the presidio of El Norte. This had been reported by one of Ugalde's soldiers, who was the sole survivor of one of the skirmishes and who arrived at the presidio by foot on April 20. With this news Captain Elguezabal himself set out the next day

---

[31] Díaz to Rengel, Guajoquilla, April 13, 1787, *loc. cit.*; Captain Juan Bautista Elguezabal to Rengel, El Norte, April 21, 1787 (cert. copy), AGN, PI 112, Expediente 1.
[32] Elguezabal to Rengel, April 21, 1787, *loc. cit.*
[33] Ugalde, Extracto y Sumario de la primera Campaña, *loc. cit.*

with forty-two men, including Ensign Granados, to confer with Ugalde in person. The Mescaleros at the presidio were upset and, having been offered peace on the one hand and attacked on the other, believed that they had been deceived.[34] According to Ugalde, he had made this second attack on April 19, in the "Sierra de la Pendencia," and his adversary was a camp of the powerful "Zendé nation," which had never previously made peace, but which had stolen Spanish horses and was now on its way to El Norte to take refuge from him.[35] It was reported to Ugarte, in Sonora, that the second attack was on Cuerno Verde's band and that it occurred on April 20, in the Cerro de la Cieneguita, a short distance from El Norte.[36]

On April 22 Captain Elguezabal and his escort arrived at Ugalde's camp, a place called Cieneguilla del Paisano. During a long and serious discussion of the problem, Elguezabal complained bitterly of the recent attack on the supposedly peaceful Mescaleros, and Ugalde responded that his final decision was to make war on them wherever he found them within the provinces under his jurisdiction, that they would be secure from his attacks only in Nueva Vizcaya. Then, in spite of Elguezabal's objections, Ugalde proceeded to attack a third "enemy" camp, in the Sierra del Movano, and then a fourth, near the Pecos River.[37] As it turned out, these were the bands under Bigotes El Bermejo and Montera Blanca, respectively, which suffered only the loss of their horses and goods.[38]

Meanwhile, Ugalde did offer to release the Mescalero prisoners he had taken in the attack on Zapato Tuerto's band, but only in exchange for other hostages. To this end he sent the captured Zapato Tuerto to the camp of the lesser chieftain Patule, now back at the presidio of El Norte, to demand two Spanish prisoners for the liberation of fourteen of his own captives, including the family of Zapato Tuerto. However, although

[34] Elguezabal to Rengel, April 21, 1787, *loc. cit.*
[35] Ugalde Extracto y Sumario de la primera Campaña, *loc. cit.*
[36] Ugarte to Ugalde, Arispe, May 18, 1787, AGN, PI 112, Expediente 1.
[37] Ugalde, Extracto y Sumario de la primera Campaña, *loc. cit.*
[38] Díaz to Rengel, El Norte, May 1, 1787, AGN, PI 112, Expediente 1.

Zapato Tuerto returned with the Spanish captives, Ugalde did not release the Mescaleros he held. Chief Patule then sent three other Mescaleros as hostages, but again without result. Fearing the effect this bad faith might have on the peace arrangements at the presidio, Captain Elguezabal then urged the Commandant-Inspector to order Ugalde to restore the families captured from Zapato Tuerto's band as well as another six Mescaleros whom he had taken in his second attack, on Cuerno Verde's band. Since this latter attack, the bands of Cuerno Verde, Bigotes El Bermejo, and Montera Blanca had not returned to the presidio, and those of Volante, Alegre, El Quemado, and Patule, which had returned, were growing restless.[39] In response to this urging and also in compliance with Ugarte's order of April 19 from Arispe, Rengel arranged for the release of the Mescaleros who had been captured in Nueva Vizcaya previously and were then held in the prison at Chihuahua and the workhouses of Encinillas. These were to be sent to Captain Díaz, presumably to be restored to their people when the peace terms were solemnized.[40]

The Commandant-Inspector was reluctant to condemn Ugalde for his attacks on Zapato Tuerto and Cuerno Verde, however, since he might not have been informed of the truce and because Díaz should never have allowed the Mescalero bands to stray so far from the presidio. The trouble, he thought, was that the environs of El Norte were unsuitable for fixed Mescalero villages. The presidio itself could not provision such a large number of families; there was a scarcity of good farming land at that place; and the site was too close to the Comanche range. To remedy the situation Rengel ordered Díaz and Elguezabal to induce the Mescalero chieftains to come to El Paso del Norte and arrange with him for their permanent residence in that vicinity. He especially recommended for their new home the abandoned town of Los Tiburcios, about fifteen miles from El Paso, which was far from the center of Nueva Vizcaya and thus less threaten-

---

[39] Elguezabal to Rengel, El Norte, May 1, 1787, AGN, PI 112, Expediente 1.
[40] Rengel to Ugarte, El Paso del Norte, May 9, 1787, AGN, PI 112, Expediente 1.

ing to its settlements. Los Tiburcios also had plentiful game and mescal nearby, excellent water for irrigation, open terrain for villages, good soil for farming, and several neighboring settlements for trading.[41]

Two of the Mescalero chiefs, Patule and El Quemado, were persuaded to go to El Paso, escorted by a party of troops under Ensign Granados. There they listened to Rengel's inducements and the conditions under which he would admit them to peace, and then, on May 17, made a formal deposition of their own. In order to gain security from the Comanches, who were still attacking them, they wished to accept Rengel's terms, which were essentially the same as Ugarte's, but they had some notable reservations. They preferred to live by hunting and gathering rather than by farming; they wanted their bands to reside in separate camps and not under the control of a single chieftain; and they wished to remain in the vicinity of the presidio of El Norte, where they felt more secure from their enemies. However, the four lesser chieftains—Cuerno Verde, Bigotes El Bermejo, Zapato Tuerto, and Montera Blanca (whose bands usually traveled together)—might come to the El Paso district, for it was within their traditional range. When asked about El Calvo and El Natagée, the two chiefs who had never arrived at El Norte with their bands, Patule and El Quemado declared that they did not know them and that they lived far from their own camping places. They did, however, single out one of the chieftains, Alegre, as the principal source of the difficulties among the Mescaleros and probably of the breach of the current peace.[42]

Although Patule and El Quemado had promised less than Rengel desired, he presented each of them with a horse and El Quemado with a suit of Spanish clothes (Patule already had one). Each of the six braves who had accompanied them was given either a hat or a shirt, and after all were fed, they left for El Norte under military escort on May 22. Rengel then wrote

[41] Rengel to Díaz, Elguezabal, and Ugarte, El Paso, April 27, 1787 (cert. copies), AGN, PI 112, Expediente 1.
[42] Rengel, deposition, El Paso, May 17, 1787, AGN, PI 112, Expediente 1.

Elguezabal, urging him to induce all the Mescaleros to come to El Paso and also to carry out all of the conditions that Ugarte had required.[43]

Ugarte had dictated supplemental instructions on February 27 and March 22, which Rengel had passed on to Díaz, and in June he urged that the Commandant-Inspector carry these out to the letter. The instructions required Díaz, among other things, to take a complete census of the Mescaleros who were gathered at the presidio, to provide them with weekly rations of corn, wheat, beans, sugar, and tobacco until they could support themselves from farming, and to distinguish the chieftains with Spanish clothing.[44] Owing to new and embarrassing circumstances, however, Díaz did not immediately comply with the new orders.

Of the eight bands of Mescaleros who had come to the presidio in peace, Díaz explained, four of them, having been unexpectedly attacked by Ugalde's troops, had abandoned their assigned campsites, joined other bands in the sand dunes and Guadalupe Mountains, and then retreated to the Sierra del Movano. Only the bands of the lesser chieftains Alegre, Volante, Patule, and El Quemado remained near the presidio, and even these were fearful of being attacked. Díaz had sent notice to the fugitive bands urging them to return and promising them protection and the restoration of their captured tribesmen, horses, and goods, but even he feared that these guarantees could not be enforced. It was owing to their all-too-justified mistrust that Díaz had delayed making the intimate inquiries necessary for a census. Nor had he issued them the specified weekly rations, believing as he did that the Mescaleros would never adjust to Spanish foods as long as there were abundant wild fruits such as mescal, datil, pitahaya, tuna, and mesquite to be gathered and deer to be hunted. From April to October the Mescaleros relied on these for food, and during the rest of the year on buffalo, which they hunted during the winter months.

[43] Rengel to Elguezabal, El Paso, May 22, 1787 (cert. copies), AGN, PI 112, Expediente 1.
[44] Rengel to Díaz, El Paso, June 3, 1787, AGN, PI 112, Expediente 1.

The Mescaleros, Díaz explained, loved the liberty and idle life in which they had been reared, and only those less than twelve years old, who might grow up under the peace terms, could ever be expected to subject themselves to cultivating the soil or to other such labor. Moreover, the only terms they would accept would be such as would allow them to live in the lands where they had been born and reared—near the mountains and springs in the vicinity of El Norte. On the other hand, they would agree never to endanger the lives and property of the Spaniards in return for the same guarantees respecting their own, and they would help capture and punish any renegades among themselves who should commit the slightest theft, so long as the innocent did not suffer for the crimes of the guilty. They would even help the troops keep their distant kinsmen, the Gileños, out of the provinces.[45]

With Ugarte's permission Díaz had offered the Mescaleros a respectable detachment of troops to escort them on their annual buffalo hunt, which he thought would take place in December and January, and thus protect them from the Comanches during that expedition. This promise had greatly pleased them. Díaz had decided not to try to reconcile an apparent rivalry between Alegre and Patule, for this discord might eventually serve the Spaniards. He had, however, attempted to distinguish the principal men of the several bands by bestowing gifts on them and their kinsmen. Alegre and Volante seemed to have the greatest authority over their tribesmen, and Alegre had been sent out to solicit the return of the fugitive bands. He was expected back any day now.[46]

The Commandant-Inspector took exception to the terms that the Mescaleros now proposed to Díaz, noting that these violated the fourth, fifth, and sixth stipulations of the original capitulation and that they would not reduce the tribe to a permanent peace. Should they persist in their new demands, he felt that the Spaniards should not be bound to their part of the agreement. Rengel

[45] Díaz to Rengel, El Norte, June 30, 1787, AGN, PI 112, Expediente 1.
[46] *Ibid.*

also worried about the effect on the Comanches of the military escort Díaz had promised the Mescaleros for their buffalo hunt, but he would consult Ugarte before making a final ruling. Meanwhile, Díaz should continue to pacify the Mescaleros, promise to return their people and goods from Coahuila, get them to join the troops as scouts against the Gileños, and maintain patrols to prevent them from engaging in raids on the settlements.[47] Ugarte approved Rengel's instructions and also the arrangements Díaz had made for escorting the Mescaleros into the buffalo country.[48] This latter proved to be a risky venture in view of the newly-formed alliance with the Comanche nation in New Mexico and Texas and the bitter enmity of those powerful warriors with all of the Apache bands.

By the end of August, 1787, the Mescaleros were so upset over Ugalde's failure to return their captured kinsmen and his continuing campaign against them that a general breakdown of the peace seemed imminent. From Sonora on April 19 Ugarte had ordered the return of these captives, and although Ugalde may not have received this written command until he returned from his campaign on August 9, he had been verbally informed of the truce by Granados on April 7 and again by Elguezabal on April 22. Shortly afterward he had sent the captured Zapato Tuerto to Patules' camp near the presidio of El Norte with his terms for the return of the fourteen Mescaleros he held; Patule had delivered him two of his own captives and three Mescaleros as hostages; but Ugalde had still failed to release his prisoners. After Ugalde returned from his campaign, Captain Díaz sent Patule under escort of a sergeant and six soldiers to obtain the release of the captives. By this time the Mescaleros had delivered nine of their prisoners, but on August 31 Patule returned with the sad news that Ugalde still refused to restore those he held. Díaz now feared that the Mescaleros were ready to revolt.[49]

[47] Rengel to Díaz, El Paso, July 30, 1787 (cert. copy), AGN, PI 112, Expediente 1.
[48] Ugarte to Rengel, Arispe, September 6, 1787 (cert. copy), AGN, PI 112, Expediente 1.
[49] Díaz to Rengel, El Norte, August 31, 1787, AGN, PI 112, Expediente 1.

Ugalde's version of the proceedings was entirely different. After attacking four supposedly hostile bands between the end of March and the second week in May, he had overtaken a fifth band in the Sierra de Guadalupe. This band had just been attacked by the Comanches and was suffering heavy losses and fleeing to the sand dunes when Ugalde struck. His forces killed the chief, captured several others, took most of their goods, and redeemed one captive. Then, after a march of several hundred miles to the north in June, he reached a large encampment of Lipiyán Apaches under a great chief who sought and was accordingly granted Spanish protection under Ugalde's terms. Returning to the south, he found and attacked still another Mescalero camp, on July 25, in the mountains forming the northern rim of the Bolsón de Mapimí. When he learned from this group that its chiefs, Patule and El Quemado, had gone to Santa Rosa, the capital of Coahuila, to seek "peace terms," he granted an armistice of fifteen days. Then, returning to Santa Rosa himself, he ended his campaign of almost seven months on August 7. According to his own reckoning, Ugalde had personally been in the field for 203 days, had marched a total of 1,011 leagues (almost 2,630 miles), had found 31 "enemy" campsites, had encountered Mescalero, Lipiyán, "Sembrador," and "Pedrero" Apaches, had killed 40 warriors, captured 220, released several of their captives, and had taken 600 horses and a considerable amount of booty, all with a loss to his own force of only 8 killed and 5 wounded.[50]

Back in Santa Rosa, Ugalde found "for the first time" the letters Ugarte had sent him from Arispe between April 19 and May 28 regarding the Mescalero truce. In three letters of his own Ugalde sought to justify his failure to abide by the *Comandante General's* orders. Praising his own campaign and long service,

[50] Ugalde, Extracto y Sumario de la primera Campaña, *loc. cit.*; Ugalde, Sumario que ha formado el Colonel Don Juan de Ugalde . . . de la Campaña que ha celebrado . . . a la Apachería India gentil, con paricularidad la Mescalera Enemiga la mas común . . . , Santa Rosa, September 13, 1787, AGN, PI 112, Expediente 1.

he declared that he had thrown the enemy Apaches into consternation and would have finished them for good had it not
been for the "incomprehensible" granting of a truce at El Norte.
He had himself refused to give asylum to the Mescaleros, who
had sought it from fear of the very sound of his name, because
of the bloody atrocities they had committed (in July of 1786) at
Sabana Grande, Gruñidora, Mazapil, Cedros, and other places.
They had sought peace at El Norte only through fear of the
rigorous and just pursuit of his own army. He did not go into
detail about this or about Ugarte's orders to restore the captive
Mescaleros except to say that he had taken them from "those
cruel assassins" in a just war, at great risk, and with the glorious
sacrifice of the blood of his own troops, and that he had acted in
the best service of God, the king, the fatherland, and even of
Ugarte.[51]

Only in respect to his attack on the Mescaleros at the northern
rim of the Bolsón de Mapimí did he explain his actions fully, and
even then he couched his explanation in flowery prose inter-
spersed with justifications, circumlocutions, and extensive gratuitous remarks. Reduced to its essence, one of Ugalde's patrols had
discovered that camp with the aid of Zapato Tuerto and took it
without a fight when the Mescaleros, about forty in number,
realized that they were confronted with his troops. When Ugalde
arrived at the scene, he was greeted by a procession of the
Indians who begged for his hand in peace, and when he learned
that their chiefs, Patule and El Quemado, were in Santa Rosa to
talk terms, he gave them an armistice of fifteen days. Then, on
his way back to Santa Rosa, he met Patule and El Quemado at
the Río de Sabinas on August 8 and gave them a two-hour lecture
charging them with their iniquities and indicating his scorn for
them. Duly intimidated, they accepted his offer for an armistice
and declared that they knew they would find no honor or security
at the presidio of El Norte, not even any food, for the Gila

[51] Ugalde to Ugarte, Nos. 11 and 12, Santa Rosa, August 11 and 12, 1787,
AGN, PI 112, Expediente 1.

Apaches were boldly attacking the settlements of Nueva Vizcaya, and the Mescaleros feared that these hostilities would be attributed to themselves.[52]

At Santa Rosa, on August 11, Ugalde summoned the two chiefs again, this time to a junta made up of "all" the Mescalero and Lipán Apaches, the provincial military officers, and the residents of the town. There he repeated his charges and threats and asked them why they had left El Norte to seek peace from him, since he had never offered it to them. Then, in view of "powerful considerations which he would explain in due time," he reluctantly gave them three months of grace in which to prove their sincerity and good conduct and to witness his own. He then presented his terms for peace, to which they agreed with demonstrations of joy and friendship, indicating that the other chiefs, including that of the "Cendés," would also accept the terms when they learned of them. The Mescaleros then asked Ugalde to allow them to bring all their families and horses from the presidio of El Norte so they might reside under Ugalde's protection. Ugalde consented to this. Then Patule and El Quemado left with some of their warriors, leaving others behind with their families. Ugalde considered it a very rare event that his most formidable and only remaining enemies had come to him to surrender without his having pursued them, which he might easily have done. His own procedure, he professed, had been in keeping with Ugarte's ideas.[53]

As conditions for the peace Ugalde had insisted that the Mescaleros recognize a single, principal chief for all of their bands, whom he would appoint; that all of their bands assemble in the land between the headwaters of the Río de Sabinas and the Paso de Longoria; that they confine their hunting to the terrain between the Río de Sabinas and the Río Grande; that they sustain themselves on game and the rations of meat, corn, sugar, and tobacco that he would issue; that they be responsible to him and

[52] Ugalde to Ugarte, No. 14, Santa Rosa, August 12, 1787, AGN, PI 112, Expediente 1.
[53] Ibid.

accept severe punishment for the slightest hostility; that they join the troops in pursuit of those who committed such offenses, each of their leaders receiving four bridled horses for this service; that they keep the peace with all of the Spaniards and with the Indians who were at peace with them; and, finally, that in three months Ugalde would determine how well they had conducted themselves.[54]

It would seem that either Ugalde was misrepresenting the facts or that he was being grossly misled by the Mescaleros, who might well have been playing the military commanders of Coahuila and Nueva Vizcaya against each other. Instead of taking their bands to Coahuila and residing there under Ugalde's protection, in accordance with his terms, the Mescaleros in fact continued to reside near the presidio of El Norte. Less than three weeks after Patule and El Quemado reportedly agreed to Ugalde's terms, Captain Díaz informed the Commandant-Inspector that there were ten Mescalero bands at the presidio, that Patule had returned from Santa Rosa on August 31 with the sad news that Ugalde had refused to deliver his captured tribesmen, that those living at the presidio were preparing to leave for their annual buffalo hunt, and that they had asked for and been granted an escort of presidial troops. Since Ugalde was still holding their kinsmen at Santa Rosa, there were symptoms of a brewing revolt, and Díaz had acceded to this request in order to forestall it.[55] Obviously, either Díaz or Ugalde had misread, or was misrepresenting, the true intentions of the Mescaleros.

Rengel approved furnishing the Mescaleros with a military escort but provided Díaz with detailed instructions for the assignment. Presuming that over 300 Mescaleros would participate in the hunt, he specified that they be accompanied by 70 or more soldiers. Captain Elguezabal was to be in command and was to see that the troops remained united at all times. The Mescaleros were to be prohibited from attacking any Coman-

[54] *Ibid.*
[55] Díaz to Rengel, El Norte, August 30 and 31, 1787 (cert. copies), AGN, PI 112, Expediente 1.

ches whom they might encounter and to confine their hunting to lands south of the Comanche range. They were also to be prevented from combining with any Gila Apaches who might have strayed that far eastward. The troops were to observe their conduct closely, and the interpreters were to spy on their activities and endeavor to overhear their secret conversations. The troops were to maintain harmony with the Mescaleros but not become so familiar with them as to lose their respect. The Indians should be induced to leave their families at the presidio as hostages for their good conduct. Experience had shown that the buffalo ranged in the northern latitudes until the freezes in December obliged them to move southward toward the Mescalero country, and Rengel thought that if the Mescaleros could delay their departure until that season, the chance of an encounter with the Comanches would be more remote.[56]

As events developed the Mescaleros and their escort did not adhere strictly to Rengel's instructions. The several bands of Mescaleros were scheduled to assemble on September 20 at a place known as Las Varas de San Juan and proceed to the hunting grounds under Captain Elguezabal and a party of 100 troops. Three bands—those of Alegre, Volante, and a lesser chief, called Joseph—accompanied the troops to the appointed site but did not find the other bands there. It was later explained that the bands under Cuerno Verde, Bigotes El Bermejo, Montera Blanca, the Lipiyán chief El Calvo, and El Natagée had waited at the rendezvous point for ten days, until September 30, and had then gone on to the north by themselves to hunt in the Guadalupe Mountains. Meanwhile the other three bands continued eastward under escort to the buffalo range between the Nueces and Colorado Rivers in Texas, where for about two months they made their kills, butchered, and prepared hides for future use. They returned to the presidio on November 30. Elguezabal reported that the Mescaleros comported themselves well during the entire expedition, and that only two incidents worth noting

[56] Rengel to Díaz, El Paso, September 7, 1787 (cert. copy), AGN, PI 112, Expediente 1.

Lipán Apache warrior.

From Emory's *Report on the . . . Mexican Boundary Survey*

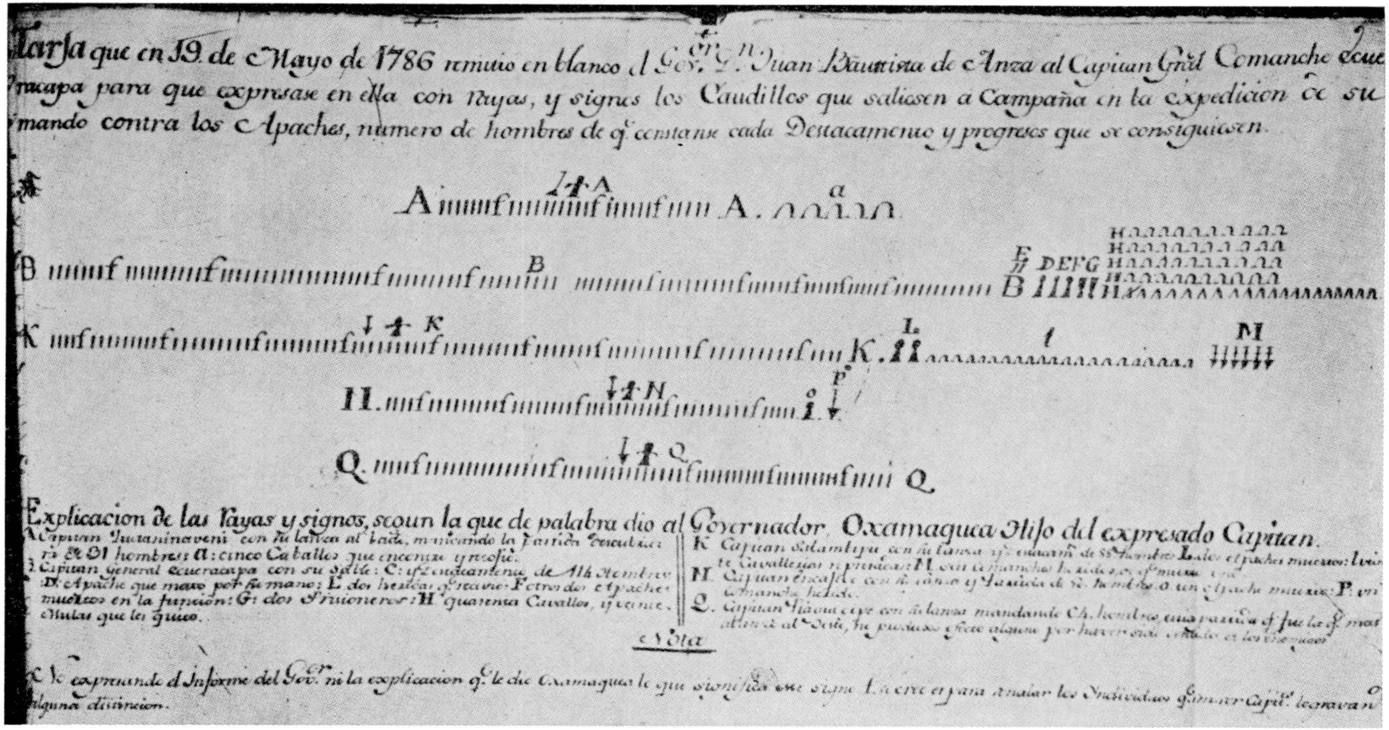

A Comanche record of a Comanche-Apache battle, 1786.

From A. B. Thomas, *Forgotten Frontiers*

occurred. One soldier was killed when his horse stumbled in a prairie dog hole and fell on him, and a demented servant of the muleteers strayed, became lost, and was found dead, pierced three times by a lance. Both the troops and the Mescaleros tried to trail the culprits, but their tracks were obliterated by those of an immense buffalo herd. On the return of the three bands and the troops, Volante and Alegre sent couriers to summon the others from the Guadalupe Mountains.[57]

Meanwhile, in Sonora Ugarte had at long last received replies from Ugalde to those orders he had issued between April 19 and May 28 respecting the Mescalero truce at El Norte. Ugalde had also sent him a summary of his campaign diary, and Ugarte was alarmed at the impression these reports would make on the new viceroy. In order to counteract the distortions he considered these to be, he wrote Viceroy Flores at great length on October 15, summarizing all of the developments in the Mescalero affair since the Mescaleros' first overtures for peace in January, and attaching certified copies of the documents in his possession that substantiated his own contentions.[58]

Instead of carrying out his cease-fire orders of April 19 and returning the Mescalero prisoners he had taken, Ugalde had continued to avoid complying with these directives even after acknowledging them on returning from his campaign. As Ugarte saw it, Ugalde had pretended that the Mescaleros had been admitted to peace during the climax of his own offensive operations against them and that the prisoners had been taken in a just war. Ugarte could not understand how Ugalde could claim credit for inducing them to seek peace by intimidation when the very order of April 19, to which he was replying, made it clear that the Mescaleros had already requested peace on January 30, well before he was operating in their territory. Nor could Ugarte conceive how Ugalde could call a just war the attacks that his forces had made on Indians who were living in good faith under the

[57] Díaz to Ugarte, El Norte, November 30, 1787 (cert. copy), AGN, PI 112, Expediente 2.

[58] Ugarte to Flores, Nos. 5 and 6, Arispe, October 15, 1787, AGN, PI 112, Expediente 1.

protection of a truce. Ignorance of the facts might have justified the first attack, he admitted, but those attacks Ugalde made after receiving Captain Elguezabal's letter were inexcusable. And in neither case should he have refused to return the prisoners and goods he had captured, in view of Ugarte's orders, especially since the Mescaleros had obligingly surrendered nine captives of their own. The report of Captain Díaz to Rengel of August 31 clearly showed that Chief Patule had gone to Santa Rosa under military escort to recover the prisoners held there, but Ugalde, feigning not to understand these circumstances, reported surprise that the bands of Patule and El Quemado had offered no resistance to his forces and that the two chiefs had come to Santa Rosa to surrender to him. The sinister impressions that Ugalde's conduct had caused among the Mescaleros was responsible for their suspicions, mistrust, and complaints, and hence their delay in establishing fixed residences under a secure peace. This peace would continue to be in jeopardy unless Ugalde complied with the promised restitution of prisoners, horses, and goods. All of this was demonstrated in the accompanying documents. If Ugalde did not co-ordinate his subsequent conduct and dispositions with those of Ugarte, who was well informed of the operations in the several frontier provinces, the obstacles to a permanent peace would be insurmountable.[59]

Ugarte only hoped that the results of Ugalde's extensive campaign corresponded with the efforts of his troops. The campaign would have been even more successful had it not destroyed the uniforms, arms, and horses of the troops, indebted the soldiers beyond their means, inactivated them, and thus delayed any further operations on their part for a long time. Ugarte thought the results were also questionable in view of Ugalde's own reports that Indian attacks were still occurring in Coahuila, Texas, and especially Nuevo Santander, and that the mission Indians had rebelled in Nuevo León. At the time Ugalde took command of these eastern provinces, there were few such attacks in Coahuila and almost none at all in Texas.[60]

[59] *Ibid.*   [60] *Ibid.*

As for the truce at the presidio of El Norte's having prevented Ugalde from completely exterminating his enemies, Ugarte explained that not only was the armistice granted before Ugalde attacked them but that its terms conformed to Gálvez's *Instrucción* of 1786 and was in the spirit of several other royal decisions. Ugarte could not have denied the Mescaleros their request simply because they had bloodied their hands in the prior assaults on Sabana Grande, Gruñidora, and other places Ugalde mentioned, and because stolen horses had been found among them, as Ugalde also reported. These Mescalero hostilities had been committed in wartime and were thus not crimes. Furthermore, the articles of the *Instrucción* of 1786 specifically required that the Apaches be conceded peace each time they asked for it as there was less harm in a bad peace than in a good war.[61]

Having dispatched this justification of his policy to the Viceroy, Ugarte issued Captain Díaz a new set of instructions for solidifying the Mescalero peace. He thought that providing the Mescaleros with a military escort for their annual buffalo hunt would alleviate some of their restlessness arising from Ugalde's attacks, but he did not believe they would cease their demands for the restoration of their captured kinsmen and goods. However, he ventured, their feelings were probably more vehemently for revenge than for sorrow over their losses, and so Díaz must assure them of the *Comandante General's* protection and determination to make up for their losses. Díaz must try to persuade them that Ugalde had acted under some misunderstanding or failure to receive Ugarte's orders, that the misfortunes were due in part to their own straying from the lands assigned to them, and that everything was being done to prevent a repetition of such mistakes. If this explanation should restore tranquility among them and induce them to keep the peace, Díaz should determine the kinship of the prisoners with those demanding their return, the amount of goods taken from them, and the names of each who suffered a loss, so that if Ugalde did not return them, some satisfactory means of compensation might be adopted.

[61] *Ibid.*

Even if the prisoners themselves should not be returned, Ugarte suggested with some cynicism that conjugal love was not so strong among barbarians that it could not be compensated by material objects. The love they professed for their children was no more intimate than that which they held for goods, and their friendships were based on even weaker principles. Thus, Díaz might promise each Indian who had lost his squaw another of his choice from those whom the Spaniards might capture from enemy tribes, and for those who might have lost children, fathers, brothers, and other kinsmen, Díaz might attempt to satisfy them with horses, mules, or other effects. Less heartlessly, Ugarte felt that these might also be offered for the goods that had been taken from them. But Díaz should be careful that the Mescaleros not pretend to greater losses while at peace than they had actually suffered.[62]

Having dissipated the rancor and suspicions of the Mescaleros and assured himself of their good faith for a permanent peace, Díaz was then to inform them that Articles 1, 2, 3, 8, 9, 10, and 11 of the capitulation required by Ugarte on February 12 remained in full force and must again be ratified by them. Article 7 was to be modified to allow the Mescaleros to come to a presidio only with the advanced permission of its commandant and to the towns only with a temporary, written license from the post commander nearest their camps. In keeping with Article 10—requiring them to present all their animals for branding—they were to be warned that they could acquire no other animals except through trade among themselves or by donation from the Spaniards. This was to induce them to raise horses and cattle themselves or to go to war against the hostile tribes and capture their livestock. In all cases they must have their own animals branded, and those not appropriately marked would be confiscated from them. In regard to Díaz's report to Rengel of June 30, Ugarte thought it reasonable that the Mescalero bands would not live together in a single town, substitute Spanish foods for their own, dedicate themselves to unaccustomed labor, accept

[62] Ugarte to Díaz, Arispe, October 30, 1787 (cert. copy), AGN, PI 112, Expediente 1.

the leadership of a single chief, or sacrifice for the common welfare their individual liberty and independence, as required by Articles 4, 5, and 6, and so Díaz should relieve them of those obligations. Ugarte counted on the effect of time and care to attract them to Spanish foods, clothing, and other commodities. Therefore they should be allowed to establish themselves, as they requested, in the mountains and around the springs near the presidio and maintain themselves there from the gathering of wild fruits and hunting of deer and buffalo, as was their custom.[63]

However, Ugarte was establishing certain specific limitations. They must report to Díaz where each band was encamped and not move to another site without his prior permission. They must not come within the line of presidios except to trade and with the requisite permission. They must renounce the Bolsón de Mapimí and all its mountains. And they must encourage their children to take up farming. In keeping with these points, the armies of Nueva Vizcaya and Coahuila would be free to operate throughout both provinces, and within the Bolsón de Mapimí, as far north as the line of presidios, and they would capture or kill any Mescalero found beyond their restricted reservations without the required written permit. In order to distinguish the men of the peaceful bands from those who continued to rob and kill, Ugarte thought it would be appropriate to have them wear a special device. This could be a circular badge made of scarlet and either blue or white cloth, about three or four inches in diameter, divided into quarters by the two colors, and sewn to their leather shirts. To prevent the enemy from appropriating the insignia from one of their victims and securing the protection it guaranteed, Ugarte suggested that a piece of antelope skin with a distinctive mark burned on it should be inserted between the badge and the shirt to which it was sewn. He felt that the vanity and inclination of the Mescaleros for anything ornamental would make them willing to wear the insignia, even though it would incriminate them if they should be caught with stolen goods or out of their prescribed boundaries.[64]

[63] *Ibid.*   [64] *Ibid.*

Ugarte insisted that the Spanish troops operate with such discretion as not to punish those who remained faithful, but he required that the Mescaleros inform the nearest military post of any intended attack or theft of which they might hear, and surrender any of their own people whom they found with stolen property. Otherwise the troops must proceed against the entire encampment with full military force. Díaz must never trust the Mescaleros. Rather, he was to maintain a careful vigilance and place paid informants among them. He might also try to form a dominant party among them, composed of those most faithful to the peace, agreeable to the Mescaleros at large, and inclined to get along with the Spaniards. This group might serve as an example to the others and keep order among all, for the establishment of such a party was a well-practiced technique and had been one of the principal means of assuring the tranquility of uncivilized tribes. Natural mistrust made the "barbarians" variable, timid, apprehensive, and susceptible to every bad impression, Ugarte believed, but when some of the principal tribesmen lived in good faith and experienced sincere and frank treatment, their own tranquility tended to dissipate the pusillanimity of the others. This had been tried and proved among the Chiricahuas in Sonora, and Díaz must now establish and maintain such a loyal nucleus among the Mescaleros. Above all, after the Spaniards had ratified the peace treaty, Díaz must employ the friendly Mescaleros in the war against the rebel bands, whether of their own kind or others, in conjunction with the troops, as specified in Ariticle 11. If Díaz could manage to bloody their hands on the neighboring Apaches once, it would keep them more securely devoted to the Spanish cause, for they would then live in fear of the vengeance of those they had aggravated.[65]

The soundness of Ugarte's new instructions was never tested. Soon after he dictated them he received the order from Viceroy Flores, dated October 8, which transferred all authority to make war on or peace with the Mescaleros from his office to that of Ugalde. Ugarte was adamant. Responding in another lengthy

[65] *Ibid.*

discourse on the alleged misrepresentations of his subordinate in Coahuila, Ugarte declared that leaving such decisions to Ugalde would produce an irremediable setback to the progress toward universal peace on the frontier. Ugarte had already offered articles of capitulation, which coincided with Flores' policy, and which he would no doubt approve. That Ugalde had concluded more important pacts with the principal chief of the Lipiyanes was gratifying, but Ugarte had long known that these Apaches were not a distinct nation from the Mescaleros. As for Ugalde's reported negotiations with a congregation of Mescaleros on the banks of the Río de Sabinas, Ugarte had already demonstrated that these were the bands of Patule and El Quemado who merely went there to reclaim their captured kinsmen, not to negotiate peace with Ugalde. In contending the contrary Ugalde was merely trying to confound matters and feign ignorance of the facts in order to erase the charge against him of insubordination. Captain Díaz, who was in charge of the peace negotiations at El Norte, was, on the other hand, an officer of prudence and sufficient will to manage this delicate matter successfully. Ugarte was also astonished that Ugalde complained that the Comanches had deprived him of the glory of defeating a band of Apaches in the Aguaje del Tabaco by destroying them before he arrived. Such a contention would make the Comanches and other so-called Nations of the North appear as enemies unworthy of Spanish assistance and support in their attacks on the Apaches. This was too absurd for further comment, and Flores had already warned Ugalde about harboring such notions. The Spaniards had concluded a solemn peace with the powerful Comanche nation in New Mexico, and Ugarte considered this and the peace with the other Nations of the North far preferable to one with the Apaches, since the Comanches could supply the means for the entire reduction or extermination of the latter.[66]

Ugarte's appeal fell on deaf ears. Not only did Flores refuse him authority over war and peace with the Mescaleros, but he also deprived him of all jurisdiction over Ugalde and the eastern

[66] Ugarte to Flores, Arispe, November 12, 1787, AGN, PI 112, Expediente 1.

frontier provinces. Dividing the Provincias Internas del Norte into two separate general commands, the Viceroy raised Ugalde's rank to that of Ugarte. Moreover, since Nueva Vizcaya was now under heavy attack by invading Gila Apaches, Flores ordered Ugarte to transfer himself at once from Arispe to Chihuahua in order to direct its defense personally.[67]

Ugalde had reported on October 22 that he had admitted to peace under specified conditions 8 chieftains and 140 other Mescaleros, adults and children, who were now assembled near the Río de Sabinas, and Flores had approved the articles of capitulation. Now, on November 21, he wanted Ugarte to demand that the Mescaleros residing near the presidio of El Norte embrace the same terms under penalty of full military prosecution. He also ordered both commandant-generals to combine their military operations in incessant patrols of the sierras and springs of the Bolsón de Mapimí so as to keep it free of enemies and thus prevent further hostilities in Coahuila and Nueva Vizcaya. Since the four eastern provinces under Ugalde's command were suffering few attacks and yet had more troops, Ugarte could count on military aid from that quarter for the more extensive province of Nueva Vizcaya. Or, at least, so the Viceroy informed him.[68]

Replying finally to Ugarte's heavily-documented refutation of Ugalde's reports and justification of his own policies, of October 15, Flores declared that he was almost convinced that the promises of the Mescaleros were false and should be depreciated and that war should be waged against them. The peace they had solicited in January had not been due to their having been intimidated by the troops, as required by the *Instrucción* of 1786, and so its acceptance amounted only to a dispensation. They had not complied with the capitulations and had not demonstrated true fear and sincere abjection. Their perfidious conduct was not a

[67] Flores to Ugarte, México, November 21, 1787 (draft), AGN, PI 112, Expediente 1.

[68] Flores to Ugarte, México, November 21, 1787 (draft), AGN, PI 112, Expediente 3.

result of Ugalde's failure to return their captive kinsmen but was rather the justification of Ugalde's attack. Flores did not excuse Ugalde's failure to respond to Ugarte's orders, and he appreciated Ugarte's own mature and judicious procedure, but the division of the commandancy-general offered the best means of reducing the Mescaleros. Ugarte should declare war on them in Nueva Vizcaya at once. They should not have been given an escort for their buffalo hunting expedition, for this violated Articles 177, 179, 180 of the *Instrucción* of 1786 and risked a breach of the peace with Comanches. Furthermore, according to Flores, the new demands of the Mescaleros were inadmissible, and those among them who wished to be friends must now assemble on the banks of the Río Sabinas with those already under Ugalde's protection. There they would not suffer the scarcities and misery that existed at the presidio of El Norte, and there they could also be watched more closely. Henceforth, no Mescalero could be admitted to peace in Nueva Vizcaya on any pretext whatsoever, and all who did not remove to the reservation on the Sabinas would be considered avowed enemies. The same would hold for any who left Coahuila without a safe-conduct pass. The troops of Nueva Vizcaya, now unembarrassed by the obligations of the pact with the Mescaleros, should engage in frequent campaigns along the frontier and into the Bolsón de Mapimí and punish all of the bands they might encounter. Flores was now ordering Ugalde to have the troops of Coahuila do likewise. Ugalde was to return the Mescalero prisoners that he had taken on his last campaign as soon as all were assembled on the Sabinas. And, finally, Ugalde was to report regularly to Ugarte on all developments in that quarter.[69]

The Viceroy's instructions to Ugalde were essentially the same as those to Ugarte, but there was one notable difference. Ugalde was to deliver his captives to the Mescaleros only if he thought it proper to do so! Also the prohibition against military

---

[69] Flores to Ugarte, México, December 4, 1787 (draft), AGN, PI 112, Expediente 3.

escorts for the Mescaleros was to apply to the Lipanes and Lipiyanes as well.[70]

Thus, in less than a year after its inception the peace at the presidio of El Norte was nullified, and the Mescaleros were left entirely to the mercies of their vindictive nemesis. Moreover, the impetuous Ugalde now held equal status with the more reasonable Ugarte. With the backing of Viceroy Flores, he was now not only vested with independent authority but, in the matter of war or peace with the Eastern Apaches, his decisions took precedence over those of the veteran Ugarte. The Mescaleros and their kinsmen would soon feel the wrath of their foremost antagonist.

[70] Flores to Ugalde, México, December 5, 1787 (draft), AGN, PI 112, Expediente 3.

CHAPTER X

THE EASTERN APACHES
1788-1791

When Ugarte received a copy, which the Viceroy had sent him, of Ugalde's articles for the capitulation of the Mescaleros in Coahuila, he was even more incensed than before over the transfer of the peace arrangements to his rival. Flores had preferred Ugalde's conditions to his own, he complained, but Ugalde had done little more than paraphrase those which Ugarte himself had imposed and change their numerical order. Meanwhile, Ugarte had added a new requirement of his own, in keeping with Flores' order of November 21. The Mescaleros at the presidio of El Norte were not to extend their wanderings into the Bolsón de Mapimí.[1]

Ugarte's most eloquent protest against the Viceroy's new policies was in response to the order of December 4, requiring him to send to Coahuila all the Mescaleros who wished peace and announcing the impending division of the commandancy-general. Referring again to his profusely documented discourses of October 15 and November 12, the contentious *Comandante General* reviewed the facts of the case and bolstered his previous defense. He had now carefully examined the pertinent requirements of Gálvez's *Instrucción* of 1786—Articles 24, 29, 36 through 48, and 195—and had found that his concession of peace to the Mescaleros had been in both the spirit and letter of these specifications. They all supported his policy of waging an active and

[1] Ugarte to Flores, Arispe, December 24, 1787, AGN, PI 112, Expediente 2.

incessant war on the Apaches for the purpose of compelling them to sue for peace, of conceding peace every time and every place they might request it, notwithstanding their known propensities for breaking it, of taking up arms again each time they did break it until they were sufficiently humiliated to request it again, of accepting their overtures even though they had broken the peace many times, of thus alternating peace and war by the maxim established in Articles 29, 43, and 44, and, notwithstanding their many treacherous acts, of preferring the bad results of such a peace to those of an open war. As Neve and Rengel had done in the past, Ugarte had carried on a vigorous and damaging war against the Mescaleros and other Apaches for three and one-half years. A solid peace had been made with the Comanches, who had then attacked the Mescaleros from the north, sometimes in company with the troops and sometimes by themselves; his own forces were battering the Apaches from the south; and, as a result, Nueva Vizcaya had been suffering less from their incursions than in the past. This was the decadent situation of the Mescaleros when eight of their chieftains requested peace on January 30, 1787. Ugarte had never believed that their overtures were due only to their being pursued by Ensign Granados. The very fact that they had sued for peace without having been intimidated by the troops proved that they were impelled by other, more powerful forces, that they were caught between two enemies of superior strength, the Comanches in the north and the presidial troops in the south. This was what the *Instrucción* of 1786 required as justification for conceding peace, and Ugarte could not have refused to grant it without evading its requirements. Nor could his subalterns have contravened his orders once they were issued.[2]

Ugarte did not apologize for the Mescaleros. Eighteen years of service in the frontier provinces had taught him the character of the barbarous tribes, how little faith could be placed in their words and offers, and what their motives were for imploring piety. He had gained a great deal of experience with their bad

---

[2] Ugarte to Flores, Arispe, January 5, 1788, AGN, PI 112, Expediente 2.

relations and ingratitudes, and he therefore had no illusions regarding their current pretensions for peace. But neither had Gálvez, whose policy was to gain as much as possible from them, realizing very well that no elements of the human species were so ferocious that they could not be civilized by some means. Ugarte's policies toward the Mescaleros were the same as those that Gálvez had established. They conformed also to Title 10, Article 1, of the *Reglamento de 1772* and to several other of the king's endorsements, notably the royal order of 1779. Ugarte had the texts of all of these in mind when the Mescaleros sued for peace, and he knew their proposals well, for he was in Chihuahua at the time and had specified the conditions for accepting them. He had done the same for the Chiricahua and Mimbres Apaches, who were now at peace, and against this background he had dictated the articles of capitulation for the Mescaleros on February 12, 1787.[3]

Ugarte's authority as *Comandante General* of all the northern frontier at that time gave his measures all the force and efficacy necessary; his subalterns obeyed them. Only Ugalde tried to elude them, and by his imprudent maneuvers and tenacious habit of contradicting orders he had managed to destroy the integrated policies of Ugarte's strategy. In spite of Ugalde's insulting conduct, Ugarte had tried to appeal to reason and to the true interests of the royal service, employing the most suave and moderate means to win his co-operation. He could easily have forced Ugalde to obey by using his full powers, and he would perhaps have gone to this extreme had Ugalde remained under his command and continued in disobedience. Flores had applauded his own conduct, and this was some satisfaction.[4]

Ugarte had later made some changes in the capitulations, partly because of the incidents resulting from Ugalde's campaign and partly because of his own realization that the Mescaleros could not comply with some of the conditions. It was necessary

[3] *Ibid.* Although the Chiricahua peace dated from September, 1786, the Mimbreño overtures did not take place until March, 1787, a month after Ugarte established the terms for the Mescalero pact.

[4] *Ibid.*

to keep in mind their peculiar ideas, customs, means of subsistence, and chain of command. Taking these into consideration had enabled the Spaniards to overcome even greater difficulties with the Comanches, and the complete success of their pacification had proved the efficacy of his strategy. In allowing the troops to escort the Mescaleros on their buffalo expedition, Ugarte had in mind dissuading them from any idea they may have entertained of wreaking vengeance on Coahuila or Nueva Vizcaya. He did not suspect even slightly that this assistance would produce the antagonism of the Comanches, which Articles 177 and 178 of the *Instrucción* of 1786 warned against. As a matter of fact, ten deputies from the Comanche nation had been in Chihuahua shortly before, to ratify the peace that had been made in New Mexico, and Ugarte had informed them of the active war, which they were required to make on all rebel Apaches, and the friendship they must maintain with those at peace and with those who were traveling under the protection of the troops. They had accepted this proposal, as could be witnessed in their joining with their former enemies—the Utes, Navahos, and Jicarilla Apaches in New Mexico.[5]

Begrudgingly, Ugarte acknowledged Flores' order to send the Mescaleros from the presidio of El Norte to the banks of the Río de Sabinas, where they could make peace with Ugalde, to deny them peace in Nueva Vizcaya on any terms, and to co-ordinate his own military operations with those of Ugalde. He would comply, but he had to point out that it would be difficult to send all the Mescaleros to Coahuila. Some would refuse to go and, if compelled to do so, would become more hostile in both provinces. It was true that Apache raids had increased in Nueva Vizcaya, but there was no absolute proof that the Mescaleros were involved, even though the new arrangement with them had freed them from their reservation near the presidio. Ugarte had permitted them to leave the presidio mainly because of the inconvenience of their residence there. If they remained docile, that was all that could be expected under the present circum-

[5] *Ibid.*

stances. He was transferring himself from Sonora to Nueva Vizcaya in order to be closer to the problem, and if necessary he would go to the presidio itself. If all of his measures should fail to keep the Mescaleros faithful, he could direct a continuous war on them more easily from that quarter. However, until he received a final decision from Flores on the matter, he would do nothing further.[6] Apparently Ugarte expected the Viceroy to reverse his determination.

Flores, however, had made up his mind that Ugalde's peace pact with the Mescaleros was more secure than Ugarte's. After concluding his seven-months campaign in August of 1787, Ugalde had supposedly received the voluntary surrender at Santa Rosa of a total of 140 Apaches under 8 chieftains. These he identified as Etol-illé, Dajat-te, Pit-syé, Echag-Ydé, Kandeviestin, and the well-known Quijiequsyá (Zapato Tuerto), El Quemado, and Patule. The terms under which he accepted them in peace were approved by the Viceroy on November 5, 1787. On March 5, 1788, the famous Lipiyán chieftain Picax-andé-Instinsle, known in Nueva Vizcaya as El Calvo, also arrived at Santa Rosa. He was accompanied by six other chiefs and fourteen principal warriors, and within five days El Calvo, too, had ratified the capitulations. On Ugalde's request, the Viceroy bestowed upon this worthy the title of *capitán grande* with a stipend of ten reales a day and authority over the six "nations" then at peace in Coahuila.[7]

Meanwhile, Ugarte thought it strange indeed that Ugalde should claim the submission of 8 "Mescalero" chieftains in Coahuila when Captain Díaz had reported that 8 were at peace at the presidio of El Norte. It was also remarkable that the 8 in Coahuila should have only 140 followers, which would amount to only 40 or 50 warriors. He therefore asked Díaz to interrogate the Mescalero chiefs at El Norte about the matter. On January

[6] *Ibid.*

[7] Flores to Ugalde, México, November 21, 1787, and January 8, 1788 (drafts); Ugarte to Diaz, Arispe, December 21, 1787; and Ugalde to Ugarte, San Antonio de Béjar, May 2, 1788 (cert. copies), AGN, PI 112, Expediente 2 and Expediente 3.

20, 1788, the officers at that presidio read aloud the 8 names that Ugalde had listed so that Volante and Alegre, in the presence of several other Mescaleros, might identify them. On hearing them, they laughed, according to Díaz, and then explained that the 5 names given in Apache were only common members of the bands of Patule and El Quemado, and that they were among those who had gone with these two chiefs to reclaim Zapato Tuerto and the other captives whom Ugalde had taken in his campaign of the previous year. Díaz then reported to Ugarte that the only chiefs known among the Mescalero, Natagée, and Lipiyán Apaches during the past decade were the 8 who had come to the presidio in peace early in 1787 (Volante, Alegre, Patule, El Quemado, Bigotes El Bermejo, Montera Blanca, Cuerno Verde, and Zapato Tuerto) and the two who had not arrived, El Calvo and El Natagée. There had been two other chiefs—Patule El Viejo, who had been succeeded by his brother Patule El Chico, and Bigotes El Pelón, now replaced by El Quemado—but these had died several years before.[8]

Reporting this interesting information to Flores, Ugarte reminded him again that it was on his own orders that Patule and El Quemado had been sent under a military escort from the presidio to reclaim their captured tribesmen from Ugalde after three of Zapato Tuerto's people had already gone to him for the same purpose, and that these Mescaleros had not "surrendered" to Ugalde from fear of his armies, as he had claimed. Alegre, Volante, and Joseph had been at the presidio with their people ever since returning from the buffalo hunt at the end of November. Cuerno Verde had arrived shortly thereafter. And Bigotes El Bermejo and Montera Blanca were expected soon. They had all honored their peace terms, and the first three were preparing to lead a party of warriors against the Gila Apaches who were invading the environs of Julimes.[9]

One of Ugarte's ulterior motives in extending an easy peace

[8] Díaz to Ugarte, El Norte, January 20 and 21, 1787, and Elguezabal to Lieut. Francisco Xavier Uranga, deposition, El Norte, January 20, 1788 (cert. copies), AGN, PI 112, Expediente 2.

[9] Ugarte to Flores, Arispe, February 7, 1788, AGN, PI 112, Expediente 2.

Chiricahua Apache shirt, thirty-five inches long.

Deerskin painting of Mexican Indians mounted on rawhide-armored horses attacking an Apache *refugium* or stronghold. This skin was sent by Father Phillip Segesser from a mission in Sonora, Mexico, to his brother in Lucerne, Switzerland.

From George E. Hyde, *Indians of the High Plains*

to the Mescaleros was to recruit them in the war against the Gileños. But now even this felicitous achievement was frustrated. On January 30, 1788, two Indians from the bands of Patule and El Quemado arrived from Coahuila at the Mescalero encampments near El Norte with an ominous message. Within two months, they said, Ugalde would declare war on them unless they brought their people to him and accepted his terms at Santa Rosa. This so upset the Mescaleros at the presidio that Captain Díaz abandoned his plans to use them against the invading Gileños. In fact, Cuerno Verde, Montera Blanca, Bigotes El Bermejo, and Joseph retired with their followers to the security of the Sierra del Movano shortly after receiving Ugalde's ultimatum. Montera Blanca and Joseph returned with their bands on February 27, and Díaz expected Cuerno Verde and Bigotes El Bermejo to do likewise within two or three days, but all were still fearful. According to Díaz, they were afraid of an attack not only by Ugalde's troops but also by the Gila Apaches, for they had spurned the many invitations of the latter to join in their forays on the settlements of Nueva Vizcaya. Díaz had assured Ugarte with testimony from the troops and magistrates at Parras and Saltillo that the recent attacks in the eastern part of the province had been made by Gileños in concert with renegade Tarahumaras and not by the Mescaleros who had left the presidio reservations.[10]

Although Viceroy Flores had ordered the Mescaleros removed from the presidio to Coahuila, Ugarte had not forced them to go and would not, he said, until he received a final decision from Flores in full consideration of his own objections to the removal. The Mescaleros had been at peace at the presidio for almost a year, and it would be contrary to equity and good faith for Ugarte to break the agreement now. The threats of Ugalde to remove them by force would only induce them to join the hostile Gileños. The residence of the Mescaleros at the presidio might well be the last hope for their pacification, and unless Flores

---

[10] Díaz to Ugarte, El Norte, January 31 and February 28, 1788 (cert. copies), AGN, PI 112, Expediente 2.

restrained Ugalde, Ugarte could not be responsible for the outcome.[11]

At long last, on April 15, 1788, Flores acknowledged Ugarte's letters of January 5 and 8, and February 7 and 17, and handed down a final resolution of the matter. In spite of Ugarte's explanations and arguments, he had found no reason to change his earlier disposition. He would never be persuaded that peace with the Mescaleros and other Apaches would be sincere and lasting anywhere, least of all in Nueva Vizcaya. Experience had proved their peace pacts to be less secure and more tragic there than elsewhere. Nueva Vizcaya was the largest populated territory on the frontier, had the most to lose, and would always be the theater of Apache hostilities. Therefore, weak deferences to the suits for peace by these bands would not diminish their attacks but only increase them, and these would inevitably complete their desolation of the province. Gálvez's system of alternating peace with war might be followed in other provinces but in Nueva Vizcaya the only defense must be the waging of the direst war on all its enemies. The heathen Apaches were the sworn enemies, but they would surrender when they had experienced the rigor of the army's incessant operations. The unfaithful Tarahumaras, being domestic thieves and therefore even more pernicious than the Apaches, would be subjugated by 100 troops, which had been sent to their villages to watch, pursue, and punish them wherever they might go. Peace with the Chiricahuas in Sonora, with the Lipanes, Lipiyanes, and Mescaleros in Coahuila, and with the Nations of the North in New Mexico and Texas would easily free the majority of the troops for the pacification of Nueva Vizcaya, and these Indian allies would aid in draining the blood of the hostile Apaches. It was Ugalde's responsibility to handle peace with the Mescaleros, Lipanes, and Lipiyanes, and these must assemble in Coahuila in order to enjoy its blessings; it was Ugarte's responsibility for the Western Apaches who were gathered in Sonora, the Navahos and

[11] Ugarte to Flores, Arispe, February 16 and March 18, 1788, AGN, PI 112, Expediente 2.

Jicarillas in New Mexico, and for those of the central portion of the frontier who were seeking it at El Paso del Norte. But war must be waged on every Apache who approached the presidios and towns of Nueva Vizcaya without a legal safe-conduct pass. Flores did not wish to consider which bands of the Mescaleros would oppose being concentrated on the banks of the Río de Sabinas or which bands of Gileños would resist being gathered in Sonora or at El Paso, and which preferred to continue their war against Nueva Vizcaya. His resolution was final, and Ugarte must now concentrate on mobilizing his troops and collaborating with Ugalde's military operations.[12]

Had the Viceroy but known what had happened in Coahuila on April 8, he would have been even more emphatic. On that date, while Ugalde was in Texas, the Mescaleros and kindred bands who had been residing under his protection suddenly abandoned their reservation, killed the soldiers who tried to restrain them, and ransacked the ranches along the line of their flight. According to reports reaching Ugalde from his subalterns in Coahuila, the Mescaleros had been provided with adequate rations, treated with kindness, and given no cause whatsoever for their sudden revolt. The event was totally unexpected, and Ugalde could only charge it up to what he considered to be their own charateristic perfidy and the weak and baseless peace pacts that they had entered into only to escape their ultimate ruin.[13]

Some two weeks after the revolt in Coahuila, Díaz received news of it from a squaw belonging to Patule's band who arrived at El Norte. According to her, the Indians assembled in peace at Santa Rosa had killed several soldiers and civilians and all had fled to the Guadalupe and Sacramento Mountains, where most of the invading Gila Apaches were gathered. She also reported that the Mescaleros had had several altercations with Ugalde over their desire to return to the presidio del Norte; that they had gone to Coahuila only to retrieve their captive kinsmen,

[12] Flores to Ugarte, México, April 15, 1788 (draft), AGN, PI 112, Expediente 3.
[13] Ugalde to Ugarte, Campo del Arroyo del Atascoso, April 13, 1788 (cert. copy), AGN, PI 112, Expediente 2.

whom Ugalde had promised to restore as soon as their bands came to him; but that Ugalde had not only refused to deliver their relatives but had also prevented themselves from returning to El Norte, maintaining them in a strict subjection with shouting and threats; and that they had remained with him only until an occasion had arisen for their escape.[14]

A few days later Díaz learned that seven soldiers had perished during the revolt at Santa Rosa; that the rebels were the bands of Patule, El Quemado, and Zapato Tuerto; and that they had gone on foot to the Sierra del Carmen; that El Calvo, El Natagée, and several Lipanes had taken advantage of the revolt to steal horses and head along the Colorado River to the Guadalupe Mountains. Alegre, Volante, and Joseph had remained at the presidio of El Norte in spite of this news, but they were visibly afraid. In fact the three had declared that as soon as the troops of Coahuila arrived, they would flee for their own security, but they would keep Díaz informed of their whereabouts and return as soon as the Coahuila troops were gone. They said that Bigotes El Bermejo and his band, who had fled when Ugalde threatened the Mescaleros at the presidio on January 20, was in the Guadalupe Mountains with the Gila Apaches.[15]

Díaz assured Ugarte that the Mescaleros at the presidio were still loyal. Some of them frowned on the revolt in Coahuila, and even though others attempted to justify it, Díaz had no reason to suspect their motives. In fact, when the news of the event first arrived in their camps, they had sent word instantly to the officer in charge of the presidial horse herd and to several civilians, and the next morning the chieftains themselves had come to the presidio to inform Díaz and warn him to gather up the civilian horses and mules, which were pastured near the river, so as to prevent their being stolen by the rebels.[16]

---

[14] Díaz to Ugarte, El Norte, April 27, 1788 (cert. copy), AGN, PI 112, Expediente 2.

[15] Díaz to Ugarte, El Norte, May 1, 1788 (cert. copy), AGN, PI 112, Expediente 2.

[16] Díaz to Ugarte, El Norte, May 3, 1788 (cert. copy), AGN, PI 112, Expediente 2.

Meanwhile, Ugarte had finally returned to Chihuahua as he had promised. He was arranging for an interview with the Mescalero chieftains residing at the presidio of El Norte, but when the news of the revolt in Coahuila arrived, he canceled it. On April 22 he ordered Díaz to urge the Mescaleros at the presidio reservation to join with the troops in the war on the hostile invaders. The plan was to attack the Gileños and renegade Mescaleros in the Sacramento and Guadalupe Mountains, and Ugarte had ordered the troops of several presidios to unite there under the command of Captain Antonio Cordero of Janos.[17] Once more, however, the enlistment of the Mescaleros as auxiliaries was thwarted.

During the first week of May Ugarte received Flores' final order of April 15, which demanded the immediate expulsion of the Mescaleros from Nueva Vizcaya. Accordingly, on May 7, he ordered Captain Díaz to carry out the unpleasant task. Díaz was to inform the Mescaleros at the presidio of the viceregal decision and require them to leave at once, denying them any excuse, pretext, or delay. He was to urge them to take advantage of Ugalde's peace offer in Coahuila and go directly to Santa Rosa without visiting any other places en route. If they failed to carry out these instructions, war was to be declared on them. Díaz was to send a party of troops a day or two after their departure to watch their movements without exposing themselves to view.[18] On May 20, Ugarte reported to the Viceroy that the expulsion had been accomplished. He wanted Flores to know, however, that the Mescaleros had shown great disappointment. Since Ugalde had still not restored their kinsmen to them, Ugarte expected them to take revenge on him at the first opportune occasion.[19]

As might have been expected, the Mescaleros did not go to Santa Rosa at all. Instead they fled to the mountains and returned from time to time to raid the settlements. By June, 1788, Nueva

[17] Ugarte to Flores, Chihuahua, April 30, 1788, AGN, PI 112, Expediente 2.
[18] Ugarte to Díaz, Chihuahua, May 7, 1788 (cert. copy), AGN, PI 112, Expediente 2.
[19] Ugarte to Flores, Chihuahua, May 20, 1788, AGN, PI 112, Expediente 2.

Vizcaya was under attack by Mescalero and Lipiyán as well as Gila Apaches, and Ugarte's troops were operating against them in shuttle forces of over 150 at a time.[20]

Meanwhile, however, some truth was emerging from the scrambled information the Spaniards had obtained regarding the relationship and identification of the Eastern Apache tribes and bands. In arranging the peace at Santa Rosa, Ugalde had specified that he was dealing with six "nations" (actually they were tribes and bands)—the Lipiyán, Lipán, Mescalero, "Sendé," "Nit-ajende," and "Cachu-ende" tribes—and that these had agreed to accept the over-all leadership of the Lipiyán chief Picax-andé-Instinsle (El Calvo), who was now christened Manuel de Ugalde and dignified by the Viceroy, on January 9, 1788, with the title of *"gran capitán."*[21] According to Antonio Cordero's more comprehensive and disinterested report some eight years later, there were then only four recognized eastern tribes of the Apache nation: the Faraones (*Yntajen-ne*, which included the Jicarillas), the Mescaleros (*Sejen-ne*), the Llaneros (*Cuelcajen-ne*, which included the Llaneros proper, the Lipiyanes, and the Natagees), and the Lipanes (*Lipajen-ne*).[22] Ugalde's "Sendé" seemingly corresponds to Cordero's *Sejen-ne* (Mescaleros); his "Nit-ajende," to the *Yntajen-ne* (Faraones); and his "Cachu-ende," probably to the *Cuelcajen-ne* (Llaneros). Therefore, instead of six "nations" Ugalde seems to have made peace with only four or five tribes—the Lipiyanes, the Lipanes, the Mescaleros, the Faraones, and perhaps the Llaneros proper, who were closely associated with the Lipiyanes under that generic designation.

At a later date Ugalde referred to Volante and Alegre as Cachu-ende (Llanero) chiefs and to Cuerno Verde, Montera Blanca, and Bigotes El Bermejo as "Sendé" (Mescalero) lead-

[20] Ugarte to Flores, Chihuahua, June 12, 1788, AGN, PI 112, Expediente 2.
[21] Ugalde to Ugarte, San Antonio de Béjar, May 2, 1788 (cert. copy), and Flores to Ugalde, México, November 21, 1787, and January 8 and 9, 1789 (drafts), AGN, PI 112, Expediente 2 and Expediente 3.
[22] Matson and Schroeder, "Cordero's Description of the Apache—1796," *loc. cit.*

ers.[23] For their part, Ugarte and his commissioner, Captain Díaz, were less discriminating. At first they reported that there were ten bands of Mescaleros, and when they learned that El Calvo was a Lipiyán chief and El Natagée, a leader of the tribe of the same name, Ugarte pretended that the Mescaleros, Natagees, Llaneros, and Lipiyanes were all, regardless of such designations, united into one "nation."[24] In view of the confusion over band and tribal relationships of the Apache nation, which still exists, the undiscriminating designations of both Ugalde and Ugarte are not surprising.

Ugarte and Díaz did correctly identify the Lipiyán chief Picax-andé-Instinsle, whom Ugalde and the Viceroy had elevated to the principal chieftainship of the Eastern Apaches, as the chief known in Nueva Vizcaya as El Calvo. Ugarte also found him to be the same whom Governor De la Concha had mistakenly identified as a Lipán when he came to New Mexico bearing a passport from Ugalde dated July 12, 1787, to seek peace for his tribesmen in that province. According to the Mescaleros at El Norte, this worthy had joined with El Natagée and several Lipanes in a raid on the presidial horse herd of Coahuila when the Mescaleros revolted there in April of 1788. However, Ugarte was now not sure that he was personally involved in that assault.[25]

When he was apprised of the Mescalero revolt in Coahuila and the failure of those expelled from Nueva Vizcaya to seek Ugalde's protective custody, Viceroy Flores was convinced that his prejudices against the Apaches were fully vindicated. On the basis of his long experience with and understanding of the "voluble character and bad faith of the barbarous Indians," he had neither approved nor disapproved the peace pacts or truces conceded to the Mescaleros. The truces had presented a difficult problem for him, but those "perfidious" Indians had resolved it completely by their "unjust" breach of the peace in Coahuila.

[23] Ugalde to Juan Antonio de Arce, Campo de la Vega del Río Grande, April 23, 1790 (copy), AGN, PI 159, Expediente 6.
[24] Ugarte to Flores, Arispe, February 7, 1788, AGN, PI 112, Expediente 2.
[25] Ugarte to Flores, Chihuahua, June 12, 1788, *loc. cit.*

In view of such an "abominable event," Flores now believed that no confidence should be placed in any of the Apache bands or tribes, and that the Spaniards, no longer working for their voluntary surrender, should exterminate or reduce them by force. Ugalde had proposed this in respect to the Mescaleros, believing that they could be conquered within two years, but Flores had no faith in any Indian who bore the generic name Apache. According to all reports, this nation was "numerous, astute, warlike, and the true destructive enemy" of the frontier provinces. There was no doubt that all of their tribes were linked by the strictest bonds of kinship, friendship, and alliance, and that they were malicious in their relations with the Spaniards and their captives. It would therefore be very difficult to disunite these tribes so they might destroy each other, for, as he understood it, the Apaches had now learned the Spaniards' most secret plans and stratagems, they knew how to evade them, they astutely overran the general defenses, and they would not lose occasion to consummate the ruin of the interior country. These were the reasons why he was ordering the immediate, vigorous, and continuous war against the Mescaleros and denying them peace in any part of the country until they were reduced by force or exterminated. Ugalde had asked him to send overseas the Mescaleros he had captured and to allow him to place in strict confinement those who tried to sue for peace. Flores saw nothing wrong with this and agreed that it be done.[26]

To the king's minister, Flores reported that Coahuila and Nueva Vizcaya were both now under attack—Coahuila from the rebel Mescaleros and Nueva Vizcaya from all Apache tribes and the unfaithful Tarahumaras and Tepehuanas, who were in league with renegade mixed-bloods. Only Texas and New Mexico were quiet. There was friendship, against his own judgment, with the Lipán and Lipiyán Apaches in Coahuila, with the Jicarillas in New Mexico, with the Chiricahuas in Sonora, and supposedly with some bands of the Mescaleros in Nueva Vizcaya, but others of this tribe had broken their pact in Coahuila. He had

[26] Flores to Ugalde, México, June 4, 1788 (draft), AGN, PI 112, Expediente 3.

chosen Ugalde instead of Ugarte to direct the war against the Mescaleros because Ugalde was situated nearer to their range and had the aid of the Lipán and Lipiyán bands who remained at peace in Coahuila. He had placed Ugarte in charge of the war against the Gileños in the west, and he was to be assisted by Rengel in Sonora, who had the support of the friendly Chiricahuas. As Nueva Vizcaya had always been the chief target of Apache attacks, no member of that nation was to be admitted to peace there, either now or in the future. On the other hand, there were powerful reasons for preserving friendship at any cost with the Comanches and the Nations of the North in New Mexico and Texas, for there were not enough troops to oppose them.[27]

Meanwhile, on May 6, Flores had ordered Ugarte to meet personally with Ugalde and reach an agreement on reciprocal military assistance, combined operations, and harmonious correspondence with each other. Ugarte did attempt to arrange an interview with Ugalde on the banks of the Río de Aguanaval, which separated their respective territories. But since Ugalde was then inspecting the troops of Nuevo Santander, Ugarte planned to go ahead with his own plans to tour the southern part of Nueva Vizcaya and set up a meeting with him while en route. Before his departure from Chihuahua he received a new order from Flores, dated June 17. This officially placed Ugalde in charge of the war against the Mescaleros and himself in command of the defense of Nueva Vizcaya from the Gileños and from other hostile attacks. It also provided that Ugarte must furnish Ugalde with troops from the presidios of El Norte, El Príncipe, San Carlos, and the light-horse company stationed at Guajoquilla. Ugarte felt that this would compromise his defense of the eastern frontier of Nueva Vizcaya.[28]

At the end of July Ugarte left Chihuahua and began his southern tour, passing through the Valle de San Bartolomé, the Real de Cuencamé, the haciendas of La Zarca and El Pasage, and the

---

[27] Flores to Valdés, México, June 24, 1788, AGN, CV 146, Fojas 442–48.
[28] Ugarte to Flores, Chihuahua, June 5 and July 10, 1788, AGN, PI 112, Expediente 2.

city of Durango, where he remained for a week in November, before he then returned to Chihuahua at the end of the year. He had apprised Ugalde of his itinerary, indicating the time and place he would be at the Río de Aguanaval or some other nearby place, and he had waited at each stop on his tour for a reply. But all he had received from Ugalde were two letters explaining that it was inconvenient for him to meet with Ugarte at that time.[29]

Meanwhile, the war went on, and Nueva Vizcaya suffered heavily from Apache attacks, whether Mescalero as Flores believed or Gileños as Ugarte suspected. In November Ugarte complained that he could not prevent the raids on the eastern settlements near the Bolsón de Mapimí because Flores had assigned troops from the companies of El Norte, El Príncipe, San Carlos, and Guajoquilla to Ugalde.[30]

In Coahuila Ugalde was preparing for an extensive campaign against the Mescaleros and other hostiles. So as to co-ordinate the operations of his own troops with those of his Indian allies, he summoned their *"gran capitán,"* Picax-andé-Instinsle. The Lipiyán chief arrived at Santa Rosa on December 31, 1788, in company with another chief of his tribe, two from the Lipanes, and nine of their distinguished warriors. During a three-day conference Picax-andé promised full military co-operation, but Ugalde became suspicious of his motives.[31] Two visits to the great camp of Picax-andé by an officer of the presidio of Aguaverde and an experienced interpreter confirmed these misgivings, for it was discovered that among the 273 tipis and 157 wickiups there were also 18 Mescalero tents and a large amount of Spanish goods, which were recognizably stolen. A Lipán chief known among the Spaniards as Casimiro informed the officer from Aguaverde that the *"Gran Capitán"* had collaborated with the Mescaleros in their raids, had received some of their stolen

[29] Ugarte to Flores, Chihuahua, July 31; San Bartolomé, August 17, September 15, and October 20; Hacienda de la Zarca, October 31; Hacienda del Pasage, November 7 and 13; Durango, November 18; and San Bartolomé, December 22 and 29, 1788, AGN, PI 112, Expediente 2.

[30] Ugarte to Flores, Durango, November 25, 1788, AGN, PI 128, Expediente 3.

[31] Ugalde to Flores, Santa Rosa, April 1, 1789, AGN, PI 159, Expediente 4.

goods, and was allied by marriage with the Mescalero chief Alegre, each having married a sister of the other. Alegre, moreover, was in Picax-andé's camp at the time of his visit.[32]

While Ugalde's disenchantment with his Lipiyán ally and namesake mounted, he soon found an opportunity to balance the loss. On February 15, 1789, an emissary sent by the Mescalero chiefs Zapato Tuerto and Patule arrived at Santa Rosa to feel out Ugalde for a renewal of their peace pact with him. Normally, Ugalde would have imprisoned the emissary immediately, as he said, but he saw a chance for a major coup and so sent him back with word that he would gladly receive all the Mescalero chiefs. Five of them took the bait, and between February 23 and March 23, 1789, Zapato Tuerto, Patule, El Quemado, and two others whom Ugalde called Dax-até and Tacolk-sú came to Santa Rosa with their bands. In long conversations with Ugalde they professed profound regret for their revolt of the previous April and a great desire for renewing their former pact.[33] Meanwhile, a Mescalero squaw from Volante's band arrived at the presidio of El Norte to dicker for peace in Nueva Vizcaya for her people, but she was turned away.[34]

On March 24, 1789, when all of the followers of the five chiefs were assembled in Santa Rosa to hear the terms for their new capitulation and over 200 troops, drawn from four companies, were inconspicuously stationed in strategic position around them, Ugalde sprang the trap. At a pre-arranged signal while Ugalde himself was addressing the Indian multitude, the troops confronted the unsuspecting tribesmen with arms at the ready. It was all over in a matter of minutes. The five chiefs, twenty-three warriors, twenty-nine squaws, and nineteen children—seventy-six in all—were made prisoner, and two other warriors were killed while attempting to resist arrest. With characteristic braggadocio Ugalde reported the bizarre proceedings in twenty-

[32] Ensign Casimiro Valdés, Diarios, San Fernando and Santa Rosa, January 11 and 21, 1789, AGN, PI 159, Expediente 4.

[33] Ugalde to Flores, Santa Rosa, April 1, 1789, *loc. cit.*

[34] Alberto Maynez to Díaz, El Norte, March 3, and Díaz to Ugarte, Chorreras, March 4, 1789 (copies), AGN, PI 159, Expediente 6.

four sheets tightly written on both sides.[35] Viceroy Flores saw nothing wrong with his procedure, promising to support his appeal for a promotion, and ordered him to send all of the prisoners under maximum security to Mexico City. From there he would send the warriors and squaws overseas.[36]

Four bands of Mescaleros—those of Volante, Cuerno Verde, Bigotes El Bermejo, and Montera Blanca—had not fallen into Ugalde's trap. About a week after their kinsmen were betrayed at Santa Rosa, these four chiefs together with the lesser leader Joseph led their bands to the presidio of El Norte, where Ugarte had been forced to expel them almost a year before, and asked to be accepted again. The commandant turned them away. Ugarte asked the Viceroy for permission to receive them in peace, but Flores, yielding to Ugalde's objections, steadfastly refused.[37]

The peace with the Eastern Apaches had now almost completely evaporated. The Mescalero bands whom Ugalde had not imprisoned were denied peace in Nueva Vizcaya, and Ugalde had turned his back on the Lipiyanes, Lipanes, Natagees, and other assorted followers of Picax-andé in Coahuila. On April 20, 1789, in fact, Ugalde asked Flores for permission to declare war on his former ally, Picax-andé. According to Ugalde, his *"Gran Capitán,"* who had been allied with him for almost two years, had been found to have encouraged the Mescalero revolt of April 8, 1788, at Santa Rosa; he had sheltered enemy Mescaleros at the very time he was promising to hunt them down; and he had received goods that they had stolen in their raids. Flores readily approved Ugalde's request for a declaration of war on the *"Gran Capitán."*[38]

Finally, after a severe drought had delayed its organization,

[35] Ugalde to Flores, Santa Rosa, April 1, 1789, *loc. cit.*
[36] Flores to Ugalde, México, April 29, 1789 (draft), AGN, PI 159, Expediente 5.
[37] Maynez to Díaz, El Norte, April 2 (copy), and Ugarte to Flores, Chihuahua, April 10, 1789, AGN, PI 159, Expediente 6.
[38] Ugalde to Flores, Santa Rosa, April 20, and Flores to Ugalde, México, May 13, 1789 (draft), AGN, PI 159, Expediente 4 and Expediente 5.

Ugalde assembled his military forces on August 12 for a 200-day campaign against the hostiles and set them in motion on August 20. As it developed, the campaign lasted more than 300 days and was a remarkable demonstration of the eastern commander's indefatigable offensive operations. Measured in miles traveled, hardships endured, and energies expended, it must be considered a major military effort. In terms of enemies killed or captured, however, it may not have been worth the price. As in past campaigns, Ugalde so exhausted his troops and horses that they were unfit for follow-up operations, and while they ranged far afield, the hostile Apaches struck the unprotected settlements of Coahuila with deadly effect.

Ugalde's forces attacked Lipiyán and Mescalero camps at the Piedras Negras crossing of the Río Grande on August 20 and others between San Sabá and San Antonio on December 29. Then came the most telling achievement of his campaign, on January 9, 1790. After a large body of Mescaleros, Lipiyanes, and Lipanes had been set upon by an overwhelming number of their ancient enemies, the Nations of the North, Ugalde's troops, with the support of 140 Comanches under seven chiefs, maneuvered the Apaches (10 chiefs and 300 warriors) into a gigantic trap at the Arroyo de la Soledad, on the Río Frío to the west of San Antonio. In a crushing attack Ugalde's troops and allies killed 2 chiefs, 28 warriors, 28 squaws, and 1 child and captured 30 women and children, 800 horses, and a large amount of booty, all with the loss of only 3 soldiers killed and 4 wounded. In lesser actions, Ugalde attacked the western Lipanes in the Guadalupe Mountains on April 10, two camps in the same range on April 11, and a band of Gileños about a day's journey from those mountains on April 19. On April 21, Ugalde arrived in the El Paso district and asked the commandant of the presidio of San Elizeario for reinforcements and aid to continue his operations in the Organo, Mimbres, and Sacramento Mountains. The commandant could spare only 30 horses and 1,200 cartridges. Until then Ugalde had never informed Ugarte of his plans or whereabouts, and the western *Comandante General* refused to issue further reinforcements or supplies.[39]

For all his hard campaigning, intrepid exploits, and boastful manner, Juan de Ugalde had only intensified the hostility of the Apaches, and his days on the frontier were numbered. His first setback came without his knowing it. In October of 1789, during the early stages of his campaign, his patron at Mexico City retired from office because of ill health. Moreover, Flores was succeeded by the Conde de Revillagigedo, who almost immediately reverted to the policies set forth by Viceroy Gálvez. Ugarte may have had some part in the undermining of Ugalde, for three months before Revillagigedo assumed office, he wrote the new Viceroy a confidential letter which damned the eastern commander's policies and operations. This letter and the new Viceroy's reply are not in the files, but something of their nature is evident in another of Ugarte's dispatches to Revillagigedo.

On November 20, 1789, Ugarte informed the new Viceroy that his confidential reply of October 28 to Ugarte's letter of July 17 had filled him with "inexpressible consolation," not only because Revillagigedo's principles for the welfare of the frontier provinces complied with the "pious intentions" of the king, but also because they corresponded with Ugarte's own. Ugarte was grateful for Revillagigedo's acknowledgment of his own dedication to the king's true intentions, and he now declared that the only way the damages to the frontier defenses could be repaired was to reincorporate Texas and Coahuila into his own general command.[40]

Meanwhile Ugalde stood condemned in Revillagigedo's mind from his own reports. Revillagigedo found Ugalde's report to

[39] Ugalde, Estado que Ynsinió extractadamente la obstilidad que sobre la Apachería Enemiga . . . ha verificado el Comandante General de las del Oriente desde el mes de Noviembre de 1786 . . . hasta la fecha, Campo de la Vega, April 23, 1790; Ugalde to Commandant Juan Antonio Arce, Campo de la Vega, April 23, 1790, quoted in Arce to Ugalde, San Elizeario, April 25, 1790 (copy); and Ugarte to the Conde de Revillagigedo, Chihuahua and Hacienda de Encinillas, April 26 and May 4, 1790, AGN, PI 159, Expediente 6.

[40] Ugarte to Revillagigedo (confidential), Chihuahua, November 20, 1789, AGN, PI 159, Expediente 6.

Flores of September 12, 1789, with accompanying documents, so diffuse that after reading it he had to have a summary made of its principal information. He was going to send this summary to the king's minister because he noted in Ugalde's elaborations a definite evidence of bad faith. Ugalde had admittedly incarcerated peaceful Mescaleros at Santa Rosa in March and had attacked them again on August 20, and this, he suspected, led to their raid on a supply train bound for the Coahuila garrisons. He also noted a contradiction in Ugalde's reports on the Lipán and Lipiyán Apaches, especially in regard to Picax-andé. In one place Ugalde had said that he placed blind trust in the *"Gran Capitán's"* followers; in another he disavowed them completely. Revillagigedo could not approve the deceit and bad faith of Ugalde nor his attempts to justify his "perfidious" treatment of the friendly Apaches, for it was in contravention of the king's requirements as expressed in both the *Reglamento de 1772* and the *Instrucción* of 1786.[41] In a confidential report to the king's minister on February 28, 1790, Revillagigedo expressed horror at Ugalde's treachery in attacking peaceful Indians protected by treaties, of his "slaughtering them in cold blood," and of his failure to submit reports during his extensive campaign. He was further horrified by Ugalde's recent plan to attack his long-standing allies, the Lipanes.[42]

Finally, in April, 1790, the Viceroy ordered Ugalde to return from his campaign immediately and surrender his command over the eastern provinces to Ugarte. The aging Ugarte was already scheduled for promotion and transfer to a less strenuous command, but until his successor should arrive, all eight of the frontier provinces were again entrusted to his authority.[43] The

[41] Revillagigedo to Valdés, No. 15, México, October 27, 1789, AGN, CV 154, Fojas 16–19.

[42] Nelson, "Juan de Ugalde and the Rio Grande Frontier, 1777–1790" (unpublished Ph.D. dissertation, University of California, 1936), 221–23, citing Revillagigedo to Valdés, México, February 28, 1790 ("Confidential Report on the Conditions of the Interior Provinces").

[43] Revillagigedo to Ugarte, México, May 25, 1790 (draft), AGN, PI 159, Expediente 6; Nelson, "Juan de Ugalde and the Rio Grande Frontier, 1777–1790," 221–23.

irrepressible Ugalde continued to keep out of touch with the new Viceroy by remaining in the field against the antagonized Apaches long beyond the allotted time for his campaign.

Meanwhile, with full assurance from Revillagigedo, Ugarte was able to return to his original Indian policy of sapping the strength of the Apache nation by making peace and alliance with each tribe that requested it. He still hoped to renew his peace with the Mescaleros, with the more recently alienated Lipanes, and also with the vagrant Faraones and Natagees.

Ugarte invited the Mescaleros to accept Spanish peace and protection once more, but with Ugalde still on campaign and operating in the vicinity of El Paso, in May of 1790, he feared that they would postpone their arrival at El Norte.[44] During the same month the Faraón Apaches of the Sacramento Mountains had come to the town of El Paso del Norte to dicker for peace, but they soon fled that vicinity when Ugalde's troops approached.[45] On May 31, two bands of Natagée Apaches in the Organo and Sacramento Mountains, under chiefs Arco and Pedro de Barrio, sent eighteen braves and two squaws to El Paso to talk terms, but while they were waiting for high water to subside so that they could cross the Río Grande, Ugalde's forces approached, and they beat a hasty retreat. As soon as Ugalde retired from that district, however, the Natagée delegation returned to press their suit, and on June 8, 1790, Ugarte authorized the authorities at El Paso to accept them in peace under proper conditions.[46]

Also on June 8 Ugarte authorized Captain Díaz at El Norte to enter into negotiations with the Mescaleros. Accordingly, Díaz summoned Volante, Alegre, and the lesser chief Joseph, who were encamped with their bands on the Conchos River, about two and one-half miles from the presidio. From them he learned of the whereabouts of the others. Bigotes El Bermejo and Mon-

[44] Ugarte to Revillagigedo, Hacienda de Encinillas, May 4, 1790, AGN, PI 159, Expediente 6.
[45] Ugalde to Revillagigedo, May 27, 1790 (extract), AGN, PI 65, Expediente 1.
[46] Ugarte to Revillagigedo, June 11, 1790 (extract), AGN, PI 65, Expediente 1.

tera Blanca were in the Sierra Rica, and Cuerno Verde and El Natagée were in the Sierra del Carmen. Mescalero couriers were then dispatched, on June 11, to the camps of these four chiefs, asking them to come to the presidio at once to negotiate. The *"Gran Capitán"* Picax-andé (El Calvo) had left with his people for the more northerly Sierra Oscura, in New Mexico, and could not be reached. Meanwhile, Díaz questioned Volante, Alegre, and Joseph, who admitted having attacked several places in Coahuila in revenge for Ugalde's mistreatment of them at Santa Rosa, but they denied having joined the Lipán Apaches in these raids or having committed any hostilities in Nueva Vizcaya. Díaz was convinced by their protestations and planned to take the chiefs to Chihuahua so that Ugarte might confer with them personally as soon as all arrived from their mountain retreats.[47]

Once more the prospects for peace with the Mescaleros were bright, but once more these were also shattered. On July 5, word reached the bands gathered at the presidio that Ugalde's troops were in their vicinity, and the bands of Volante, Alegre, and Joseph fled forthwith. Díaz managed to overtake them the next day, but they refused to return until Ugalde and his troops had retired from the area. According to Díaz, Ugalde's presence had also discouraged Bigotes El Bermejo, Montera Blanca, and El Natagée from coming to the presidio, although Joseph had promised to go out and try to bring them in.[48]

Ugarte was anxious for Díaz to get all the Mescaleros and associated bands assembled at El Norte so that peace could be made with all in unison. He ordered Díaz to inform them that war would be waged on all who remained at large. It had been rumored for some time that Patule, El Quemado, and Zapato Tuerto, together with a prominent warrior named El Zaragate, had died while imprisoned by Ugalde at Santa Rosa. A captive taken by the Mescaleros had confirmed this, but Ugarte was unable to establish whether they had been the victims of vio-

[47] Díaz to Ugarte, El Norte, June 15, 1790 (cert. copy), AGN, PI 159, Expediente 6.
[48] Díaz to Ugarte, El Norte, July 10, 1790 (cert. copy), and Ugarte to Revillagigedo, Villa de San Gerónimo, July 30, 1790, AGN, PI 159, Expediente 6.

lence or illness. The Mescalero bands still held other captives, and Ugarte ordered Díaz to obtain their release, either by voluntary surrender or ransom, as soon as the several bands reached the presidio.[49] Viceroy Revillagigedo had drawn up terms for the capitulation of the Mescaleros and sent these to Ugarte on July 7. Ugarte found them to be in complete accord with his own proposals. In the matter of the required exchange of prisoners, Ugarte was asking the governor of Coahuila for a special report on the Mescaleros whom he might have in the jails there, indicating the names of those who had been justly captured in war and those who had been involved in the recent raids on the settlements of Nueva Vizcaya. This latter, he admitted would be difficult to ascertain, especially since the Mescaleros at the presidio had declared positively that those hostilities had been committed by a party of Gila Apaches rather than Mescaleros.[50]

One condition that was to be required—that the Mescaleros extend military assistance to the Spaniards against hostile Apaches —had already been met by August of 1790. The Gila Apaches, whose raids in Nueva Vizcaya had long been blamed on the Mescaleros, were found to be camped in the Sierra Mojada, to the east of the Bolsón de Mapimí. Díaz led a party of troops and Mescalero auxiliaries against them, found them in the heights of the sierra, and with the Mescaleros leading the assault, forced them to abandon their position. One Gila warrior was killed, another one and two children were captured, and more than 200 loads of horsemeat, 200 hides, and several other articles were seized and burned by the Mescaleros. The seasonal rains having erased the tracks of the fleeing Gileños and the troops being short of provisions, no further pursuit was practical. On their return to the presidio, Díaz took the Mescalero participants to Chihuahua, and there Ugarte rewarded them for their service with suitable gifts.[51] By September 10 the Mescaleros had accom-

---

[49] Ugarte to Díaz, Chihuahua, July 20, 1790 (cert. copy), AGN, PI 159, Expediente 6.

[50] Ugarte to Revillagigedo, Villa de San Gerónimo, July 30, 1790, *loc. cit.*

[51] Ugarte to Revillagigedo, Chihuahua, August 27, 1790, AGN, PI 159, Expediente 6.

panied Díaz's forces in four separate attempts to dislodge the Gileños from the Bolsón de Mapimí.[52]

Meanwhile, Alegre, Volante, Cuerno Verde, Bigotes El Bermejo, and Montera Blanca had rejoined the followers of the lesser chief Joseph at the presidio of El Norte, and so by September 10 all the Mescaleros and their immediate associates from other tribes had reassembled at the presidio with the exceptions of the elusive El Calvo and El Natagée.[53] With this accomplishment Ugarte now turned his attention to the Lipán Apaches. Ugalde, who had not only wrecked negotiations with the Mescaleros, but who had also driven the Lipanes from their former alliance with the Spaniards, had been relieved of his command in April. However, by remaining in the field, he had kept out of touch with other authorities and therefore had not received the Viceroy's orders suspending him until the end of July. At that time he was reportedly encamped with his troops at the abandoned presidial site of La Babia and had retired from his long and reckless campaign.[54] Now that Ugalde was officially relieved of his duties and the eight frontier provinces were reunited under one command, Ugarte decided to transfer himself to Santa Rosa and direct the restoration of the Lipán alliance in person. To add military support to his persuasive efforts, he ordered Captain Díaz to meet him there with seventy troops and twenty-five Mescalero warriors. However, Díaz and the Mescalero auxiliaries, being engaged against the Gileños in the Bolsón de Mapimí, were unable to respond until September.[55] Moreover, a number of other developments caused Ugarte's well-laid plans again to go awry.

When Díaz and his troops with Volante and his Mescalero warriors reached a watering place about twenty miles short of Santa Rosa, he met with the most disconcerting news. A Mescalero scout named Vicente, whom he had sent ahead to Santa

[52] Ugarte to Revillagigedo, Chihuahua, September 10, 1790, AGN, PI 159, Expediente 6.

[53] *Ibid.*

[54] Revillagigedo to Ugarte, México, August 11, 1790 (draft), AGN, PI 159, Expediente 6.

[55] Ugarte to Revillagigedo, Chihuahua, September 10, 1790, *loc. cit.*

Rosa with 5 soldiers, returned and reported that the dreaded Ugalde was at that headquarters and that all the Mescaleros imprisoned there had died from lack of food. These alarming tidings so horrified Chief Volante and his warriors that they fled immediately, supposedly to report the tragedy to their families and kinsmen at El Norte. Díaz, fearing what effects this might have on the some 300 Mescaleros there with only 50 troops to control them, set off in hot pursuit. He overtook Volante and 13 of the fugitives in the Sierra del Carmen, but the others reached the presidio ahead of him. A complete panic there was averted, however, not only by Díaz's timely arrival but also by the previous departure of most of the Mescaleros, who had set out on their annual buffalo expedition and were therefore without news of the tragedy at Santa Rosa.[56]

The Mescalero buffalo hunt, nevertheless, had its own unfortunate consequences. Ugarte had expressly prohibited Díaz from furnishing the Indians with a military escort for this expedition, by order of October 16, for Viceroy Revillagigedo had previously forbidden it, but the order did not reach the presidio until four days after the escort had departed. Since the forty troops were then some 200 miles distant and also because Díaz did not want to upset the Mescaleros traveling with them by reversing his policy and thus indicating to them that something was awry at the presidio, he did not recall the escort.[57] He did, however, permit Volante and his band to join the hunt. When they left on October 29, he promised to send them six squaws whom Ugarte had released from captivity at Coahuila, as soon as they should arrive at the presidio. The squaws, accompanied by an interpreter, Francisco Pérez, arrived on November 3, and a week later they were sent along Volante's trail, hoping to overtake him on the Colorado River of Texas or in the great sand dunes nearby, where they could assist in the skinning and butchering operations. When they arrived in the sand dunes, however, the accompanying Pérez became lost in a blinding snowstorm

---

[56] Díaz to Ugarte, El Norte, October 26, 1790, AGN, PI 224, Expediente 1.
[57] Ibid.

and, hoping to indicate his whereabouts, fired his musket several times. The squaws, mistaking the signal, thought Pérez was being attacked by Comanches. Fleeing along Volante's trail, they reached his camp on the Nueces River on November 28. Under the impression that the interpreter had been killed by Comanches, Volante and his warriors, accompanied by the escorting troops, set out to find him. At a short distance along the river they encountered a band of Comanches, and Volante's incensed warriors attacked before the troops could intervene. Three Comanches were killed and several men, women, and children were captured, but Lieutenant Ventura Montes, in command of the escort, was able to restrain the Mescaleros from pursuing those who escaped. Montes and Volante then sent couriers to the presidio to inform Díaz of the encounter, and Díaz, of course, became alarmed. He felt certain that the Comanches who escaped had seen that their Mescalero assailants were accompanied by Spanish troops. Realizing that the alliance with the Comanches was fundamental to the entire Indian policy, Díaz offered a most bizarre proposal to rectify the tragic blunder. He suggested that the Comanches be formally invited and permitted to take revenge by attacking the Mescaleros when they returned to the presidio! Meanwhile he planned to ransom and return the captive Comanches, but this promised to be somewhat difficult. They had already been apportioned out among several Mescalero bands.[58]

Ugarte, as sole commandant-general on the frontier, was still attempting to arrange a reconciliation with the Lipán and Lipiyán Apaches, whom Ugalde had alienated. In June, 1790, he had

[58] Díaz to Ugarte, El Norte, December 19, 1790, AGN, PI 224, Expediente 1. By the time Díaz's report and recommendations reached the *Comandante General*, Ugarte had been replaced. His successor vetoed the suggestion of allowing the Comanches to attack the Mescaleros at the presidio, but he did manage to restore most of the captives. By the middle of March, 1791, ten Comanches, including the daughter of the exalted Ecueracapa and two other important persons, had been returned to their nation with the annual caravan from Chihuahua to New Mexico. The Mescaleros still held one squaw and three or four babies, whom they were rearing, but four other squaws had escaped from them and fled to their homeland. Brigadier Pedro de Nava to Revillagigedo, Saltillo, March 18, 1791, AGN, PI 224, Expediente 1.

ordered Governors Miguel Emparán of Coahuila and Manuel Viamonde of Nuevo León to concede peace to the rebellious Lipanes if they should request it, granting them just terms if they should cease hostilities in all of the provinces and restore whatever Spaniards they might have captured. Although they had not yet been punished for their attacks, Ugarte thought they might request peace in order to escape a punitive expedition, which he was then preparing to send against them, as well as to enjoy once more the security of a Spanish alliance.[59]

In September Ugarte had decided to hold up the formalization of the peace pact with the Mescaleros until he had learned of the dispositions of the Lipanes. Two of the Mescalero chiefs, Volante and Alegre, had sent emissaries to the Lipanes with an offer of amnesty, but Ugarte had since learned that the Lipanes had attacked the supply train of the presidio of Río Grande, killing two noncommissioned officers and twenty soldiers and making off with about one hundred horses and mules.[60]

Ugarte had arrived at the *villa* of Monclova on October 10 and sent word to Captain Díaz to bring his seventy troops and twenty-five Mescalero auxiliaries to Santa Rosa. If it were agreeable to the Mescaleros, Ugarte would go to the *villa* of San Fernando and parley with the Lipanes there. As he explained to the Viceroy, he had still not put the terms of the Mescalero peace in writing, for he wanted these articles of capitulation to serve both them and the Lipanes, and he was awaiting the agreement of the latter.[61]

Captain Díaz's hasty retreat to the presidio of El Norte to stave off a panic among the Mescaleros had prevented his supporting Ugarte militarily in Coahuila. Then, to make matters worse, the Mescalero emissaries carrying Ugarte's peace offers to the Lipanes had failed to find them. Therefore Ugarte decided to move from Monclova to San Fernando and send other couriers

[59] Ugarte to Governors Miguel Emparán and Manuel de Viamonde, Chihuahua, June 16, 1790 (cert. copy), AGN, PI 159, Expediente 6.

[60] Ugarte to Revillagigedo, Chihuahua, September 10, 1790, *loc. cit.*

[61] Ugarte to Revillagigedo, Monclova, October 13, 1790, AGN, PI 159, Expediente 6.

from there to feel them out and offer them a firm choice of peace or war.[62]

This may have had the desired effect. On October 26, three days before Volante left the presidio of El Norte to join the buffalo hunt, a Lipán brave and his squaw arrived in his camp. The two had been sent by the upper branch of their tribe, they said, to learn from the Mescaleros the terms of their peace with the Spaniards, how secure it was, and whether the Upper Lipanes might be admitted under the same terms. The Upper Lipanes, it was understood, were all encamped between the Sierra de Sacramento and the Sierra Blanca. Volante brought the Lipán couple to Captain Díaz and arranged to leave in two days, accompanied by the Lipán brave and a party of Mescaleros, to find the Lipanes, explain the conditions of peace that Ugarte had proposed, and then report to Ugarte at San Fernando on their reaction to the terms.[63]

Since the Lipanes were encamped between the distant Blanca and Sacramento Mountains and Díaz had sent emissaries to negotiate with their chiefs, Ugarte decided to suspend his military operations against them. He hoped that their chiefs would meet with him at either Santa Rosa or San Fernando to discuss the capitulations before his own successor arrived to take over the negotiations.[64]

By November 27 Ugarte was optimistic about peace in both Coahuila and Nueva Vizcaya. Díaz had reported that the delay of the Lipanes in meeting Ugarte in Coahuila was involuntary on their part and was due to their having had to travel a long distance to the Nueces River to find game for their sustenance. Ugarte had sent a Lipán prisoner whom he had found at San Fernando to inform his tribesmen of the procedure they would have to follow when the new commandant-general arrived, and this, he thought, was all that they were waiting for before formal-

[62] Ugarte to Revillagigedo, Monclova, October 19, 1790, AGN, PI 159, Expediente 6.
[63] Díaz to Ugarte, El Norte, October 26, 1790, AGN, PI 224, Expediente 1.
[64] Ugarte to Revillagigedo, San Fernando, November 6, 1790, AGN, PI 224, Expediente 1.

izing the capitulations. While the Upper Lipanes had solicited peace through the Mescaleros, many bands of the Lower Lipanes still recognized a peace they had made at San Antonio, in Texas, although others of this division did not and continued to attack in both Texas and Coahuila. Ugarte wanted to unite both branches under the same peace.[65]

On December 9 Ugarte was able to report that one of the Lipán chiefs with several braves had arrived at San Fernando, apparently in humility and good faith, and that others who were not far away were expected shortly. They were coming in from their hunting expedition in the Sacramento and Blanca Mountains, where the Mescaleros from El Norte had found them and induced them to accept Ugarte's offer. Encouragingly, there had now been no Lipán attacks in the eastern provinces for three months.[66] Within a few days two more Lipán chiefs and several braves had presented themselves to Ugarte at San Fernando and demonstrated their fidelity and recognition. These then left again to seek others so that all, or the greater part, of the tribe might meet the new commandant-general at Santa Rosa and recognize him as the one with whom they would have to keep the peace. Ugarte's own march to Santa Rosa had been delayed by the arrival in San Fernando of eight Comanche braves and four squaws on December 13. Ugarte felt obliged to stay on and entertain these allies, especially since they were led by Soxay, a brother of the great Ecueracapa.[67] Soxay and his party had come to retrieve their comrades who had been captured by the Mescaleros during the buffalo expedition.

When Ugarte turned over the commandancy-general to Brigadier Pedro de Nava at the end of 1790, peace with the Lipanes was all but concluded. Fearing the armies that Ugarte had marshalled at San Fernando to punish them for their previous

---

[65] Ugarte to Revillagigedo, San Fernando, November 27, 1790, AGN, PI 159, Expediente 9.

[66] Ugarte to Revillagigedo, San Fernando, December 9, 1790, AGN, PI 159, Expediente 6.

[67] Ugarte to Revillagigedo, San Fernando, December 13, 1790, AGN, PI 159, Expediente 6.

breach of the peace, the Lipanes had come in to that town and to Santa Rosa. There they agreed to abide by the three principal capitulations that Ugarte had demanded. In the first place, they undertook to return all the captives whom they had taken from the Spaniards, in return for all the Lipán prisoners, except those who had been baptized, whom the Spaniard held. In the second place, they would deliver to the Spaniards the members of their tribe responsible for any further raids, so that these might be suitably punished. And finally, the Lower Lipanes would live in peace in the lands between San Antonio and Laredo, and the Upper Lipanes would reside quietly in the environs of San Fernando and the presidio of Río Grande, where the Spaniards could watch their movements. Under these conditions Ugarte had conceded them the peace they requested, and he felt that it would be true and permanent so long as the Spaniards kept faith with their own obligations. He had arranged for emissaries from the Lipanes of the Texas frontier to present themselves to Brigadier Nava and ratify the agreement, and he would have had the representatives of the Coahuila Lipanes do likewise if they had been at hand. These, however, had remained in their camps to protect their families from an expected attack by the Comanches.[68]

For a time it seemed as though the Lipiyán and some of the affiliated Natagée Apaches would also return to the fold before Ugarte left office. While the Mescaleros from El Norte were on their buffalo expedition in the late fall of 1790 they had discovered a large number of Lipanes butchering buffalo on the bank of the Nueces River, but these had retreated in the direction of Coahuila as the Mescaleros approached. Then, on December 10, as the Mescaleros and their military escort were returning from the hunt, they were joined at the Colorado River by Chief El Natagée and his family. El Natagée then sent word to the presidio of El Norte that the rest of his band was with that of Picax-andé (El Calvo) on the slopes of the Sierra de Sacramento,

[68] Ugarte to Revillagigedo, Villa de Monclova, January 5, 1791, AGN, PI 159, Expediente 6.

that they wished to enter into the Mescalero peace pact, that he was now on his way there, and that he and Picax-andé would come to El Norte to negotiate if the Spaniards would recognize Picax-andé as the principal chief of all the associated bands. Captain Díaz also learned that Picax-andé and El Natagée had among their people several Lipanes who had recently joined them. Since the Mescalero bands of Volante, Alegre, Joseph, Montera Blanca, Bigotes El Bermejo, and Cuerno Verde all recognized the superiority of the great Lipiyán chief, Díaz decided to accept him as their principal chief whenever he and El Natagée should arrive at the presidio. He realized that Volante and some others would harbor some resentment of this selection, but he knew that they also had too much respect for Picax-andé to voice their disapproval.[69]

Picax-andé did not come to the presidio of El Norte until Ugarte had left the frontier for his new position at Guadalajara. However, the Mescalero peace, which Ugarte had renewed in June of 1790, remained in effect for at least two years with the bands of Volante, Alegre, Joseph, Bigotes El Bermejo, Montera Blanca, Cuerno Verde, and two new chiefs, Dayel and Esquinoye, who were now in residence near the presidio. There were complaints from Coahuila that the Mescaleros were raiding in that province, but in an investigation conducted in June of 1792, several officers and enlisted men at El Norte testified that their conduct had been exemplary. There appeared no reason to suspect any of the chiefs except, perhaps, Cuerno Verde. He had been away from the presidio for five months, and it was possible that he had participated in raids during that time. But none of the officers and men had noticed any horses or mules among the Mescaleros that did not carry their legitimate brands nor any clothing or other effects that might have been stolen. It had been alleged in Coahuila that the Mescaleros had obtained firearms from the soldiers at El Norte in exchange for stolen goods, but there was no evidence to substantiate this. The warriors had been furnished arms when employed with the troops in regular

[69] Díaz to Ugarte, El Norte, December 19, 1790, AGN, PI 224, Expediente 1.

military operations against hostiles, but these had been collected afterwards, and the accounts showed none to have been missing.[70]

The peace that Ugarte had finally achieved with the Eastern Apaches was less than perfect. As long as the Mescaleros remained in residence at El Norte the authorities in the neighboring province of Coahuila continued to attribute to them all of the Indian trouble they experienced. As in the past, they were to charge the officials of Nueva Vizcaya with tolerating, concealing, and protecting Mescalero breaches of the peace.[71] Nor were the pacts of long duration. But as Gálvez and Ugarte had well understood from the beginning, an insecure peace was better than open war. It gave the frontier settlers a temporary respite from the terrors of the past, and it brought the Apaches themselves one step closer to civilization and thus to a peaceful coexistence with their neighbors.

[70] Nicolás Villaroel, declaration, El Norte, June 23, 1792, and Nava to Revillagigedo, Chihuahua, August 2, 1792, AGN, PI 170, Expediente 1.
[71] Nava to Revillagigedo, Chihuahua, July 19, 1792, AGN, PI 170, Expediente 3.

CHAPTER XI

SUMMATION

In assessing the contribution of Jacobo Ugarte as commandant-general of the Provincias Internas del Norte, it should first be noted that his administrative authority was much reduced from that of Teodoro de Croix, who first held that office. Although formally invested with the same powers, Ugarte was placed under viceregal supervision from the very beginning. Furthermore, a few months after he assumed active command he was relieved of almost all duties except those relating to military and Indian affairs. Viceroy Bernardo de Gálvez's *Instrucción* of 1786 also divided the frontier command into three districts with Ugarte in full charge of one of them and in only nominal control over the other two. When Gálvez died in November of 1786, Ugarte automatically became independent of viceregal supervision, but only for a few months. He was subjected to it again when Manuel Antonio Flores was invested with the same powers that Gálvez had exercised. In 1788 Viceroy Flores divided the frontier administration into two separate commands, and Ugarte was left with authority only over the western provinces. This restriction endured until the Conde de Revillagigedo succeeded Flores in 1789, discharged the commandant-general of the eastern provinces in 1790, and placed Ugarte temporarily in full command of both divisions. It is not without some significance that the greatest progress in the pacification of the hostile Indians was made during the few months, in 1786–87 and in 1790, in which

Ugarte was the sole commandant-general of the Provincias Internas.

In view of Ugarte's earlier stormy relations with Viceroy Antonio de Bucareli and Commandant-Inspector Hugo O'Conor during his governorship of Coahuila, it would appear that he was by nature resentful of superior authority, especially since he exhibited a similar recalcitrance as commandant-general during the viceregency of Flores. On the other hand, however, his relations with Viceroys Gálvez and Revillagigedo were exceptionally cordial. Ugarte's characteristic peevishness was apparently a resentment of unacceptable policy rather than of superior office. He agreed with the basic tenets held by Croix, Gálvez, and Revillagigedo but opposed those of Bucareli, O'Conor, and Flores.

In his relations with colleagues of equal or nearly equal rank Ugarte again encountered kindred and hostile spirits. Juan de Ugalde, both before and after his promotion to equal command of the eastern provinces, and Felipe Díaz de Ortega, the intendant of Durango, both pursued policies that frustrated Ugarte's administration. Yet, he was able to work smoothly with Joseph Antonio Rengel, the commandant-inspector, and that veteran seems to have brooked no resentment at all of Ugarte's having replaced him as commandant-general.

From his inferior officers Ugarte enjoyed more respect and co-operation than he accorded some of his own superiors, and he was not ungrateful. Captain Domingo Díaz, of the presidio El Norte, had been in rank for eighteen years and had not always used the best of judgment as Ugarte's peace commissioner during the negotiations with the Mescaleros. Nevertheless, before leaving office Ugarte urged his promotion to the rank of lieutenant colonel. Díaz, he said, had performed an important service in keeping the Mescaleros relatively peaceful, and when treasury funds for the purpose were not forthcoming, he had footed the bill personally.[1] Captain Antonio Cordero, of the presidio

---

[1] Ugarte to Revillagigedo, Chihuahua, August 27, 1790, AGN, PI 84, Expediente 1.

of Janos, had campaigned indefatigably against the Western Apaches and had served as Ugarte's commissioner for the Mimbreño peace. Ugarte placed him in temporary command of the western provinces in 1790, when he transferred himself to Coahuila to supervise the peace arrangements with the Lipanes. The unusually able Juan Bautista de Anza also worked in perfect harmony with Ugarte, both as governor of New Mexico and later as military commandant of Sonora, and especially during the successful negotiations with the Comanches and Navahos. In both 1786 and 1787 Ugarte recommended him to the king for special consideration.[2]

Throughout the Spanish service the promotion and patronage of individuals were frequently based on personal kinship, and nepotism was rampant. Ugarte, however, prided himself on having only one relative in the colonial service. José Joaquín de Ugarte, a nephew, came to the northern frontier in June of 1786, shortly after his uncle became the commandant-general. He arrived as a lowly cadet and remained as such for at least three years. Commandant-Inspector Rengel listed him for promotion in 1788, but Ugarte passed him over in favor of another candidate. On the basis of seniority José Joaquín was eventually promoted to ensign; but his uncle, although favorably impressed with his service, refused to advance him further. When the young man was again proposed for promotion, Ugarte deferred to the judgment of the viceroy.[3] In view of his cavalier attitude toward superior orders and his own financial obligations, Ugarte was unusually circumspect in passing on the merit of a kinsman.

Following the policy that Croix had initiated, Ugarte attempted to improve frontier defenses by withdrawing the presidios from the outer line established by the *Reglamento de 1772* and placing them nearer the settlements that actually needed

[2] Ugarte to the Marqués de Sonora, Chihuahua, December 21, 1786, and February 1, 1787, translated in Thomas, *Forgotten Frontiers*, 364-66.

[3] Cordero to Flores, Janos, August 14, 1788; Flores to Valdés, México, October 22, 1788; and Ugarte to Flores, San Bartolomé, September 17, 1788, AGN, CV 147, 62–76; Ugarte to Revillagigedo, April 16 and October 27, 1790, AGN, PI 84, Expediente 1.

protection. He did not, however, count alone on this more immediate military coverage to discourage Apache raids. Against the opposition of the intendant of Durango he continued to send troops in pursuit of the marauders and to mount regularly-scheduled offensive expeditions into their distant mountain retreats. Although such campaigns temporarily reduced the forces protecting the settlements, Ugarte considered them essential, for they impressed the enemy with the military might of Spain and with the punishment they might invariably expect for continuing their hostilities. He also felt it necessary to keep the Apaches off balance, even on the defensive, and to continue inflicting casualties so as to reduce their military strength. Like Gálvez, he believed that a continuous harassment was essential in inducing them to sue for peace. Long experience had impressed Ugarte with the futility of waging war on the wily Apaches with Spanish troops alone, and to offset their elusive maneuvers in terrain that favored their primitive tactics, he counted heavily on Indian auxiliaries and allies who were equally cunning. Serving with the troops or attacking independently, these warriors invariably inflicted more casualties on the Apaches than did the presidials themselves.

Ugarte's grand strategy was to reduce the enemy by dividing them against each other, by forming alliances with every band or tribe that sued for peace, and by arraying these against those who remained hostile. For a time, in 1787, large segments of every major Apache tribe except the Gileños had sued for peace, and against those remaining at large in the mountains along the Gila River Ugarte had mobilized a seemingly overwhelming force to converge on them from three directions. Closing in from the southwest was the army of Sonora, composed of presidial troops with the support of Pima, Opata, and Chiricahua auxiliaries; from the northeast came New Mexico's garrison force bolstered not only by Pueblo auxiliaries but also by Ute, Comanche, and Navaho allies; and from the southeast advanced the more numerous presidials of Nueva Vizcaya in the expectation of aid from the newly-allied Mescaleros. Although the main body of Gila warriors slithered out of this gigantic trap, the triple-jawed vise did take its toll, and the prospect of its continuous operation might well have induced the recalcitrants to reconsider the advantages of a peace. Unfortunately, however, Viceroy Flores and Commandant-General Ugalde, having no faith in the Mescaleros, chose this critical time to disrupt their new alliance in Nueva Vizcaya. Ugarte protested repeatedly but in vain, and the Mescaleros, responding to the betrayal, resumed their former hostilities. Their uprising distracted the offensive operations of the troops, freed the Gileños from military pressure from that quarter, and laid Nueva Vizcaya wide open to the vengeance of those warriors. Seizing the offensive, the Gila Apaches ransacked the countryside of that province and forced Ugarte to recall his troops for defensive operations.

In his dealings with the hostile Apaches Ugarte was bound first by the *Reglamento de 1772* and then the *Instrucción* of 1786, which superseded it and which was more compatible with his own policy. Eventually, however, he was further restricted by the more vindictive requirements of Viceroy Flores. It had been the general practice to offer no quarter to Apache warriors, for they neither offered nor asked for it themselves. In each encounter the troops attempted to kill as many of these as they could and, so as to authenticate their reports of casualties inflicted, sent Ugarte the ears or heads of their victims. At the same time they were under orders to spare Apache women and children whenever possible, merely taking them prisoner. Ugarte then dispatched them to the interior, where the viceroy distributed them among private citizens who were supposed to take them into their homes, care for them, educate them, and convert them to Christianity or, at least, to a peaceful and civilized way of life.

When Apache warriors surrendered voluntarily, as they frequently did so as to become reunited with their captured families, it was Ugarte's policy to accord them all the freedom and status of those whose entire bands had entered into a peace treaty. Flores, however, ordered that such voluntary surrenders be treated as prisoners of war taken in combat, that is, imprisoned or sentenced to hard labor in the interior. Ugarte seems to have complied with this directive except in one notable instance. In the case of the renegade Chiricahuas, whose kinsmen were at peace at Bacoachi and in active alliance with the Spaniards, Ugarte accepted those who surrendered with the same honors and privileges he accorded their loyal kinsmen.

Realizing that the principal objective of the Indian wars was the ultimate pacification of the frontier, Ugarte increased the budgets of the provinces sufficiently to cover the mounting costs of subsidizing those who made peace. He was particularly careful to maintain the friendship and loyalty of the tribes who had been reduced for many years—the Pimas and Opatas of Sonora, the Tarahumaras in Nueva Vizcaya, the Julimeños and the Lipán Apaches in Coahuila, the Caddoan nations to the north of Texas, and the Pueblos, Utes, and Jicarilla Apaches in New Mexico. In the same spirit he issued detailed instructions for the perfection of the peace that had been more recently negotiated with the Comanches and Navahos. Where he differed most from previous commandant-generals, and also from Viceroy Flores, was in his ready acceptance of similar arrangements with the normally hostile Apache bands, many of whose pretensions were far from sincere. These traditional enemies had time and again sought a truce merely to obtain respite from the harassment of Spanish troops and of Comanche and Caddoan warriors, to gain temporary trading privileges for the few Spanish goods they craved, to receive food rations when game was scarce, and perhaps to obtain information on the disposition and movement of troops operating against their kinsmen. Viceroy Flores was forever suspicious of this latter ruse. Ugarte, however, held with Gálvez's conviction, that an Apache peace of any quality was preferable to the devastations of war, that in each truce the seemingly incorrigible marauders would learn something more of the advantages of peace and would become somewhat more addicted to the trade goods, food allotments, and gifts, which only the Spaniards could dispense, and that in the long run a subsidized peace would go further toward achieving total pacification than would an all-out war. If the Apaches broke the peace, as Ugarte expected they would, he knew that once they felt the sting of renewed military prosecution, they would seek it again, and perhaps with a little more sincerity.

In his attempt to debilitate the Apache nation, Ugarte promoted friction among its loosely-knit tribes and bands, insisted on military assistance from those who sought peace against those who remain hostile, and required that the former terminate their hostilities in all of the provinces. His treaty formula also called for an exchange of prisoners, the surrender of defectors from the Spanish cause, punishment for those who broke the peace, an enforcement of fair-trade practices, the branding and registration of Indian as well as Spanish livestock, and the residence among the treaty bands of Spanish interpreters who were at once translators and informers. At first he also required that each band seeking peace settle down in a permanent village near a presidio, submit to the inquiries of a census taker, dedicate itself to agriculture, and either accept Christianity or elect and be responsible to a single superior chieftain. When it became clear that the Apaches rejected these requirements as a gross violation of their cherished freedom, Ugarte modified his demands. Nevertheless, he still insisted that they keep the presidial captains informed of their place of residence, that they not enter the settled areas without prior permission, and that they at least encourage their children to take up farming. He also yielded to some Apache demands. When the Mescaleros asked for Spanish troops to escort them on their annual buffalo hunt into Comanche territory, Ugarte readily accommodated them, hoping in this way to gain their confidence and also to prevent them from clashing with the more faithful allies to the north. Both Flores and Revillagigedo prohibited this practice, and it did lead to some unfortunate incidents with the Comanches, but Ugarte was always able to make amends and retain the confidence and loyalty of the more powerful Comanche nation. Interestingly enough, Ugarte's requirements for the permanent Comanche

276

peace were more rigorous than those for the more transitory pacts with the Apaches, even though he valued the former peace above all others. He seems to have realized that the Comanche desire for peace was much more compelling than was that of the Apaches.

Some bands of every Apache tribe on the frontier eventually sought peace during Ugarte's administration, and this—rather than the annihilation of the nation—was his principal objective. In the spring of 1787 some 3,000 Mescaleros, 283 Chiricahuas, and more than 800 Mimbreños sued for peace. Meanwhile approximately 3,000 Navaho Apaches were consolidating the pact they had negotiated the previous year. For a time, therefore, Ugarte had gained the alliance of some 7,000 formerly hostile Apaches, most of whom were now aligned against those remaining obdurate.[4] Although all the Mimbreños and half the Chiricahuas soon fled their reservations, and the Mescaleros were forcibly expelled from theirs by viceregal order, Ugarte was able to restore almost all to peace and to bring still others under Spanish control in 1790. This became possible after Revillagigedo replaced Flores, removed the impetuous Ugalde from his command, and restored Ugarte to control over all eight of the frontier provinces. Without losing the valuable alliance with the Comanches, who boasted 6,000 warriors, Ugarte renewed the Mescalero peace, increased the number of friendly Chiricahuas to more than 200, and received the surrender of several hundred Mimbreños and a lesser number of Faraones and Gileños. He also restored to the fold the Lipán tribe, which Ugalde had antagonized. When Ugarte turned his command over to Pedro de Nava at the end of 1790, the frontier was far more tranquil than when he arrived in the spring of 1786.

Before Ugarte left the frontier, moreover, most of his policies had been vindicated. His Indian policy, formalized by Gálvez

[4] Figures on the Mescaleros, Chiricahuas, and Mimbreños at peace appear in Ugarte to Díaz, Arispe, December 21, 1787, and Ugarte, Extracto, Arispe, July 15, 1787 (cert. copies), AGN, PI 112, Expediente 2. For the Navahos see Garrido y Durán, Relación, Chihuahua, December 21, 1786 (cert. copy), AGN, PI 65, Expediente 9.

in the *Instrucción* of 1786 and then shattered by the hard-line requirements of Flores, was reaffirmed in 1790 by Revillagigedo. Ugarte's insistence upon a united command for the frontier army was honored, at least temporarily, when he and his successor were restored to authority over all eight of the provinces. Then, for a time, even his recommendation that the commandancy-general be made independent of viceregal control was carried into effect. From 1793 until 1812 the Provincias Internas were again autonomous and under a single command.[5]

Nor did Ugarte's obsession with the Apache problem and personal authority blind him to other considerations of frontier defense and development. At the beginning of his administration, before his command was divided, he envisioned a system of roads that would bind the several provinces of the vast frontier more closely together. His plan was to link Texas with New Mexico and Louisiana, and New Mexico with Sonora and California so as to promote an exchange of information, a reciprocity of assistance, and a development of common interests. Then, as soon as peace was secured with the Comanches, who

---

[5] Like Ugarte, Pedro de Nava (1790–1802) was given temporary command of the eastern provinces along with his regular appointment to the western command until Juan de Ugalde's successor, Ramón de Castro (1791–93), arrived. Then, by royal order of November 23, 1792, effective the following year, the two divisions (excluding Nuevo León, Nuevo Santander, and California) were formally reunited under Nava, who was also then freed from viceregal control. In the succeeding administration of Nemesio Salcedo y Salcedo (1802–13) the Provincias Internas were again divided into two separate commands, by royal decree of May 30, 1804, but political considerations prevented the enforcement of this change until 1812, when the Spanish colonial war for independence made it and also the resubjection of the region to the viceregal office a military necessity. Meanwhile, in 1808, Manuel Antonio Cordero was named "Second Commandant General" of the eastern division and was succeeded in that capacity by Bernardo Bonavia y Zapata (1809–10). After the division of the command and its reduction to viceregal authority were effected by royal order of May 1, 1811, confirmed in the following year, Bonavia y Zapata became commandant-general of the western division (1813–17) and was succeeded by Alejo García Conde (1817–21). Meanwhile the eastern division was placed in the hands of Simon Herrera, who was killed shortly afterwards and replaced by Joaquín de Arredondo (1813–21). See Faulk, *The Last Years of Spanish Texas*, 20–21; Ralph E. Twitchell, *The Spanish Archives of New Mexico*, II, 325–42, *passim*.

dominated the plains separating the three first-named provinces, he gave active attention to the project.[6]

To what extent Ugarte actually initiated the series of explorations that followed is not clear, but he did provide the pathfinders with instructions; and although no prosperous trade resulted immediately from the undertakings, he did supervise the discovery of several routes that were feasible for commerce. Pedro de Vial, a Louisiana Frenchman, blazed a circuitous trail between San Antonio, Texas, and Santa Fe, New Mexico, in 1786–87, which Joseph Mares, an inactive New Mexican corporal, shortened in the latter year. Vial then explored a route from Santa Fe to Natchitoches, Louisiana, and from thence another to San Antonio, both in 1788, before returning to Santa Fe along Mares' trail in the following year. In 1792, after Ugarte had left the frontier, Vial opened still another road, from Santa Fe to San Luis de Ylinueses (St. Louis, Missouri).[7] An indirect route from Santa Fe to Arispe, Sonora, which Anza had explored in 1780, was shortened in part in 1788 by Ugarte's Captain Manuel de Echeagaray and his Sonoran army while campaigning against the Gila Apaches, but this more direct road was not completely scouted until 1795. Then Captain José de Zúñiga, of the presidio of Tucson, reached the Pueblo of Zuñi and sent a party on to Santa Fe.[8]

Meanwhile, in October of 1788, Ugarte began to express a nervous concern for his own political and financial security. At that time, while recklessly contesting policy with Viceroy Flores, and again in May of 1789, as his own term was drawing to a close, he brought his plight to the attention of the crown. In two long memorials bolstered with voluminous documentation, he

[6] Ugarte to Flores, San Bartolomé, January 5, 1789, AGN, PI 183, Expediente 7.

[7] Most of the essential documents for these explorations appear in AGN, PI 183, Expediente 7. For a full account see Abraham P. Nasatir and Noel M. Loomis, *Pedro Vial and the Roads to Santa Fe.*

[8] George P. Hammond (ed.), "The Zúñiga Journal, Tucson to Santa Fe: The Opening of a Spanish Trade Route, 1788–1795," *New Mexico Historical Review*, Vol. VI (January, 1931), 40–65.

attempted not only to justify his policies but also to gain an extension of his term and a promotion in military rank to field marshal. These two favors he requested in view of his long service, considerable achievements, and also his precarious financial situation.[9] In March of 1790, when he addressed Flores' successor, he revealed that, owing to insufficient salary, he had never expected to free himself from debt until he began to draw the salary of a commandant-general and that even then he could hope to do so only by stringent economizing.[10] Neither the king nor the new viceroy was willing to extend his term, however, and he was shortly transferred to a more comfortable but less rewarding position in the south.

Ugarte's new assignment had almost all the earmarks of a promotion. On March 1, 1790, he was named president of the the royal audiencia at Guadalajara and intendant of the royal treasury of Nueva Galicia. Five days later he was awarded the higher military rank, which he had requested, of field marshal, and also the administrative title of commandant-general of Nueva Galicia. Although obviously disappointed in being removed from the frontier command, Ugarte may very well have taken solace in these exalted new titles and in the sovereign's confidence in him, which these implied, had only his salary been improved. As it was, his pay was drastically reduced, from 20,000 pesos a year to a paltry 8,000 pesos. He received the news of his new positions and salary in June of 1790.[11]

Meanwhile, on March 24, twenty-three days after Ugarte was assigned to Guadalajara, Pedro de Nava was appointed to succeed him, and Ugarte was directed to remain in active command until Nava's arrival on the frontier. In view of the considerable expenses that Ugarte still faced for his march to Coahuila to arrange a peace with the Lipán Apaches, he begged the viceroy

[9] Ugarte to Valdés, San Bartolomé, October 6, 1788, and to the King, Chihuahua, May 8, 1789, AGN, PI 77, Expediente 1 and Expediente 11.
[10] Ugarte to Revillagigedo (confidential), Chihuahua, March 12, 1790, AGN, PI 84, Expediente 1.
[11] Ugarte to Revillagigedo, Chihuahua, June 16 and 18, 1790, AGN, PI 84, Expediente 1; Revillagigedo to Valdés, Mexico, June 26 and July 10, 1790, AGN, CV 157, 295–96, 335.

to keep his current salary in force until he reached Guadalajara.[12]

It was after Ugarte had completed his business in Coahuila, turned his command over to his successor, and briefed him verbally on matters still pending in the Provincias Internas that he submitted his final report on the state of the frontier provinces. On January 5, 1791, he wrote the viceroy from Monclova a somewhat exaggerated summary of the situation. During his four and two-thirds years in command, he declared, he had achieved peace with all the hostiles on the frontier. In Sonora the Chiricahuas were still living in peace at Bacoachi and were even clamoring for ministers to catechize them; the ever restless Seris were quiet once more; and the province had been made so safe from attack that even women could walk along its roads without fear. In Nueva Vizcaya some bands of the barbarous Gileños were now residing quietly near the presidio of Janos and were little by little imitating the Spanish way of life; the entire Mescalero tribe, exhausted by military prosecution and reduced to an even more perfect tranquility near El Norte, had accepted the obligation of aiding the troops against the remaining hostiles; and the province itself was so secure that the settlers who had abandoned their lands on the San Pedro and Conchos Rivers had now returned to them. God, he said, had permitted him to relieve the suffering inhabitants of Coahuila from the depredations of the Lipán Apaches, and the province had now known peace for more than four months. Texas was enjoying a tranquility never previously experienced, and New Mexico had a true peace with all the tribes in its jurisdiction. In the several provinces during the period of his command, his troops had reduced the enemy's numbers by 1,776, including those who had been either killed or captured. In addition, he said, many other hostiles had been fatally wounded but, having fallen in precipitous terrain or having been removed by comrades from the field of battle, they did not enter into the official count, for the troops had been unable to collect their heads or ears. Likewise, many

[12] Ugarte to Revillagigedo, Chihuahua, September 1, 1790, AGN, PI 84, Expediente 1.

captives were not included in the toll, such as those taken recently in Sonora after the expiration of his term but by forces he had dispatched beforehand.[13]

In all his operations, Ugarte declared, his aim had been the best service to the king and to the public, and to this end he had never stinted in providing funds, even from his own pocket. This liberality together with the frequency of and distance involved in his official travels had forced him to contract personal debts amounting to more than 60,000 pesos. In spite of past promotions and salary increases he had been unable to unburden himself from these obligations, and now that his pay had been reduced to a meager 8,000 pesos a year, he would find it still more difficult. Being a man of honor, he said, he was unable to devise other sources of income, and so he was asking the viceroy to bring his plight to the attention of the king. He hoped that his majesty would grant a continuation of his current salary.[14]

Revillagigedo expressed his full satisfaction with the state of the Provincias Internas as Ugarte had reported it and also with the zeal, honor, unselfishness, and effectiveness with which he had discharged the duties of his office. He had already recommended Ugarte to the king and would do so again.[15]

The records examined for this study do not indicate whether or not Ugarte retained his former salary for the two and one-half months between December 30, 1790, when he surrendered his frontier command, and March 14, 1791, when he assumed office at Guadalajara. His importunities, however, seem to have had some result, for when he began to exercise authority in Nueva Galicia, it was with the military rank of lieutenant general.[16]

Ugarte's administration at Guadalajara is beyond the scope of this study, but a summary of his accomplishments there does reinforce the strong indication that his long career in the royal

[13] Ugarte to Revillagigedo, Monclova, January 5, 1791, AGN, PI 159, Expediente 6.
[14] Ibid.
[15] Revillagigedo to Ugarte, Mexico, January 26, 1791 (draft), AGN, PI 159, Expediente 6.
[16] Luis Pérez Verdía, Historia particular del Estado de Jalisco desde los primeros tiempos de que hay noticia hasta nuestros días, I, 463.

service was more notable in administrative than in purely military achievement. Ugarte was at his best behind a desk. His eight and one-half years as president of the audiencia, intendant, and commandant-general of Nueva Galicia constituted a period of enlightened public improvement following a long era of degeneration. It was under Ugarte that New Spain's second university, the *Real Universidad Literaria de Guadalajara*, was inaugurated in 1792, with Ugarte himself naming the first nine-member faculty; that the printing press was introduced to the province in 1793; that the *Hospital de San Miguel de Belén* was moved into better quarters and reformed administratively by Ugarte's personal intervention; that city planning and street paving were undertaken in Guadalajara; that the first regular coach service was established between that city and the viceregal capital; and that indigo, flax, and hemp began to be cultivated in the province of Nueva Galicia.[17]

Ugarte's lengthy career in the royal service—sixty-six years and three months—ended on August 20, 1798. His death in office on that day was mourned by all classes of society.[18] Neither his ailment nor his age at the time appear on the pages of the provincial history, and no portrait or statue commemorates his progressive administration. Even the record of his burial is brief and formal. With the marginal heading of "The Very Excellent Sr. President Don Jacobo Ugarte y Loyola," the entry states only that on August 21, 1798, he was buried in the Metropolitan Cathedral of Guadalajara after the customary vigil, mass, and administration of the Holy Sacraments.[19]

Perhaps the most notable monument to Ugarte was the persistence on the northern frontier of the Indian policy that Gálvez had so wisely enunciated and which he had so assiduously pursued. The Indian problem itself survived him, but so also did the methods he had adopted for its solution. Although an adequate history of the problem after 1790 remains to be written,

[17] *Ibid.*, 463–81.
[18] *Ibid.*, 481; Villa, *Historia del Estado de Sonora*, 138–39.
[19] Libro de entierros, No. 14, Foja 5, Archivo de la Parroquía del Sagrario Metropolitano de Guadalajara (notarized copy in my possession).

scattered sources and records do indicate that Ugarte's policies were continued in the main and that their enforcement did result in a diminution of Apache hostilities during the last decade of the century. Several bands, representing almost every Apache tribe, had been induced to settle down in reservation-like villages near the presidios and, although these groups seldom kept the peace faithfully or for long, the system offered a welcome respite from the wholesale slaughter and destruction of the past. And the continuous military prosecution of the more obdurate tribesmen by both Spanish troops and Indian allies did reduce the hostiles numerically and left the eventual outcome of the struggle no longer in doubt.

In the west the Chiricahua Apaches, who formerly ransacked the Sonora frontier, had been considerably debilitated. In 1796 several of their bands were still living at peace near Bacoachi and Janos while others, remaining at large in their mountain strongholds but numerically much reduced, confined their raids largely to the Navaho and Moqui villages of western New Mexico.[20]

Although the Tontos, or Coyoteros, were mainly still at large in 1796, their range was remote from the settlements, and some groups had taken up peaceful residence near Tucson.[21]

The Gileños proper, generally considered the most warlike and sanguinary of the Apache tribes and a persistent menace to both Sonora and Nueva Vizcaya, had been reduced by repeated punitive expeditions to a quarter of their former strength. Some were living quietly at Janos in 1796, but most of the tribe remained hostile. One group of Gila Apaches had been admitted to peace in New Mexico during Ugarte's administration, in July of 1790, and with Spanish assistance had actually settled down on the Río Grande south of Sabinal to a livelihood of farming and stock raising, but the experiment lasted only a few months. In the fall of the year they withdrew to their former mountain haunts, and in spite of the governor's efforts, they had still not

[20] Matson and Schroeder, "Cordero's Description of the Apache—1796," *loc. cit.*

[21] *Ibid.*

returned four years later. Gileño bands, although frequently protesting their desire for peace, continued their depredations on New Mexico to the end of the century.[22]

In 1794 the Navahos were occupying ten established villages in western New Mexico, pasturing large herds of cattle, horses, and sheep, harvesting abundant crops, trading blankets and other textiles to the Pueblo and Spanish settlements, and repeatedly waging war on the hostile Gila and Mimbres Apaches. So valued was their alliance to the Spaniards that when they complained of mistreatment by the *alcade mayor* of Laguna, the governor deposed that officer and denied him further access to the Navaho towns. No serious break with the Navahos occurred until 1796, when they rose up and again allied with the Gileños. Although they submitted to a shaky peace from time to time in the succeeding years, the Navahos were never again as faithful as during the previous decade.[23]

The formerly numerous Mimbreños were divided into two groups by 1796. The upper branch had been conquered and was living on reservations in Nueva Vizcaya, at Janos and Carrizal, while the lower branch, although still raiding in New Mexico, had been reduced by military prosecution to less than one-half its former strength.[24]

At El Paso the Faraón peace was an uneasy one. Owing to the dispersed habitat of that tribe and to the insufficiency of troops to patrol its extensive range, even those who settled near El Paso were suspected of disloyalty in 1792. The Spanish commandant of that post recommended the waging of a general war on the uncommitted Faraones in order to restore respect in those

[22] *Ibid.*; Elizabeth Ann Harper John, "Spanish Relations with the *Indios Bárbaros* on the Northernmost Frontier of New Spain in the Eighteenth Century," (unpublished Ph.D. dissertation, University of Oklahoma, 1957), 160–62, 174.

[23] Donald E. Worcester (ed.), "Advice on Governing New Mexico, 1794," *New Mexico Historical Review*, Vol. XXIV (July, 1949), 236–54; Matson and Schroeder, "Cordero's Description of the Apache—1796," *loc. cit.*; John, "Spanish Relations with the *Indios Bárbaros* on the Northernmost Frontier of New Spain in the Eighteenth Century," 172–74.

[24] Matson and Schroeder, "Cordero's Description of the Apache—1796," *loc. cit.*

at the reservation. The tribe was still numerous in 1796. Most of the bands were still raiding in New Mexico and Nueva Vizcaya, in concert with the Mimbreños and in spite of previous peace arrangements, while only a few bands remained settled, now near the presidio of San Elizeario.[25]

In the east the Mescaleros were still residing near the presidio of El Norte in 1792. Reportedly, they were demonstrating good faith, respect, gratitude, and even kindness toward the Spaniards, but some individuals were suspected of having absented themselves occasionally, on the pretext of hunting game, to commit thefts and acts of violence in the interior of Nueva Vizcaya and in some of the eastern provinces as well. They had not engaged in open hostility at that date, but ever since they had been admitted to peace at El Norte, every robbery and damage suffered in Coahuila had been attributed to them by the authorities of that province. Officials there also continued to charge those of Nueva Vizcaya with dissimulating, tolerating, and protecting Mescalero raiders. By 1796 the Mescaleros had broken their peace completely and were raiding both Coahuila and Nueva Vizcaya. The Spaniards then declared an open war on them, which was still raging in 1799.[26]

The Lipán Apaches, who had renewed peace with Ugarte and Nava in 1790 and 1791, broke it again when Ramón de Castro, the new commandant-general of the eastern provinces, seized and held a number of their emissaries at San Fernando and Santa Rosa. In February of 1792 they reopened negotiations with Nava at El Norte. Nava believed that the bands who had remained aloof from Ugarte's peace really desired it and would seek it in good faith, even though they had not been subjected to rigorous military pressure, for they had been under heavy attack by the Comanches and Nations of the North. In 1796 they

[25] *Ibid.*; Cordero to Nava, El Paso, July 20, 1792, AGN, PI 170, Expediente 2.

[26] Nava to Revillagigedo, Chihuahua, July 19, 1792, and Nava to Viceroy Miguel Joseph de Azanza, Chihuahua, July 23, 1799, AGN, PI 170, Expediente 5, and PI 112, Expediente 2; Cordero to Nava, El Paso, July 20, 1792, *loc. cit.*; Matson and Schroeder, Cordero's Description of the Apache—1796," *loc. cit.*

separated themselves from the hostile tribes out of respect for the Spanish troops and were reportedly acting in good faith, but both the upper and lower branches of the tribe were still at war with the Comanches over control of the buffalo range. In February of 1798 several Lipán groups made peace at the presidio of San Juan Bautista del Río Grande, but, posing as Faraones and Llaneros, they shortly resumed their errant ways. By 1799 the Spaniards were prosecuting an open war on them in an effort to reduce them to a more faithful peace.[27]

The more vagrant Llaneros (Natagees, Lipiyanes, and Llaneros proper) were still attacking Spanish settlements in 1796, usually in union with the Mescaleros and Faraones, but these raids were infrequent.[28]

Of all the non-Apache nations, the most important to the Spanish policy of pacification was that of the Comanches. The peace negotiated in 1786 with the Oriental branch in Texas was less perfect than that arranged in the same year with Jupes, Yamparicas, and western Cuchanticas in New Mexico. In 1792 Ecueracapa, the principal chief of the latter groups, led 100 of his braves, armed for the occasion with forty Spanish carbines, against the Lipán, Lipiyán, and Llanero Apaches along the Nueces and San Sabá Rivers in Texas. His party attacked some of their bands near El Paso, where they were soliciting peace, took 13 captives and several horses, and, on its return to New Mexico, received the congratulations of the governor. In 1794 another Comanche war party, operating in the vicinity of the Lipán encampments, stole several horses from the presidio of San Juan Bautista and committed several other slight offenses along the Coahuila frontier, but the New Mexican governor merely reprimanded the chieftains and warned them against a repetition of such acts. Throughout the rest of the century the Comanches continued to co-operate with the Spaniards in cam-

[27] Nava to Revillagigedo, Chihuahua, February 10 and June 6, 1792, AGN, PI 170, Expediente 3; Nava to Azanza, Chihuahua, July 23, 1799, *loc. cit.*; Matson and Schroeder, "Cordero's Description of the Apache—1796," *loc. cit.*
[28] Matson and Schroeder, "Cordero's Description of the Apache—1796," *loc. cit.*

paigns against the hostile Apaches, but the governors of the eastern provinces continued to launch complaints against them. In 1799 the governor of Nuevo León reported to the viceroy that Comanches had stolen animals from San Juan Bautista and from several places in Texas. So as to force them to keep a more faithful peace, he recommended that a war be waged against the Comanches with the same rigor that it was being made on the Lipán and Mescalero Apaches. Commandant-General Nava, however, minimized the thefts and damages that the Comanches may have committed since 1786 and scorned the notion that 700 troops from Texas and Coahuila with their limited auxiliaries could deal militarily with the 2,000 warriors of the Eastern Comanches, not to mention their potential allies—4,000 Jupe and Yamparica Comanche warriors in New Mexico and 7,000 Caddoan braves to the north of Texas. He insisted upon continuing the policy of tolerating minor infractions, merely reprimanding the chieftains whenever such were committed and threatening to deprive them of the gifts that they regularly received at San Antonio. Nava had ordered the governors of Texas and Coahuila to follow this policy, and, he said, it had produced the desired effect. On several occasions the Comanches had made restitution of stolen goods, submitted to the punishment of the thieves, and still remained loyal. Nava criticized the local inhabitants of Texas and Coahuila for leaving their animals in the fields unattended and not reporting thefts in time for the troops to recover the losses. He also advised the governor of Nuevo Santander not to send troops after Comanches who happened to invade his jurisdiction while pursuing the Lipán Apaches. Just as in Ugarte's time, the Comanches continued throughout the century to exert even more pressure on the hostile Apaches than did the Spanish troops themselves. They—along with the Nations of the North—continued to constitute Spain's most formidable weapon in the control of the vagrant Apaches.[29]

[29] John, "Spanish Relations with the *Indios Bárbaros* on the Northernmost Frontier of New Spain in the Eighteenth Century," 167–68, 171–72; Nava to Azanza, Chihuahua, July 23, 1799, *loc. cit.*

In general, there was a conviction among the Spaniards by 1796 that the cruel and bloody war with the Apaches was coming to an end and that this was due not to the former policy of enslavement and annihilation but to the wise one of combining pressure with enticement and allowing those who ceased hostilities to live in peace.[30] The reservation system, which formed an essential part of this policy, however, was hardly ideal for either side. According to one cursory study of the problem, the villages established for peaceful Apache bands drained the funds of the royal treasury, the energies of the presidial troops, and the patience of the civilian inhabitants. The cost of seed, tools, rations, and gifts continued to mount; the eternal vigilance of the soldiers over the restless resident Apaches strained their nerves and resources; the extra tax burden required to support these new wards of the government was resented by the Spanish settlers; and the preferential treatment accorded the newly-reduced Apaches embittered the already-pacified Indian inhabitants. Yet, in spite of the cost to the crown, the fatigue of the troops, and the imposition on the civilian population, the reservation system did reduce the problem of frontier defense to a matter of routine patrol and police action, and from 1790 to 1810 the settlements there enjoyed a considerable respite from hostilities and an opportunity to develop economically.[31]

The collapse of the reservation system seems to have coincided with the outbreak in 1810 of the Mexican revolution for independence from Spain. To meet this all-consuming crisis, Spanish administrators weakened the northern defenses by diverting troops and funds to the centers of rebellion. The remaining presidial forces, their ranks thinned and their pay reduced, resorted to unlicensed and exploitative trade with the tribes. Finally, when commanding officers cut the rations of the resident Apaches and assigned them to field work, some fled their reservations; and when presidial commanders were able to launch only

[30] Matson and Schroeder, "Cordero's Description of the Apache—1796," *loc. cit.*

[31] Park, "Spanish Indian Policy in Northern Mexico, 1765–1810," *loc. cit.* See especially pages 342–43.

halfhearted campaigns against the renegades and to entice them back only by allowing them to keep the plunder they had taken, greater numbers were emboldened to desert. During the years after 1810 both the peace and the reservation system disintegrated, and the independent national government of Mexico, which was created in 1821, had to begin all over again.[32]

Pending a more intensive study of the last years of Spain's attempt to control the Apaches, it may be said that peace by subsidization was never secure and that the terrible loss of life and property was only temporarily reduced, but also that more Apaches than ever before tasted the tempting fruits of tranquility, protection, and economic support. At worst, Ugarte's policy allowed the two races on the northern frontier to take a short step forward along the lengthy and tortuous trail to peaceful coexistence. This, of course, brought the Apaches a step closer to the white man's civilization—a tragic turn for their own way of life but seemingly an inevitable one in the relentless march of human history.

[32] *Ibid.*

SOURCES CONSULTED

MANUSCRIPT MATERIALS

I. Archival Records

Archivo General de Indias, Seville, Spain. Microcopy at The Bancroft Library, Berkeley, California.
Legajos: Audiencia de Guadalajara 272, 287, 301, 416, 515, and 521.
Archivo General y Público de la Nación, Mexico City, Mexico. Microcopy at The Bancroft Library and at the University of Texas Library, Austin, Texas.
Ramos: Correspondencia de los Virreyes, *Tomos* 137, 139, 140, 142, 146, 147, 151, 154, and 157; (second series) 19 and 28. Provincias Internas, *Tomos* 12, 15, 24, 65, 76, 77, 78, 79, 84, 102, 112, 127, 128, 129, 159, 170, 183, 224, and 254.
Archivo de la Parroquía del Sagrario Metropolitano, at Guadalajara, Mexico (notarized typescript).
Libro de Entierros, No. 14.
New Mexico State Records Office, Santa Fe, New Mexico. Spanish Archives, Archive 961a.

II. UNPUBLISHED STUDIES

John, Elizabeth Ann Harper, "Spanish Relations with the *Indios Bárbaros* on the Northernmost Frontier of New Spain in the

Eighteenth Century." Ph.D. dissertation, University of Oklahoma, 1957.

Nelson, Al B. "Juan de Ugalde and the Rio Grande Frontier, 1777–1790." Ph.D. dissertation, University of California, 1936.

PUBLISHED MATERIALS

I. Documentary Sources

Alessio Robles, Vito (ed.). *Diario y derrotero de lo caminado, visto, y observado en la visita que hizo a los presidios de Nueva España Septentrional el Brigadier Pedro de Rivera.* México, 1946.

Bolton, Herbert E. (ed.). *Athanase de Mézières and the Louisiana-Texas Frontier, 1768–1780.* 2 vols. Cleveland, Ohio, 1914.

Gálvez, Bernardo de. *Instrucción formada en virtud de Real Orden de S.M., que se dirige al Señor Comandante General de Provincias Internas Don Jacobo Ugarte y Loyola para gobierno y puntual observancia de este Superior Gefe de sus immediatos subalternos.* México, 1786.

González Flores, Enrique, and Almada, Francisco R. (eds.). *Informe de Hugo O'Conor sobre el estado de las Provincias Internas del Norte, 1771–1776.* México, 1952.

Hammond, George P. (ed.). "The Zúñiga Journal, Tucson to Santa Fe: The Opening of a Spanish Trade Route, 1788–1795," *New Mexico Historical Review,* Vol. VI (January, 1931), 40–65.

Kinnaird, Lawrence (ed.). *The Frontiers of New Spain: Nicolás de Lafora's Description, 1766–1768 (Quivira Society Publications, XIII).* Berkeley, California, 1958.

Lafora, Nicolás de. *Relación del viaje que hizo a los presidios internos situados en la frontera de la América septentrional perteneciente al Rey de España.* Ed. by Vito Alessio Robles. México, 1939.

Matson, Daniel S. and Schroeder, Albert H. (eds.). "Cordero's Description of the Apache—1796," *New Mexico Historical Review,* Vol. XXXII (October, 1957), 335–56.

Reglamento e instrucción para los presidios que se han de formar en la línea de frontera de la Nueva España, resuelto por el Rey Nuestro Señor en cédula de 10 de Setiembre de 1772. Madrid, 1772.

Reglamento para todos los presidios de las provincias internas de esta Governación. México, 1729.

Thomas, Alfred B. (ed.). *After Coronado: Spanish Exploration Northeast of New Mexico, 1696–1727.* Norman, University of Oklahoma Press, 1935.

———. *Forgotten Frontiers: A Study of the Spanish Indian Policy of Don Juan Bautista de Anza, Governor of New Mexico, 1777–1787.* Norman, University of Oklahoma Press, 1932.

———. *The Plains Indians and New Mexico, 1751–1778: A Collection of Documents Illustrative of the History of the Eastern Frontier of New Mexico (Coronado Cuarto Centennial Publications,* XI, ed. by George P. Hammond). Albuquerque, University of New Mexico Press, 1940.

——— (trans. and ed.). *Teodoro de Croix and the Northern Frontier of New Spain, 1776–1783.* Norman, University of Oklahoma Press, 1941.

Velasco Ceballos, Rómulo (ed.). *La administración de D. Frey Antonio María de Bucareli y Ursúa, cuadragesima sexto virrey de México (Publicaciones del Archivo General de la Nación,* XXIX, XXX). 2 vols. México, 1936.

Worcester, Donald E. (ed.). "Advice on Governing New Mexico, 1794," *New Mexico Historical Review,* Vol. XXIV (July, 1949), 236–54.

———. *Instructions for Governing the Interior Provinces of New Spain, 1786, by Bernardo de Gálvez (Quivira Society Publications,* XII). Berkeley, California, 1951.

II. Secondary Studies

Alessio Robles, Vito. *Coahuila y Texas en la época colonial.* 2 vols. México, 1938.

Atienza, Julio de. *Nobiliario español: diccionario heráldico de apellidos españoles y de títulos nobiliarios.* Madrid, 1959.

Bancroft, Hubert H. *History of Mexico*. 6 vols. (*The Works of Hubert Howe Bancroft*, IX–XIV). San Francisco, 1883–88.

————. *History of the North Mexican States and Texas*. 2 vols. (*The Works of Hubert Howe Bancroft*, XV–XVI). San Francisco, 1886.

Bobb, Bernard E. *The Viceregency of Antonio María Bucareli in New Spain, 1771–1779*. Austin, Texas, 1962.

Bolton, Herbert E. *Texas in the Middle Eighteenth Century: Studies in Spanish Colonial History and Administration*. Berkeley, California, 1915.

Brinckerhoff, Sidney B. and Faulk, Odie B. *Lancers for the King: A Study of the Frontier Military System of Northern New Spain*. Phoenix, Arizona, 1965.

Castañeda, Carlos E. *The Mission Era: The Passing of the Missions, 1762–1782* (*Our Catholic Heritage in Texas, 1519–1936*, IV, ed. by Paul J. Foik). Austin, Texas, 1939.

Chapman, Charles E. *The Founding of Spanish California: The Northwestward Expansion of New Spain, 1687–1783*. New York, 1916.

Faulk, Odie B. *The Last Years of Spanish Texas, 1778–1821*. The Hague, 1964.

————. "Spanish-Comanche Relations and the Treaty of 1785," *Texana*, Vol. II, No. 1 (Spring, 1964), 44–53.

Forbes, Jack D. *Apache, Navaho, and Spaniard*. Norman, University of Oklahoma Press, 1960.

————. *Warriors of the Colorado: The Yumas of the Quechan Nation and Their Neighbors*. Norman, University of Oklahoma Press, 1965.

Harper, Elizabeth Ann. "The Taovayas Indians in Frontier Trade and Diplomacy, 1719–1768," *Chronicles of Oklahoma*, Vol. XXXI (Autumn, 1953), 268–89.

Henao, Jesús María, and Arrubla, Gerardo. *History of Colombia*. Ed. by J. Fred Rippy. Chapel Hill, North Carolina, 1938.

Jones, Oakah L., Jr. *Pueblo Warriors and Spanish Conquest*. Norman, University of Oklahoma Press, 1966.

Moorhead, Max L. "The Presidio Supply Problem of New Mexico

in the Eighteenth Century," *New Mexico Historical Review,* Vol. XXXVI (July, 1961), 210–29.

———. "The Private Contract System of Presidio Supply in Northern New Spain," *Hispanic American Historical Review,* Vol. XLI (February, 1961), 31–54.

Nasatir, Abraham P., and Loomis, Noel M. *Pedro Vial and the Roads to Santa Fe.* Norman, University of Oklahoma Press, 1966.

Nelson, Al B. "Campaigning in the Big Bend of the Rio Grande in 1787," *Southwestern Historical Quarterly,* Vol. XXXIX (January, 1936), 200–27.

———. "Juan de Ugalde and Picax-andé-Ins-tinsle, 1787–88," *Southwestern Historical Quarterly,* Vol. XLIII (April, 1940), 438–64.

Park, Joseph F. "Spanish Indian Policy in Northern Mexico, 1765–1810," *Arizona and the West,* Vol. IV (Winter, 1962), 325–44.

Pérez Verdía, Luis. *Historia particular del Estado de Jalisco desde los primeros tiempos de que hay noticia hasta nuestros días.* Second edition. 3 vols. Guadalajara, Mexico, 1951–52.

Powell, Philip W. *Soldiers, Indians, and Silver: The Northward Advance of New Spain, 1550–1600.* Berkeley and Los Angeles, University of California Press, 1952.

Reeve, Frank, "Navajo-Spanish Diplomacy, 1770–1790," *New Mexico Historical Review,* Vol. XXXV, No. 3 (July, 1960), 200–35.

Richardson, Rupert N. *The Comanche Barrier to the South Plains Settlement.* Glendale, California, 1933.

Thomas, Alfred B. "San Carlos, A Comanche Pueblo on the Arkansas, 1787," *Colorado Magazine,* Vol. VI, No. 3 (May, 1939), 79–91.

Twitchell, Ralph E. *The Spanish Archives of New Mexico.* 2 vols. Cedar Rapids, Iowa, 1914.

Villa, Eduardo W. *Historia del Estado de Sonora.* Second edition. Hermosillo, Mexico, 1951.

Wroth, Lawrence C. "The Frontier Presidios of New Spain: Books, Papers, Maps, and a Selection of Manuscripts Relating to the Rivera Expedition of 1724–1729," *Papers of the Bibliographical Society of America*, Vol. XLV (1951), 191–218.

Zamacois, Niceto de. *Historia de México desde sus tiempos mas remotos hasta nuestros días.* 18 vols. Barcelona and México, 1877–82.

INDEX

Acoma, *pueblo* of, New Mexico: 195
Agave: 6
Aguaje de las Cruces: 213
Aguaje del Cíbolo: 213
Aguaje del Pabelloncito: 213
Aguaje del Tabaco: 233
Aguanaval River: 77, 251–52
Agua Salada, Navaho village of, N. M.: 179n.
Aguaverde, *presidio* of, Coahuila: 33–34, 37, 90n., 252
Agua Zarca, place in Nueva Zizcaya: 105
Alamo, *hacienda* of, N. Viz.: 90n., 206
Alegre (Mescalero chief): 202, 213, 217–20, 226–27, 242, 246, 248, 253, 258–59, 261, 264, 268
Alonso (Mescalero chief): 204
Altar, *presidio* of, Sonora: *see* Santa Gertrudis de Altar
Alvarado, Pedro de: 10
Anaelo, *hacienda* of, N. Viz.: 90n., 206
Antel (Chiricahua warrior): 192
Antelope: 6–7, 207, 231
Antonio El Pinto (Navaho chief): 174–76, 179–80, 197–98, 198n.
Anza, Juan Bautista de: governor of N. M., 45–46, 68, 143–62, 174–82, 186, 197, 272, 279; governor of Son., 49, 51, 55, 57, 59; military commandant of Son., 193–96, 272
Apaches: habitat, 3–4, 6, 170–74, 200–203; culture and characteristics, 3–8, 14, 170n., 203, 219; government and tribal affiliations, 3–4, 7, 170–71, 200, 218, 248; warfare, 7–8, 13–15, 26–30, 34–41, 46, 48, 56, 84, 99–109, 147, 164–65, 212, 250–52, 272–74, 289; peace negotiations and pacts, 14–15, 38, 41, 46, 76–77, 84, 116, 118, 134–38, 166, 186, 211–12, 271–77; war casualties, 85, 105, 113, 134, 174–75, 185, 189–91, 195, 222, 255, 281; Spanish policy toward, 115–42; ransomed from Comanches, 150, 160; *see also* Chiricahuas, Faraones, Gileños, Jicarillas, Lipanes, Lipiyanes, Llaneros, Mescaleros, Mimbreños, Mogollones, Natagées, Navahos, Pedreros, Salineros, *and* Tontos (Coyoteros)
Arco (Natagé chief): 258
Arispe, *villa* of, Son.: 48, 52, 59, 90n., 91, 93, 182–84, 186, 188, 192, 211, 217, 222, 234, 279
Arive, valley of: 53
Arizona, state of: 3, 172–73
Arkansas River: 146, 148, 162
Arredondo, Joaquín de: 278n.
Arriola, Gregorio: 69
Arrows: 7, 49, 91, 127
Arroyo de Guachuca: 52
Arroyo de la Pendencia: 26
Arroyo de las Nutrias: 52
Arroyo de la Soledad: 255
Arroyo de Terrenate: 52
Arsenals: 93–94

297

Asguegoca (Chiricahua chief): 173, 185, 194
Asguenitesy (Chiricahua chief): 173, 185
Atanasio (Chiricahua warrior): 194
Audiencia: of Nueva Galicia, 41, 61, 280, 283; of México, 42, 60, 72
Aydiá (Chiricahua chief): 192
Aysosé: *see* Isosé
Aztecs: 10, 11

Bachimba, mission of, N. Viz.: 108n.
Bacoachi, *pueblo* and presidial company of, Son.: 56, 90n., 96n., 188–89, 193; Chiricahua congregation at, 183–88, 191, 196, 212, 275, 281, 284
Bahía del Espíritu Santo, *presidio* of, Texas: 90n., 96n.
Ballenilla, Ignacio: 69
Barri, Felipe: 46
Baserac, *pueblo* of, Son.: 55
Bavispe, *pueblo* and presidial company of, Son.: *see* San Miguel de Bavispe
Berroterán, Joseph de: 35n.
Big Bend region: 26, 38
Bigotes El Bermejo (Mescalero chief): 202, 213, 216–18, 226, 242–43, 248, 254, 258–59, 261, 268
Bigotes El Pelón (Mescalero chief): 242
Boca Tuerta (Lipán chief): 38
Bolsón de Mapimí: 26, 222–23, 235, 252; Apache refuge in, 26–27, 36, 109, 206, 214, 231, 234, 237, 261
Bonavia y Zapata, Bernardo: 278n.
Bonilla, Antonio de: 52
Borica, Diego de: 68, 104
Borrados: 131, 139
Bows: 7, 91–92, 127
Bucareli, Antonio María de: 25, 28, 30, 34–37, 39–40, 42–43, 45, 59, 72n., 132, 271
Buenavista, *estancia* and *mesa* of, Son.: *see* San Rafael de Buenavista
Buenavista, *presidio* of, Son.: *see* San Carlos de Buenavista
Buenos Aires, Argentina: 73
Buffalo: 9, 14, 41, 167–68, 202–203, 207, 213, 219–21, 225–27, 229, 231, 235, 240, 242, 262, 265–67, 276, 287
Busanic, valley of, Son.: 53

Cabello, Domingo: 144
Cabello Largo (Lipán chief): 38
Cabeza Rapada (Comanche chief): 154
Cabezón, Navaho village of, N. M.: 179n.
Cachu-ende: 248; *see also Cuelcajen-ne*
Caddoan nations: 8, 275; *see also* Nations of the North
Calabazas, *pueblo* and mission of, Son.: 54
California, province of: 37, 59, 69, 74–75, 78, 88, 90n., 129; road to, 49, 52, 54, 57–58, 143, 278
Camino Real: 170; *see also* Caravan
Camisa de Fierro (Comanche chief): 154
Canadian River: 147
Cannon: 91, 93–94
Carabinas (Carbines): 90–92, 155, 287
Caravan: 155–56, 168, 200, 263n.
Carlos (Chiricahua warrior): 194
Carrasco, José Manuel: 106–107, 111, 190
Carrizal, *presidio* of, N. Viz.: *see* San Fernando de Carrizal
Carrizo, mission of, Coah.: 40
Carrizo, Navaho village of, N. M.: 179n.
Casa-Fuerte, Marqués de: 15
Casanova, Manuel: 100–102, 104–105
Casas Grandes, *pueblo* and mission of, N. Viz.: 109
Casimiro (Lipiyán chief): 252
Castro, Ramón de: 278n., 286
Cattle: 59, 126, 190, 231; Apache theft of, 6, 8, 40, 202; Navaho possession of, 179
Cebolleta, Navaho village of, N. M.: 179n.
Cedros, *hacienda* of, N. Gal.: 206, 223
Cendés: 224; *see also Sejen-ne*
Century plant: 6
Cerro, Navaho village of, N. M.: 179n.
Cerro Chato, Navaho village of, N. M.: 179n.
Cerro de la Cieneguita: 216
Chacoli, Navaho village of, N. M.: 179n.
Chamy (Chiricahua chief): 173, 185
Charles III (king of Spain): 67
Chavarría, valley of: 88n.

Index

Index

Manteca Mucha (Lipán chief): 38

Mapimí, mining town of, N. Viz.: 108 & n., 109

Mares, Joseph: 279

Matamoros, Joseph: 68n.

Mayos: 128

Mazapil, mining town of, N. Gal.: 206, 223

Medina, Roque de: 68

Medina River: 26

Merino, Manuel: 68n.

Mescal: 6, 209, 213, 218–19

Mescaleros: 27, 48, 120, 125, 131, 146, 155, 161, 203; habitat, 6, 200–202, 211, 220; campaigns against, 36, 85, 130, 186, 206–207, 235, 286, 288; at peace, 84–85, 133, 140–41, 143, 184, 191, 193, 198, 204–69, 271, 273, 277, 281, 286–87; raids by, 108, 129, 200, 202, 206, 274; as auxiliaries, 140, 189, 191, 198, 203–205, 221, 247, 260–61, 264, 268–69, 281; military escort for, 168, 220–21, 229, 235–36, 242, 262–63, 267, 276; chiefs, 202, 241–42; numbers, 212; deaths at Santa Rosa, 262

Mesquite: 219

Mexico City, Mexico: Aztec capital, 10; capital of New Spain, 12, 43, 45, 57, 59–60, 63, 66, 72, 80, 84, 94, 97, 99, 117, 129, 132, 134, 151, 191, 195, 254

Michoacán, province of: 169

Militia: 87; of Sonora, 38; of Coahuila, 38–39; of New Mexico, 165, 189

Mimbreños: habitat, 4, 143, 170, 172; trade at El Paso, 130; at peace, 133, 140, 184–87, 198–99, 211, 239 & n., 277, 285; raids by, 172–73, 191, 285–86; chiefs, 172; campaigns against, 185, 188–91, 198; as auxiliaries, 199

Mimbres Apaches: see Mimbreños

Mines: 11–14, 56, 128

Missionaries: 17, 29, 32, 50, 55, 57–58, 67, 118, 129, 196; Franciscans, 13, 52; Jesuits, 13

Missions: 9, 12–13, 26 & n., 29, 40, 53–55, 57, 116–18, 128–29, 139, 204, 228

Mixtón War: 10

Mobile company: see Compañía Volante

Mogollones: 129, 170

Monclova, presidio of, Coah.: 26, 31, 34, 36, 98; troop strength, 30, 90n.; relocation of, 33, 37

Monclova, villa of, Coah.: see Santiago de Monclova

Montera Blanca (Mescalero chief): 202, 213, 216–18, 226, 242–43, 248, 254, 258–59, 261, 268

Monterey, presidio of, Alta California: 90n.

Monterrey, Conde de: 13

Montes, Ventura: 273

Montezuma: 10

Moqui, pueblo of, N. M.: 9, 130, 164, 172–73, 284

Mountains: see Sierra

Mules: 126, 155, 246, 268; eaten by Apaches, 4, 203; stolen by Apaches, 34, 40, 99–100, 102, 106, 202, 264; presidial requirements, 91–92, 95, 98, 169; Indian possession and loss of, 111–12, 191, 195, 206; gifts of to Indians, 230

Muñoz, Manuel: 204–205

Muskets: 26, 27, 90–93, 127–28, 157, 175, 263

Nadadores, pueblo of, Coah.: 34

Naguiagoslan (Mimbreño chief): 172

Namiquipa, pueblo and mission of, N. Viz.: 90n., 108

Natagées: 155, 161, 202, 211n., 248, 254, 267, 287; habitat, 6, 27; chiefs, 242, 258; at peace, 258

Natanijú (Mimbreño chief): 172, 186–87

Natchitoches, military post of, Louisiana: 279

Nations of the North: 8–9, 116, 120, 125, 130–31, 140, 143–44, 233, 244, 251, 255, 286, 288; see also Caddoan nations, Iscanis, Kichais, Taovayas, Tawakonis, and Wichitas

Nava, Pedro de: 266–67, 277, 278n., 280, 286, 288

Navaho: 4, 9, 113, 130, 140, 155, 172, 240; kinship, 4, 170 & n., 173; habitat, 4, 170, 173–74; at peace, 133,

Index

qués de Croix, Juan Manuel Flores, Bernardo de Gálvez, Matías de Gálvez, Conde de Monterrey, Conde de Revillagigedo (the Elder), Conde de Revillagigedo (the Younger), Luis de Velasco, *and* Marqués de Villamanrique
Vildósola, Joseph Antonio: 49, 51
Villa Guerrero, Coah.: 26
Villamanrique, Marqués de: 12
Villa Unión, Coah.: 26
Vinniettinen-ne: see Tontos
Vizcaya, province of, Spain: 20
Volante (Mescalero chief): 202, 213, 217, 219–20, 226–27, 242, 246, 248, 253–54, 258–59, 261–65, 268
Voluntarios de Cataluña, company of: 87, 90n.

War with England (1779–83): 57–58, 75, 120, 144, 174
Wichitas: 8, 146
Wyoming, state of: 146

Yagonglí: *see* Ojos Colorados
Yamparicas: 146, 148–49, 157–59, 167, 287–88
Yaqui River: 55–56
Yaquis: 128
Yastasitasitan-ne (Apache god): 6
Yco-Yndixle: *see* Volante
Yntajen-ne: see Faraones
Yucca: 6
Yumas: colony among, 49, 57–58; massacre of, 58–59, 128
Yupes: *see* Jupes
Yutagen-ne: see Navahos

Zacatecas, *ciudad* of, N. Gal.: 11, 13
Zacatecos: 11–12
Zapato Tuerto (Mescalero chief): 202, 213–14, 216–18, 221, 223, 241–42, 253, 259
Zendé: *see* Sejen-ne
Zuñi, *pueblo* of, N. M.: 195, 279
Zúñiga, José de: 279
Zuñis: 9, 165, 172

The Apache Frontier has been set on the Linotype in eleven-point Caledonia with two-point spacing between the lines. Hand-set Goudy Handtooled was selected for display to complement the character of Caledonia.

The paper on which this book is printed bears the watermark of the University of Oklahoma Press and is designed for an effective life of at least three hundred years.